From Pies to Paella

By

Peter Haworth

©Peter Haworth 2018

All rights reserved. No part of this publication may be reproduced, stored in a retrieval system or transmitted by any means, electronic, mechanical, photocopying or otherwise without the prior consent of the author.

DEDICATION

Little did I think when I first started to catalogue our Premier League exploits way back in 2009 that nine, soon to be ten years on, I would still be dedicating several hours a week to this task. Through all that time my long-suffering wife Julie has had to put up with my dramatic mood swings which are an inevitable part of a Burnley Premier League season. For her it has meant long solitary hours with only 'Vera' and 'Casualty' for company, whilst I search desperately to find the right words to describe another Claret & Blue adventure. Who else then could I dedicate this, the fourth Premier League Diary to but her.

Also, she has been known to complain that she very rarely gets a mention in the books. To address that matter I have hereby made sure that she not only gets a mention, but also that it is at the very forefront of the book!

To my wife Julie. God bless her.

ACKNOWLEDGEMENTS

Once again, I am majorly indebted to two old friends without whom this book would never have seen the light of day. That may have been a good thing I hear some of you say. Well, that's as maybe but here it is and you dear reader have paid good money to have the privilege of reading it.

In no particular order (I've heard that on Britain's Got Talent!) firstly I would like to thank my pal of more years than I care to remember, Steve Calderbank. Steve now an émigré in Wragby, Lincolnshire, despite having no interest in football whatsoever, has provided the technical know-how necessary to transform this collection of ramblings into the finished magnificent glossy manuscript you now hold in your hands. His work on producing the cover demands special mention as my indecision on some aspects almost caused him a major meltdown. Still, all's well that ends well, and I'm sure he will get his rewards in heaven.

The second award for 'Outstanding Dedication to Duty' must go to ex work colleague and mate, Ed Skingsley. Ed is now very much an accomplished author in his own write (see what I did there) having published a number of books about his own team, Preston North End. I like to think that my humble little offerings have served as an inspiration to Ed in convincing him to commit his thoughts to print. Ed has been responsible for proof reading this latest masterpiece and once again has not been shy with the red ink and sarcastic comments. Many thanks Ed for fitting this work in amongst all your other projects.

My thanks for the book foreword goes to ex Claret Derek Scott who follows in a growing line of former players who have been kind enough to add a few words. Derek a loyal servant to the club for over a decade (1974-85) made his first team debut as a 17-year-old in April 1975. Playing initially at right back and later as a midfielder. In total he made 364 appearances (356 starts/8 substitute) scoring 31 goals in all competitions. Probably his most memorable goal coming in the 2nd Leg Milk Cup Semi-Final victory over Liverpool at Turf Moor in 1983. 'Scotty' was transferred in 1985 for a sum of £20,000 to near neighbours Bolton Wanderers and went on to enjoy a career that saw him play in all four divisions of the Football League.

A special mention here to Veronica Simpson, currently employed as a receptionist at Turf Moor, who also fulfils the role of Co-ordinator/Secretary of the Former Players Association. Veronica was instrumental in press-ganging Derek Scott into his literary duties. I may well be looking to make use of her services when Book 5 is due to 'hit the streets'.

Once again Tony Scholes, editor of the fans website 'Up the Clarets', has been of tremendous assistance in promoting the series of Premier League Diaries and championing my cause on many fronts. Thank you, Tony it is much appreciated.

Similarly, fellow Clarets author Dave Thomas for his assistance and promotion of the books through his Facebook page.

On the same note, a thank you to Burnley FC Chief Executive Officer, Dave Baldwin, for his assistance in retailing some copies of the previous volume, 'There's No Place Like Home' through the club shop. Hopefully, this facility will also be available to this edition.

Last but not least, a massive thank you to Sean Dyche, his management team and all the players for making 2017/18 once again a season to savour. What a fantastic achievement to qualify for Europa League competition after a gap of 50 years.

Truly unbelievable! What's next?

Contents

DEDICATION 3
ACKNOWLEDGEMENTS 4
FOREWORD 8
INTRODUCTION 10
AUGUST 18
SEPTEMBER 34
OCTOBER 56
NOVEMBER 74
DECEMBER 95
JANUARY 2018 141
FEBRUARY 171
MARCH 197
APRIL 219
MAY 246
ON REFLECTION 258
WHAT'S NEXT 274

FOREWORD

Welcome to this the fourth of Peter Haworth's Premier League season reviews.

It's my turn to follow in the footsteps of some illustrious former colleagues, Martin Dobson, Colin Waldron and Jim Thomson, in being kindly asked by Peter to write the foreword for this his latest offering.

My love affair with this great club began way back in 1971 when I signed schoolboy forms, and I am still here, a resident of this great town, dare I say, some 47 years later. To say I have experienced highs and lows, both as a player and as a supporter during that time would be a gross understatement.

My family connections to the club need no introduction, everything football wise has been well documented, but now I am proud to say that both my sons and their children, my grandchildren, attend Turf Moor as supporters, such is the special bond with this club.

We managed, for the first time to retain our Premier League status in 2016-17, but no one could have predicted what was to happen in the next season 2017-18. Once again, the football pundits had us down as big relegation favourites, but Sean Dyche and his team were having none of that.

A great start, mediocre middle, and a great finish resulted in Burnley Football Club finishing an unbelievable 7th in the Premier League. The team with the smallest budget had worked miracles, achieving European qualification for the first time in over 50 years.

How did they do it?

The manager demands determination, organisation, team spirit and a great togetherness. Not just from his team, but also the terraces, all these things together are a potent force.

Many opponents left Turf Moor having surrendered points they thought they would take home, they should have done their homework correctly, there is nothing more dangerous than a wounded animal.

As a player, I was at Burnley for 11 years, I am a former captain of this club, a fact I am proud to tell visitors on the ground tours I do every match day. Former Turf Moor legend Peter Noble once said before a game; *"Right all of you, this is what you do, look after your team mates and they will do the same for you"*. These were the words of a true leader.

That togetherness can take you a long way, you won't win every game, but it won't be for the lack of effort put in trying, this ethos runs through the club so strongly today. Sean Dyche's mantra of 'maximum effort is the minimum requirement' should be the moral in any vocation.

I'm sure you will enjoy Peter's latest offering as much as his previous seasons reviews, let's look forward to the new season and UP THE CLARETS !!!

Derek Scott - Burnley FC, 1974-1985

INTRODUCTION

After the Clarets successful retention of their Premier League place for the first time at the third attempt... a quandary! Having committed to write the first Premier League diary following the Championship final play-off victory in 2009, I believed this would be a one-off affair. However, confounded by the resilience and resolution of Sean Dyche's battlers, my writing career developed into a more ongoing project. With the completion of what had now become a trilogy in 2017, I am faced with the dilemma of whether I have the stamina and desire to continue the project. Will there be a Volume 4?

Clearly, as you are currently reading this, the answer is yes! How could I disappoint my myriads of readers globally by failing to continue my review of yet another unexpected, but thoroughly deserved, shot at the big time. Following our two previous short stays, and our third triumphant season what comes next for Burnley FC? Will the increased finances available from an extended stay in the top league allow us to consolidate our position, or will it prove once again too great a challenge?

There's no doubt that to achieve survival will be as difficult a task this time as it was last. In 2016/17 we managed to finish above Watford, and the three relegated sides Hull City, Middlesbrough and Sunderland. Two of the three doomed sides started the season in chaotic fashion. Hull City with a newly appointed untried manager in Michael Phelan, and an owner trying desperately to sell the club, exercised very little pre-season planning and their recruitment was unsurprisingly shambolic. Sunderland having lost their saviour Sam Allardyce and having appointed a 'shell shocked'

David Moyes were in similar disarray. Middlesbrough with the eminently unlikeable Aitor Karanka in charge, and ideas above their station, seemed to believe that large amounts of money would buy survival. A reported salary of £100,000/week went on loan striker Alvaro Negredo which bought them a less than impressive nine Premier League goals for the season. Mr Karanka departed before the curtain fell but too late for their slide to be arrested.

It's fair to say that with these three in turmoil for much of the season, and Swansea City, Crystal Palace and Watford also having some difficult periods, our survival chances were significantly improved. However, the league this time looks a more difficult proposition. Coming up from the Championship are Newcastle United, a club with massive support, an extremely experienced manager in Rafa Benitez, and a wealthy if reluctant owner, Mike Ashley. If they can get their act together they may well survive. Likewise, Brighton & Hove Albion, again well-supported and seemingly not short of cash. If they can adapt quickly to life at the top they should have the resources to make a good fight of it. That leaves only Huddersfield Town, a club of similar stature to ourselves as the bookmaker's relegation favourites.

Once again it has been a summer of financial madness as transfer fees and player's wage expectations spiral alarmingly out of control. Ridiculous sums, the highest being reported as £197m for Neymar da Silva Santos Junior for his move from Barcelona to Paris Saint-Germain are surely undermining the long-term survival of the game. This along with reputed wages of £500k/week!!!

In England, the major clubs are similarly afflicted by this inflationary spiral with reported fees in the region of

£75m and £50m being paid by the Manchester clubs for Romelu Lukaku and Kyle Walker respectively. Where does all this leave 'little old Burnley?' Well, as always it leaves us as they say, between a rock and a hard place. In an effort to maintain our position at the top table we are being asked to fork out increasingly large transfer fees, but more worryingly inflated salary contracts that run for lengthy periods.

As expected, players are either coming out of contract or nearing the end, with the inevitable loss of potential transfer value. Unsurprisingly key defender Michael Keane is one such and moves to Everton for a fee rumoured as £25-30m. He has been a very good player for us and I'm sure nobody begrudges him the opportunity to further his career. Another stalwart of recent campaigns George Boyd, he of the flowing locks, turns down the offer of a new one-year contract and departs to Sheffield Wednesday for a longer-term offer. Also leaving is Tenday Darikwa, who due to the impressive form of Matt Lowton, has found first team opportunities very limited.

The first new face coming in to replace some of these departees is a young full-back Charlie Taylor from Leeds United. Charlie had been a reported target last summer but his club refused to sanction a move. Now he joins as an out of contract player but Leeds are due a payment because of his age. Fortunately, after protracted wrangling this sum is agreed without the necessity of going to a tribunal. Next in is experienced striker Jonathan Walters joining from Stoke City. He is shortly followed by Swansea City's Jack Cork, an ex-loan player for the Clarets from his Chelsea days. Two weeks later the trio are joined by another Stoke City player Phil Bardsley, who covers the vacancy left by Darikwa's departure. The new additions are largely viewed as solid if not spectacular, but of course that is the Burnley way.

Away from the football for a moment, readers of my previous diaries will be acquainted with my ongoing anecdotes from my association with a Lancashire based walking group, Lancashire Dotcom Walkers. There exists within the group various factions based on geographic domicile. By far the largest and most antagonistic (in a friendly rivalry sort of way) are the Burnley Contingent and the Preston and south Ribble Mob. During the course of the year various challenges are contested between the factions. One such being the Annual Bowls match, Burnley v Rest of the World. That's no mean feat for a town the size of Burnley to be considered worthy enough of taking on the whole of the world!

Tuesday July 18th marked the date for this annual battle of wits, guile and stamina, but unfortunately, I have to report that once again we, the Burnley Contingent, came away defeated by a score of 10-4. As is usually the case with this fixture, the opposition took up serious training on the bowling greens of the Preston area some weeks ahead of the match. Whereas the Burnley lads and lasses had not rolled a bowl in anger since the last contest, 12 months ago. Needless to say, our training had consisted of tactical discussions over foaming pints in the hostelries of Burnley. Once again it was a tale of plucky amateurs versus cocky professionals. Fear not our time will come!

It was during this occasion that Jim (Skipper of the Yard) from the Preston mob attempted to revive the annual bet which had been struck between him and myself. This wager going back three years, had revolved around the relative league positions of the two teams, Burnley and Preston North End (PNE) at the end of each season. If as a result of their endeavours during the season both teams would start the next campaign in the same division, Jim would be the benefactor. If on the other hand, they would be in different divisions I would claim the prize. Let me at this juncture point out that the sum involved had on the previous two occasions been £10, and the proceeds been donated to a local charity of the winner's choice. So, it's hardly a life changing speculation by any means.

However, Jim obviously upset by his loss following our promotion in the 2015/16 season, and having had to suffer the humiliation of handing over the 'dosh' at Turf Moor, declined to take on the bet for 2016/17. Furthermore, NONE of his fellow Prestonians had the courage to take up the cudgel, and the bet lapsed for last season. Obviously, they knew the chances of the Clarets being relegated were slim, and the prospect of North End being promoted non-existent. Now, clearly buoyed by some misguided pundits' predictions, Jim is keen to once again throw down the gauntlet. It doesn't seem right somehow to be able to unilaterally skip years on the bet when you don't' fancy it, and revive it when you do. Even Jim's staunch ally, the unfortunately named Chris McCann, can see the validity of my reluctance. I think I'll make them sweat a bit!

Back to the football and an unbeaten run in the meaningless pre-season friendlies, meaningless that is apart from the victory at Preston North End, ended in bizarre fashion. The last two fixtures were home games against European visitors. The first being an entertaining and absorbing run-out against Spanish La Liga outfit Celta Vigo, ending in an amicable 2-2 draw. The final fixture saw German team Hannover 96, newly promoted to Bundesliga 1, as visitors to the Turf a week ahead of the season's opener at Chelsea.

In the week preceding the game rumours were rife of approximately 600 German supporters making the trip, and indications that some of these were pretty unsavoury characters. The rumours proved well founded indeed as our vociferous and hostile visitors took up their position in the Cricket Field stand, separated by a thin yellow line of stewards, from home supporters in the same stand. An entertaining enough first half was drawing to a close when a Hannover defender unceremoniously dumped Clarets striker Andre Gray on the deck. Clearly angered by this Andre made his feelings known to the German, and the ensuing handbags at ten paces was quickly quelled by the referee.

However, this triggered something considerably more ugly than 'handbags' in the stand as the German fans surged at the home support, with evil and brutal intent. Fortunately, quick action by stewards and police prevented a coming together, but seats were torn out and hurled as weapons by the marauding Germans. Ironically from the resultant free kick awarded for the foul on Gray, Ben Mee headed the Clarets in front. Justice if ever I saw it! Suffice it to say after an extended half time break, presumably whilst the police assembled reinforcements, the game was abandoned on account of crowd safety concerns. Next time, can somebody please explain to Hannover 96 the meaning of 'friendly'!

With the 'friendlies' out of the way it's the final week before the real thing starts. In typical Burnley fashion, the club manages to stir up controversy by selling a major striking asset Andre Gray, three days ahead of the opener. I think it's fair to say that Gray split opinions among the fans on his ability as a Premier League striker. Some saw him as an essential weapon for his pace and power, others saw him as having poor ball control, no heading ability and a sometimes disinterested attitude.

Approaching the final year of his contract, and showing no willingness to sign a new one on the terms allegedly being offered, the club were in somewhat of a dilemma. Should they retain his services for the last year of the contract and let him leave for free next summer? Or should they try and recoup the money paid on his initial transfer and attempt to find an equal or better replacement? It was a no-brainer really, and as soon as somebody came along offering what the club considered an acceptable fee, he was gone. Andre will now further his career at rivals Watford for a fee rumoured to be £11.5m potentially rising to £18.5m with add-ons.

Once again, the Clarets are awash with money, a far cry from the days of near extinction in the 1980's. However, spending that money is proving a more difficult task. Selling clubs are aware that we have in this window raked in large sums for Michael Keane and now Andre Gray, and are raising their valuations of their own players accordingly. We are about to enter another challenging season without two of our key players from last time, and as yet no sign of replacements. The more excitable posters on the Up the Clarets website messageboard are already venting their frustrations. Calm down lads, there's a long way to go.

So, things have certainly livened up as we enter the last week of pre-season and then to top it off… an away draw at arch enemies Blackburn Rovers (spit) in the 2nd round of the EFL Cup. If anybody had asked me what was the worst possible fixture for ourselves, I would have nominated this one without doubt. A relatively meaningless competition, hooliganism on the night a good bet, a highly charged atmosphere guaranteeing a physical encounter, and bragging rights at stake. Although our once illustrious neighbours are currently languishing in League 1, let us hope that presumably an opportunity to give some squad members meaningful game time, doesn't end in tears.

That's enough of the pre-amble let's get down to the serious business. Bring on Chelsea at the Bridge!

AUGUST

Game 1 Saturday 12th August 15.00 – Chelsea v Burnley

What a way to start a season! First game away to the reigning league Champions! And what chance for 'little old Burnley'? One of our main attacking threats sold three days before the opener, and our opponents having the luxury of a newly acquired £70m striker bench warming. However, as they say, 'It's a funny old game'. Who would have predicted what was to follow?

Going into this game I had a certain degree of calmness not usually associated with these fixtures. Usually I am dreading a battering and having to suffer the tedious humiliation heaped upon us by Match of The Day (MOTD) pundits. Not so today, and I think the main reason was that a defeat today, putting things in context, would not be a disastrous result. Last season's opener, a home fixture against Swansea City, was a game where we could reasonably have expected to take a point. A late goal for the Swans meant we came away empty handed from the first fixture, as we had in all previous attempts.

Today there were no such expectations, away to the Champions, and with only one away victory in the previous campaign, and that coming at the eighteenth attempt, could surely mean only defeat. So, nil points after the first fixture would be no worse than last season, and we would have fulfilled one of our most difficult away challenges. I am also of the impression that the best time to play the 'elite' teams is early in the season before they find their rhythm. Furthermore, our opponents seem to be a little 'out of sorts' with themselves. Manager Antonio Conte feels let down by the lack of incoming transfer activity (despite the signing of £70m Alvaro Morata). Their main weapon, Diego Costa, is in dispute with the club and threatening legal action! Injuries and suspensions rule out Victor Moses, Eden Hazard and Pedro. I suppose now is as good a time as any to catch them.

And that is exactly how it turned out! The Clarets start with a strange looking 4-5-1 formation. Sam Vokes is the lone striker with a central midfield three of Jeff Hendrick, Steven Defour and ex Chelsea youngster Jack Cork. Flanking this trio are wide men Robbie Brady and Johan Berg Gudmundsson (JBG). The defence are the usual culprits, Matt Lowton, Ben Mee and Stephen Ward, with James Tarkowski taking the centre back vacancy created by Michael Keane's departure.

It's a steady start and we don't look at all overawed by the occasion in front of a large home crowd. Marcus Alonso finds himself first man in the book, yellow carded for a bad challenge on Ward. It doesn't take long for the action to heat up further as on 14 minutes ex Clarets loanee, and now Chelsea captain Gary Cahill, heads for an early bath! On a foray upfield Cahill loses control of the ball and in an attempt to win it back lunges studs upwards into Defour. A clumsy if not malicious challenge that leaves referee Craig Pawson no alternative than to dismiss him. Shortly afterwards Cesc Fabregas collects a needless booking for cynically and ridiculously applauding Pawson's award of a free kick to the Clarets.

Now it's game on, and our illustrious hosts are rocked on 24 minutes as Sam Vokes turns Matt Lowton's right wing cross into the bottom left hand corner of the goal. What a fantastic start, now only 66 minutes to hang on! Wait a minute! Who said anything about hanging on? On 39 minutes, the impressive Clarets extend the lead with a magnificent strike by Stephen Ward following a clever build up. Now I'm starting to get dizzy as the shockwaves from Stamford Bridge reverberate around the football world. However, these magnificent Clarets are not done yet and following a free kick move down the right, Defour's pinpoint cross is headed home by the imperious Vokes. What a turn up for the books!!!

Half time arrives with a 3-0 lead for the massive underdogs and what is more it's thoroughly deserved. Burnley are in top form and have turned in probably their most impressive 45 minutes under Sean Dyche's tutelage. In contrast, the Champions are in total disarray. The BBC MOTD commentator sums it up in his text commentary by saying 'Burnley have been absolutely superb.'

Now I have been a Burnley supporter for more years than I would care to mention so I know just what is coming next. Three up against 10 men, it can only mean one thing, we are on the verge of implosion. Surely our hosts after a good old fashioned half-time 'bollocking' are going to come at us, big-time.

However, as the second half progresses despite their improved performance we are eating up time nicely. Chelsea are pressing but we are soaking it up. On 59 minutes, a decisive move by the Champions as they introduce Morata at the expense of the ineffectual Michy Batshuayi. The pressure is mounting and there are bookings for Robbie Brady and Ben Mee. Then on 69 minutes a breakthrough as the much more effective Morata heads home a perfect cross from Willian.

Now the tension is racking up a notch! On 75 minutes, Scotty Arfield is introduced to the fray in place of JBG, and by

77 minutes has found his name in the referee's notebook. Surely though it's all over as in the 81st minute Fabregas collects his second yellow card for a nasty challenge on Jack Cork and he's off! Nine minutes to go, a two-goal lead, and the opposition down to nine men. What could go wrong? As all followers of Burnley FC know, plenty!!!

With Chelsea now throwing all caution to the wind, unbelievably the lead is down to one goal as in the 88th minute David Luiz, probably lucky still to be on the pitch after a typical undisciplined performance, fires home from a Morata headed pass. Surely not, we are not going to be denied at this late stage. There's still time for Robbie Brady to hit the post from a free kick with the keeper well beaten. In the end it matters not as after five added minutes the referee blows time and unbelievably WE HAVE DONE IT!

That result sets up a most enjoyable Saturday evening for all of a Claret persuasion. Nay not just Saturday but the whole of the next week I would imagine. How nice to be first game shown on MOTD and listen to the glowing praises heaped on the Clarets, by none other than Alan Shearer!

It's an unexpected bonus three points that gets the season off in fine style. Last season we took eighteen away games to get a victory, this time we have done it in one, and at the home of the Champions. That is two away victories in the last three Premier League games, let's hope that particular monkey is finally off our back.

Result – Chelsea (Morata 69, Luiz 88) 2 - 3 (Vokes 24,43, Ward 39) Burnley

Burnley Team

Heaton, Lowton, Mee, Tarkowski, Ward, Gudmundsson (Arfield 75), Hendrick, Cork, Defour (Walters 75), Brady, Vokes

<u>Subs Not Used</u> – Pope, Long, Taylor, Westwood, Barnes

Chelsea Team

Courtois, Rudiger, Luiz, Cahill, Azpilicueta, Fabregas, Kante, Alonso, Willian, Boga (Christensen 18, Musonda 90=2), Batshuayi (Morata 59)

<u>Subs Not Used</u> – Caballero, Kenedy, Tomori, Scott

Attendance – 41,616

Season To Date – Played 1, Won 1, Drawn 0, Lost 0, Goals For 3, Goals Against 2, Points 3

League Position after Game 1 – 6th

After that sensational start to the campaign, which certainly had the town of Burnley buzzing, the first home fixture of the new season sees us host West Bromwich Albion. It doesn't seem five minutes since we last played the Baggies here in a game which practically guaranteed our Premier League survival. In fact, it was little over three months since the 2-2 draw at the Turf. On that occasion Sam Vokes netted both Burnley goals, and the currently rampant striker will no doubt be looking to add to his tally.

Game 2 - Saturday 19th August 15.00 – Burnley v West Bromwich Albion

The first home game of the season and a return to the usual pre-match rituals. The ceremonial donning of the 'lucky charms', reinforced with the lucky Clarets Polo shirt and on this occasion Baseball Cap. Then off to the Talbot for a couple of pints of Moorhouses' Premiership Bitter. The team news arrives duly on time courtesy of the BBC Sports App, and to no' one's surprise we are unchanged. Visitors West Bromwich Albion will field new signing and 'one of our own' Jay Rodriguez as their main striker.

Before kick-off rumours are rife that we have at last been successful in our pursuit of Leeds United striker Chris Wood. It appears that a fee of £15m plus add-ons has been agreed between the clubs and he will not feature for Leeds in the teatime game at Sunderland. Apparently a medical is scheduled for Sunday and the signing, should this be passed, will be confirmed on Monday.

On a dry but cool day with a stiff breeze, it feels at times more like November than August and the cap is going to be more useful keeping my head warm than shading it from the sun. In fact, a Bob Cap might have been more appropriate. Anyway, no chance of anybody suffering heat exhaustion in this one.

It's a quiet start and quickly apparent that both teams adopting similar formations are effectively cancelling each other out. WBA are sitting deep and allowing us plenty of possession, but as usual they are proving very difficult to break down. The first half is a game of little goalmouth action with the occasional missed half chance mainly by the Clarets. Perhaps, the most obvious one being a missed close-range header by Ben Mee from a set-piece situation. Half time reached and the game is unsurprisingly goalless.

The second half starts in the same vein but with the visitors showing a little more attacking intent. This is mainly due to Matty Phillips who is proving to be a threat as he operates in a wide right position. The usually calm and collected Stephen Ward is finding him more than a handful and this is curtailing our full back's attacking forays.

However, we seem to have weathered the storm and normal service towards the Albion goal is being resumed. That is until the game changing introduction of WBA striker Hal Robson-Kanu. He goes immediately into the central striking role with the largely ineffectual Jay Rodriguez pushed out wide left. Almost from the outset Robson-Kanu's more physical approach is creating a more potent threat. Then on 71 minutes a telling blow from the recently introduced striker. A hopeful punt upfield is flicked on by Phillips and some woeful defending by the Clarets presents Robson-Kanu with an opportunity which he despatches past Tom Heaton with some aplomb.

There's still sufficient time to save something from this game and Sean Dyche responds on 79 minutes with a double substitution. Jon Walters and Ashley Barnes join the fray at the expense of the two wide men Robbie Brady and Johann Berg Gudmundsson. The chances of salvaging something are further increased on 83 minutes as chief protagonist Robson-Kanu sees red for a nasty elbow in the face of Matt Lowton and exits stage left. This is the signal for a more direct approach and the visitors defence is given a thorough examination as crosses are flung into the box at every opportunity. Once again chances are created but unfortunately frittered, and after four added minutes the referee calls time and we taste defeat for the first time in this campaign.

It's not exactly a case of 'after the Lord Mayor's show' but the result is certainly disappointing and probably undeserved. Profligacy in front of goal is costly in this league, and the statistic of 20 shots with none on target certainly bears this out. It wasn't a bad display but it once again revealed that there are no easy games and any points gained will be hard won. The team received generous applause at the end, the crowd appreciating a good effort that on another day may well have reaped some reward.

Result – Burnley 0 – 1 (Robson-Kanu 71) West Bromwich Albion

Burnley Team

Heaton, Lowton, Mee, Tarkowski, Ward, Gudmundsson (Barnes 79), Hendrick, Cork, Defour, Brady (Walters 79), Vokes

Subs Not Used – Pope, Long, Taylor, Westwood, Arfield

West Bromwich Albion Team

Foster, Nyom, Dawson, Hegazi, Brunt, McClean (Robson-Kanu 63), Livermore, Field (Rondon 85), Barry, Phillips, Rodriguez

Subs Not Used – Myhill, Wilson, Harper, Leko, Chadli

Attendance – 19,619

Season To Date – Played 2, Won 1, Drawn 0, Lost 1, Goals For 3, Goals Against 3, Points 3

League Position after Game 2 – 13th

On Monday 21st the Clarets confirm their fifth major signing, or sixth if goalkeeper Adam Legzdins is included, of this transfer window as Chris Wood joins from Leeds United. He appears to be the player most coveted on Sean Dyche's wish list and is seen as the replacement for the recently departed Andre Gray. Welcome aboard Chris!

EFL (Caraboa Cup) Round 2 – Wednesday 23rd August – Blackburn Rovers v Burnley

As I believe I have said many times in the past, this is a fixture which I am not now overly enamoured with. Back in my youth, a long time ago I hear many say, I would look forward to the keen local rivalry this game would have generated. Unfortunately, over the years the fixture has been hijacked by the 'lunatic fringe'. Alcohol soaked individuals out to cause as much mayhem as possible, all done supposedly in the name of their respective team. Will tonight be different? Once again a major Police operation is in place to preserve order. How sad!

Anyway, to the game. It's a slow start by the Clarets not surprisingly as the team shows eight changes from Saturday's starting eleven. Out goes goalkeeper Tom Heaton, and three defenders, Matt Lowton, Ben Mee and Stephen Ward. In midfield we lose Johann Berg Gudmundsson, Steven Defour and Jeff Hendrick, whilst upfront Sam Vokes is rested. Replacing them are Nick Pope, Phil Bardsley, Kevin Long, Charlie Taylor, Scott Arfield, Ashley Westwood, Ashley Barnes and Jon Walters.

So, its starting places for new boys Bardsley, Taylor and Walters, but new record signing Chris Wood only signed on Monday, has to settle for a seat on the bench. That's a lot of changes but it still looks like a side more than capable of winning this one.

The first 15 minutes are probably best forgotten as the new team finds its shape. However, around the 20 minute mark Barnes draws a good save from the Rovers keeper David Raya and suddenly we have lit the blue touch paper. From this point in and for the rest of the first half the Clarets proceed to take their hapless hosts apart. On 27 minutes, Robbie Brady is the provider for Jack Cork to head the opening goal.

Shortly before half time new signing Wood gets his first taste of Burnley action replacing the injured Walters. Then just before the end of the first period the Clarets extend the lead, this time with the roles reversed. Cork provides the assist for Brady to create his own bit of magic and put the game surely beyond the reach of the increasingly ragged Rovers.

Understandably it's a much quieter second half, Burnley are happy to see the game out, whilst the hosts despite substitutions are incapable of troubling them. Chris Wood on his debut could have had a hat-trick but on this occasion, goes home empty handed. Hopefully he is saving all the goals for the more meaningful encounters yet to come.

The game ends in a comfortable 2-0 victory. The match statistics are pretty comprehensive, Blackburn with three attempts, none on target, ourselves with 13 attempts, nine on target. I think that about sums it up.

The evening is marred as usual by some predictable unsavoury incidents from the spectators, notably a pitch invasion from a Rovers thug following the first goal resulting in an assault on Ashley Westwood. Our own fans were not entirely blameless, one being arrested for setting off a flare which injured a nine-year-old boy following the second goal. Still that is that one out of the way and hopefully a draw against less antagonistic opposition in the next round.

Unfortunately, that's not to be as the Third Round draw, made bizarrely in Beijing at 4.15 am, pairs us with none other than equally hostile near neighbours Leeds United. Talk about out of the frying pan and into the fire!

Result – Blackburn Rovers 0 – 2 (Cork 27, Brady 45+4) Burnley

Burnley Team

Pope, Bardsley, Tarkowski, Long, Taylor, Brady (Gudmundsson 78), Cork, Westwood, Arfield, Walters (Wood 43), Barnes

<u>Subs Not Used</u> – Heaton, Lowton, Mee, Defour, Vokes

Blackburn Rovers Team

Raya, Williams, Ward, Mulgrew, Caddis, Feeney (Conway 45), Smallwood, Whittingham (Samuel 66), Chapman, Antonsson, Gladwin (Bennett 45)

<u>Subs Not Used</u> – Graham, Leutwiler, Evans, Doyle

Attendance – 16,313

That victory over the 'auld enemy' certainly set me up for my annual August Bank Holiday weekend in the Lincolnshire village of Wragby. It's a chance to visit old friends who have retired to the Lincolnshire flatlands, and this year we will be joined by my daughter Stephanie and her partner Tom. With a good weather forecast all seems set fair for a boozy weekend of fun and frivolity.

Well the trip certainly didn't disappoint with some lovely walks, excellent Greek food from a pub in Nettleham and a visit to Woodhall Spa, before commencing the journey home on Sunday afternoon. The enjoyment of course was heightened by the unbroken sunshine for three days with temperatures in the mid-twenties centigrade, a rarity indeed in this awful rain affected summer. Additionally, my stress levels felt the benefit of a blank Saturday for the Clarets as the away trip to Wembley Stadium, the temporary home of our hosts Tottenham Hotspur, was re-scheduled to Sunday afternoon.

Game 3 - Sunday 27th August 16.00 - Tottenham Hotspur v Burnley

Leaving Woodhall Spa around 2.30pm I'm reckoning that, with a bit of assistance from the 'Traffic Gods', I should be hopefully around Radio Lancashire's reception area by the start of the second half. Fortunately, on this occasion the A1(M) going North flows smoothly, apart from the obligatory few mile crawl, this time around Barnsdale Bar. Still in good shape I make the service station at Hartshead Moor in time for a quick comfort break and in time for second half commentary.

Tuning the radio to 95.5 FM it's quickly apparent that Radio Lancashire's airwaves don't yet reach this far-flung outpost of civilisation. Undeterred I switch to Talksport on the AM frequency. All I'm getting here for several minutes is chat concerning Arsenal's inept defending at Liverpool, and

Chelsea's mastery over Everton. Yes, the same Chelsea who not so long ago were taken apart by 'little old Burnley' but who are now once again 'Masters of the Universe'. Conte's crisis, what crisis?

Still I suppose it's a good omen that we are hearing little about our game as it suggests that the expected pounding at the hands of Harry Kane and Dele Alli et al, has not yet materialised. Indeed, as I leave the service area the news is that the half-time score from Wembley is 0-0. I'll settle for that.

Hitting the motorway, I ask Julie to once again try our home station for second half coverage. A big mistake! True to form after not listening for half a game, in which we perform admirably, as soon as I tune in we go a goal behind. A sloppy effort at that! A cross into the box deflects off a player wrong footing Ben Mee who fails to clear and the ball drops invitingly for Alli to fire home. He's not my favourite player I have to admit, and I can visualise the smirk from this distance.

Still, it's not the Burnley way to let heads drop and with plenty of time to go it's not game over. However, it might not be game over, but it seems to be for me as the car radio goes into the most annoying habit of switching frequencies between 95.5 and 103.9. One minute I get coverage from Wembley, next I get 20 minutes of bloody Gerald Jackson's 'Unforgettable' programme. It's definitely unforgettable for me!

The goal unsurprisingly gives the hosts added confidence and their stuttering performance notches up a gear. They are making a number of chances but resolute defending, great goalkeeping and uncharacteristic misses from the usually reliable Kane mean as we approach the final period, we are still in it.

New signing Chris Wood, on as a 57th minute substitute for Johann Berg Gudmundsson, is suddenly beginning to get half-chances as the game opens up. On 81 minutes, a master stroke as Sean Dyche replaces the tiring Steven Defour, with the fresh legs of Ashley Westwood. As Spurs settle for their solitary goal the Clarets start to push forward and the crowd becomes edgy.

By now I am approaching home, the radio signal has thankfully stabilised, and as I turn on to my drive, it's a stoppage time GOAL! Almost causing me to drive into the front door, Chris Wood has latched on to a brilliant through ball from Robbie Brady to level the scores. What a way, and what a game for the new man to score his first Burnley goal. We safely see out the last couple of minutes and for the second Premier League away game running it's an incredible result.

Who would have believed that a team that managed only one away victory last season, would start this one with a win at the Champions, and a deserved draw at the runners-up. Add the spiritually uplifting midweek victory at Blackburn to those two, and it's no wonder Burnley fans are euphoric.

Result – Tottenham Hotspur (Alli 49) 1 – 1 (Wood 90+2) Burnley

Burnley Team

Heaton, Lowton, Mee, Tarkowski, Ward, Gudmundsson (Wood 57), Arfield, Cork, Defour (Westwood 81), Brady, Vokes (Barnes 57)

<u>Subs Not Used</u> – Pope, Long, Taylor, Bardsley

Tottenham Hotspur Team

Lloris, Trippier, Alderweireld, Vertonghen, Davies, Dier, Dembele (Sanchez 90+3), Son Heung-min (Sissoko 70), Alli, Eriksen (Winks 88), Kane

<u>Subs Not Used</u> – Vorm, Walker-Peters, Oakley-Boothe, Janssen

Attendance – 67,862

Season To Date – Played 3, Won 1, Drawn 1, Lost 1, Goals For 4, Goals Against 4, Points 4

League Position after Game 3 – 10th

After the Tottenham Hotspur game, the fans focus switches to the rapidly approaching closure of the summer transfer window. After 11.00 pm on the 31st August the window will 'slam shut' until January 2018. If there are no further additions to, or for that matter departures from, the squad will stay as is until the season's half-way point. As usual most fans have their own ideas as to what or whom are required, and the fans website messageboards are crammed with rumours, suggestions and downright guesses.

It's a popularly held feeling that the prime target should be a centre back as this seems, since the departure of Michael Keane, to be the area least well covered. However, despite various names being bandied about, cometh the hour and no suitable candidate available at the right price is forthcoming. Indeed, the only incoming player is yet another striker, Nahki Wells from Huddersfield at an undisclosed fee but rumoured to be £5m. A bit of a strange signing this, and I think fair to say underwhelming to many supporters. There's no doubt though that Nahki will bring something a little different to our striking options and I for one wish him well in his time at Turf Moor. At £5m in today's inflated transfer market, he may well just turn out to be a first-rate bargain buy.

Thankfully, no senior players leave the club ahead of the deadline, although one or two from the development squad go out on loan deals to lower league clubs to hopefully get some first team experience. Rumours of bids for Ashley Barnes are reportedly rejected and this popular wholeheartedly committed player remains a Claret for the immediate future.

The annual wager referred to earlier in the piece, i.e. the bet between myself and North Ender, Jim (Skipper of the Yard) is once again re-instated after missing a season last time round. For Jim to take the spoils both Preston North End and Burnley must start season 2018/19 in the same division, for myself to win the two teams must be in different ones. Jim seems to feel that we do not have the necessary depth of squad to succeed in our survival quest this time. I myself am more confident than I have ever been that our goal can be achieved, and believe the current squad more than capable. Jim even has the temerity to suggest that North End may even take the Clarets place in the Premier League at the end of this campaign. I shall treat that notion with the contempt it deserves!

A blank weekend coming up as Premier League action gives way to International World Cup qualifiers. So, an eventful and encouraging August comes to an end, and we look forward to the resumption of hostilities with struggling Crystal Palace on Sunday 10th September.

SEPTEMBER

September 5th not only marks the resumption of Tuesday Dotcom walks, but more importantly…it's my Pearl wedding Anniversary. Yes, 30 years of wedded bliss! Back then in 1987, I was a strapping young buck, and my wife Julie a ravishing young beauty. I have to say, not much has changed in those respects - but for Burnley FC things could hardly be more different.

May 1987 saw the Clarets, very much 'down at heel', gain victory in the final game of a tortuous season to ensure their Football League survival. The triumph, in the now famous 'Orient Game', saved our team from dropping out of the league of which they had been one of the 12 original founder members. Failure on that day would quite possibly have meant extinction for our famous old club. From that point on began a steady rebuild of the club from its foundations, to the point where now 30 years on we sit proudly in 10th position of arguably the best league in the world. What a transformation! How fitting that on that fateful day in 1987 Lincoln City should be the team that ultimately took the drop, and that now after three decades they have once again reclaimed their place in the Football League.

Today's Dotcom walk is a scheduled gentle re-introduction following the summer recess. An approximate five-miler, from Hurst Green around Stonyhurst College, is today's planned outing to whet the appetite for the bigger challenges ahead. Needless to say, it rained! Not just gentle summer rain but a deluge of biblical proportions. What an omen for the start of the walking year! Still it was a great opportunity to meet up with old friends and re-ignite the local football rivalries. Conspicuously absent on this occasion was

'Blackburn John' who I was particularly looking forward to discussing our recent 'walkover' victory with. He is purported to be on holiday... we will see! He can't hide forever.

Thank God, we are getting back to normal football this weekend. Watching England labour through the qualifying stages of a World Cup group is like being in a scene from Groundhog Day. Managers come and go, players come and go, but still the action on the pitch is less than inspiring. Sideways, backwards and a bit of time-wasting thrown in, it's all now too familiar. Roll on the 'blood and guts' of Premier League action.

The fact that the upcoming weekend game is re-scheduled for Sunday lunchtime to accommodate Sky TV, affords my wife and myself the opportunity to arrange a brief meet with daughter Stephanie in Harrogate. Stephanie's birthday is fast approaching, and as she will not be coming to Burnley on the date - having a prior booking in Scotland - my wife Julie is taking the chance to indulge her in a little birthday shopping. I say little but nothing about Stephanie's birthday shops is ever little. Anyway, after coughing up for lunch for four, Steph's partner Tom having decided to join the party, I am not in the mood for further expenditure.

Tom and I decide, despite the threat of heavy rain, that we will be better suited enjoying a stroll around Valley Gardens and environs whilst the girls attempt to empty the shops. A strange thing as we enter the gardens as Tom, in a rather mysterious manner, announces he has something of a delicate nature to ask me. Intrigued I bid him to go ahead. At which point he drops the bombshell, somewhat old-fashioned, of asking my permission for Stephanie's hand in marriage!

Momentarily taken aback, and not wishing to appear at first-hand too keen, I tell him I will have to consider the matter. After a suitable wait, all of five seconds, I tell him he can have her hand, and for that matter, the rest of her, with my pleasure. On the way home, I break the news to my wife Julie, who is quietly overjoyed, and we pass the rest of the journey contemplating the financial consequences. Will she accept the proposal apparently to be put in the next couple of weeks? Time will tell, keep reading for the outcome!

Game 4 - Sunday 10th September 13.30 – Burnley v Crystal Palace

A most traumatic experience for me today as I make my way to the game. Leaving home early, and forsaking the pub, I have a pre-match rendezvous arranged with fellow author Dave Thomas. Dave has been having problems obtaining a copy of my third Premier League diary 'There's No Place Like Home' via the Amazon website. So much so that he has cancelled the order and we have come to an agreement that we will meet outside Turf Moor and swap copies of our respective recent publications.

All is going well, apart from the annoying rain, as I near the meeting point at approximately 12.50, 40 minutes ahead of kick-off. Something prompts me to check in my pocket for my Season ticket card. Horror of horrors, there's a card there alright, but it's the wrong one! Instead of gaining me access to the game, it will admit me to the recreational facilities at St Peter's Health & Leisure Centre!

What to do? I must press on and make the rendezvous with Dave, exchange the books, then leg it back to the car about a mile away and drive home. I estimate that this, coupled with finding a car parking space on my return, will mean missing a substantial chunk of the first half. Fortunately, on relating this tale of catastrophe to Dave T he suggests that if I 'come clean' at the ticket office they will print me a paper ticket to gain access. On joining the queue for tickets, I am questioned by a steward as to the nature of my visit to the office. On telling her my tale of woe she assures me that the office will be able to oblige. I am surprised and somewhat heartened that others in the queue have committed the same 'faux-pas'. Suffice it to say that after a very amicable encounter with the ticket office, my day is saved and the need for a return journey avoided. Well done Ticket Office, and well done Dave T!

So, with my nerves settling I'm in good time to take my seat and await the action. It's not long before I'm joined by my next seat neighbours and we indulge in a short pre-match discussion about our team's prospects today. We are both agreed that with our visitors enjoying a dismal start to the campaign, three games, three defeats, no goals scored, our chances by the law of averages are not good. A further spanner is thrown in the works as we lose the toss and are obliged to play the first half attacking the Jimmy McIlroy stand - not our favoured opening direction.

How negative were those feelings? And how wrong as within three minutes we have the lead! A sloppy back pass from Lee Chung-yong is manna from heaven for on fire new Clarets striker Chris Wood. Striding on to it, and with the Palace keeper advancing out of goal, he calmly despatches his shot with unerring accuracy into the 'onion bag'. One up in quick time, just what the doctor ordered. Surely the cue for our demoralised visitors to cave in. Don't you believe it, the game ratchets up a gear and the visitors attack with sustained vigour.

They carry a potent physical threat up front with man mountain Christian Benteke an ever-present aerial threat. Palace are throwing lots of crosses into the box but our defence is holding firm. The pressure is resulting in a fair number of corners for the visitors and the feeling is that one of these will be our downfall. Having said that we are at this stage not without threat ourselves, and from an excellent left-wing attack, Sam Vokes is close to extending the lead with a header narrowly glanced wide of the far post.

The game continues in the same vein with some desperate defending and goal-line clearances from the Clarets until on 36 minutes a potential disaster. Goalkeeper Tom Heaton rises to catch yet another Palace cross but in doing so falls awkwardly over the attendant defenders. A bad landing ensues and Tom is clearly in some distress as a stretcher is called. Fortunately, this is not required and he rises to his feet to be substituted acknowledging the cheers of the fans. An opportunity now arises for Tom's understudy to take a rare opportunity to display his goal minding talents…

It's not long before he's called into action and the young keeper makes a fine save that will do his confidence no harm at all. Half time is reached with the lead still intact but a feeling that a difficult 45 minutes is yet to come.

This indeed proves to be the case, our opponents pressing but our defence resolute. There's precious little attacking threat now from the Clarets and the end seems a long way away. Benteke for once manages to escape the clutches of the once again impressive James Tarkowski but is thwarted by an excellent save from Nick Pope.

The substitutions begin as we try to close the game out and the Eagles attempt to salvage something from the day. On is Ashley Barnes for the tiring Vokes but the formation remains 4-4-2 when perhaps an extra body in the midfield would have been beneficial. Ashley is his customary mix of abrasive industry and occasional skilfulness. A well worked shooting opportunity giving him the chance to fire in a curling left footer, destined for the corner of the net, before a diving stop from Wayne Hennessey in the visitor's goal.

That would surely have sealed the game but it's still a mainly rearguard action for the Clarets. Again, some excellent defending and goal-line clearances keep the lead intact. Nearing full-time the miss of the match as Palace centre back Scott Dann inexplicably guides his header wide from close range. Thank God for that, and after three added minutes it's all over and a relieved Burnley can celebrate their first home points of the season.

Clearly not at our best today, but with the resilience to hold a lead against consistent pressure, it augurs well for the season. Only four games gone and the points tally already up to seven. Only 33 more required for safety! Man of the Match today for me, Jack Cork a faultless midfield exhibition, closely followed by James Tarkowski. A valuable win that takes us up to eighth in the table sitting just above next week's formidable opponents, Liverpool at Anfield.

Result – Burnley (Wood 3) 1 – 0 Crystal Palace

Burnley Team

Heaton (Pope 36), Lowton, Mee, Tarkowski, Ward, Gudmundsson, Cork, Defour (Westwood 82), Brady, Wood, Vokes (Barnes 64)

Subs Not Used – Bardsley, Long, Arfield, Walters

Crystal Palace Team

Hennessey, Ward, Fosu-Mensah, Dann, Schlupp, MCarthur (Riedewald 81), Cabaye, Puncheon, Townsend, Benteke, Lee Chung-yong (Lumeka 65)

<u>Subs Not Used</u> – Speroni, van Aanholt, Kelly, Milivojevic, Kaikai

Attendance – 18,862

Season To Date – Played 4, Won 2, Drawn 1, Lost 1, Goals For 5, Goals Against 4, Points 7

League Position after Game 4 – 7th

In some ways a lucky win, but in others not so. News coming from Sean Dyche in the after-match press conferences is that goalkeeper and club captain Tom Heaton, has suffered a suspected dislocated shoulder. Early indications are that recovery time may well be 10-12 weeks! Tom is such an important player to us that this is a major blow. A chance now for young Nick Pope to show what he is made of.

Tom is not the only person who had something to rue after the day. Crystal Palace manager Frank De Boer was sacked on Monday following the game. What lunacy, the guy had only been in the job for four Premier League fixtures! Admittedly, all had been lost, and without a single goal scored, but give the bloke a chance! It's a cut-throat business for sure is football management, but I don't think Burnley FC would treat their manager in such a cavalier fashion.

Away from the football, Tuesday 12th September offers a bit of a diversion from the usual Dotcomers type walk. Ever trying to educate us and instil a little culture this week's excursion will start with a visit to The King's Lancashire

Regiment Infantry Museum at Fulwood Barracks, Preston. This will be followed in the afternoon with a short walk round rural Fulwood taking in the Ladywell Shrine, and a walk past, but not too close to, David Moyes palatial residence. I have to say the guided tour of the Infantry Museum was extremely interesting and informative, and I would recommend a visit to anybody interested in military history.

Fortunately, in this late summer of monsoon rain conditions, the weather managed to stay fine for what was billed as a 3.5-mile walk, but which I actually measured as five. Mr Moyes has certainly done well for himself with the house, largely hidden from view, accessed via a long tarmac driveway through ancient woodland. It was reputedly purchased by himself for £3.8m in 2006 and is currently believed to be once again on the market. I was of course obliged to appease the North End contingent, by having my photo taken outside the gates. It will go in my collection along with similar outrages taken at the Tom Finney statue, and Finney Lane in Croston.

Friday afforded me the opportunity for a little bit of book promotion for Volume 3 of the Premier League Diaries, 'There's No Place Like Home', with a slot on Radio Lancashire's afternoon show. Once again, I have to thank Dotcom Leader Bob Clare for the use of his many contacts in the media. Thanks to Bob's friendship with John "Gilly" Gillmore I had been invited in as a studio guest. I must confess to feeling a little nervous as I made my way to Blackburn for the 2.00 pm slot, made even more so on arriving and learning that "Gilly" would not in fact be doing the show. However, not to worry as the stand-in presenters, Nishma Hindocha and Carl Hartley, quickly made me feel relaxed and comfortable.

Carl, being a Bolton Wanderers fan, allowed me to land a few 'cheap shots' at our now impoverished neighbours and I also managed a few jibes at Blackburn Rovers. Overall a new and ultimately pleasurable experience for me. Unfortunately, I was goaded by the presenters into describing on-air, my wife as a Clarets jinx. Thinking that she was working at the time I thought I would get away with it. Wrong again, my mother-in-law had heard the interview on her way home and alerted my wife who tuned in at the office. Thankfully she took it in good spirit and I live to tell the tale.

Book promotion done, now just sit back and wait for the sales to go through the roof. Everything nicely set up now for another big test for the Clarets on Saturday as we enter the cauldron of Anfield.

Game 5 - Saturday 16th September 15.00 – Liverpool v Burnley

Well. What can I say! The Clarets, who last season could best be described as hopeless away from home, have only gone and done it again. For the third successive away fixture, we have taken points from a team that finished in last season's Premier League top four. Yes, the opening away games against three Champions League sides have resulted in a return of five points from a possible nine. That is incredible! Our last season's total away points of seven are almost equalled after only three games. We now fear no-one.

Once again, a challenge that on paper appeared a total mismatch, has proved to be nothing of the sort. Liverpool's squad of international superstars, assembled at a mind-blowing cost, have failed to defeat the warriors of Turf Moor. Adding to the magic, this achieved with a rookie goalkeeper making his first full Premier League start. It's a great time to be a Claret.

The game can I suppose be likened to last season's encounter at Turf Moor, where Liverpool bossed the possession and shots at goal statistics, but came away defeated 2-0. This time a similar score on the statistics front but a game ending in a 1-1 draw. Liverpool manager, Jurgen Klopp, must hate the sight of Burnley. Having said that he is always very gracious in his comments and respectful of our performances.

Not unexpectedly Liverpool started the game on the front foot and with their array of attacking talent including the likes of, Philippe Coutinho, Roberto Firmino, Mohamed Salah, and Daniel Sturridge, must have fancied their chances of an early goal. However, this didn't materialise as the Clarets ruthlessly efficient defensive unit shielded Nick Pope in goal with its customary reliability.

Indeed, it's our heroes who take the lead as the Reds defensive frailties are once again exposed. A high ball out to the left wing is won in the air by Robbie Brady who heads it into the box. A sandwich, consisting of two Liverpool central defenders and Chris Wood, miss the ball but as it lands striding into the area is Scott Arfield. Cool as a cucumber Scotty despatches a side-foot shot into the corner of the net and we unbelievably lead on 27 minutes.

Unfortunately, we are unable to hold our precious lead for long, and on 30 minutes it's all square as Salah, a thorn in our side this half, swivels and fires past a helpless Nick Pope. To the home fans this is surely the cue for the expected goal avalanche. However, a combination of fine saves and resolute defending keeps the score level at the break.

The second half is much of the same again, Liverpool pushing hard and firing in plenty of attempts at goal, the Clarets soaking up the pressure and looking for an opportunity to spring a surprise. That chance almost comes with the game entering the final phase.

From a needlessly conceded corner, Ben Mee wins the ball in the air only to see Joel Matip clear off the line. From the resulting corner, it's deja-vu as Mee again outjumps the defence to see his header saved at the post by Simon Mignolet.

From that point Liverpool throw the 'kitchen sink' at us but fine goalkeeping by our new hero Nick Pope keeps the Reds at bay. One brilliant save from Dominic Solanke, almost at the death, has pundit and former top goalkeeper Peter Schmeichel describing it as the 'Save of the Day'. What a joyous day for our Pope, perhaps aided on occasion by divine intervention. He gets his moment in the spotlight with a TV interview on Match of the Day, and boy did he deserve it!

Once again, a magnificent team performance and a triumph for the battling underdogs. Next up two home games this week, Leeds United in the EFL Cup, followed by a Premier League fixture against newly promoted Huddersfield Town. After that its back to Merseyside and a visit to Goodison Park the home of Everton. Can we keep the unbeaten away run going? I certainly wouldn't be betting against it.

Result – Liverpool (Salah 30) 1 – 1 (Arfield 27) Burnley

Burnley Team

Pope, Lowton, Mee, Tarkowski, Ward, Gudmundsson (Barnes 60), Cork, Arfield, Defour (Westwood 87), Brady, Wood (Vokes 87)

<u>Subs Not Used</u> – Legzdins, Bardsley, Long, Walters

<u>Liverpool Team</u>

Mignolet, Alexander-Arnold, Matip, Klavan, Robertson, Milner, Can, Coutinho (Solanke 78), Firmino (Oxlade-Chamberlain 79), Sturridge, Salah

<u>Subs Not Used</u> – Karius, Moreno, Lovren, Henderson, Wijnaldum

<u>Attendance</u> – 53,231

<u>Season To Date</u> – Played 5, Won 2, Drawn 2, Lost 1, Goals For 6, Goals Against 5, Points 8

<u>League Position after Game 5</u> – 7th

If you cast your mind back a few paragraphs you will recall my little conversation with daughter Stephanie's partner Tom. Well, I can confirm that as of Sunday 17th September he is no longer to be regarded as a partner, but will become in the near future, son-in-law Tom. The proposal was put during a short break in Scotland and gleefully accepted. Both sets of parents are highly delighted, and the news caps off a great weekend.

Only problem now, there's a wedding to pay for. I have suggested as a venue Burnley Registry office, with a pie and pea reception at Plumbe St. Miners Club. I doubt somehow that I will get away with that! Still, as yet there's no date fixed so I can breathe easier for a while.

It's Tuesday 19th September and for Stephanie it's her birthday and the last day of her travels in Scotland. For me it's an early start for the Dotcom walk which this week is from Burton in Kendal to Hutton Roof Crags. It's a long trip for the

Burnley contingent but the prospect of some decent weather and fantastic views make the one hour plus journey well worthwhile. A lovely walk in mostly bright sunshine and over mostly well drained limestone terrain, measures out at seven miles. Just time for a beer, Tirrill's Golden Ale, at Longlands Inn & Restaurant at Tewitfield before a quick return trip in time for tea and the Turf.

EFL (Caraboa Cup) Round 3 – Tuesday 19th September 19.45 – Burnley v Leeds United

I've had a long day and all that fresh air has made me a little sleepy as we drive home from Cumbria. Fortunately, Ed 'Sherpa' Walton is at the wheel so there's a chance for a few minutes shuteye. I won't need much rocking tonight so we definitely want a result in 90 minutes, none of that extra-time malarkey.

As expected, lots of changes from both teams as they take the opportunity to give squad members a run-out. Burnley make seven, the survivors from Saturday being Nick Pope, James Tarkowski, Scott Arfield and Johann Berg Gudmundsson (JBG). Our visitors go two better with nine changes following their weekend defeat at Millwall.

It was a fairly lively start from the Clarets attacking the Cricket Field End which is housing 2000+ highly vociferous Tykes. They seem to be venting their spleen every time our left back, Charlie Taylor, late of Leeds United, touches the ball. Taylor seems pretty relaxed about it all and is enjoying some good runs and crosses from the left flank. An early goal would be nice just to quieten the away support.

However, despite our dominance and a number of chances, we are unable to finish any off. Leeds for their part are posing little threat, although the lively and somewhat niggly Kemar Roofe, looks a bit of a handful. I can't really recall a save of note for Nick Pope in the first half, but the sides go in level at half time. During the interval, I remark that the last thing I want is extra time and penalties, and this seems to be the general consensus of opinions.

The second half continues in similar vein but the clock rolls relentlessly on with no sign of a goal. Then a telling substitution by the visitors with the introduction of Hadi Sacko on 60 minutes, taking up a right wing position his pace and trickery start to prove problematic from the off. As I begin to fear we are in for a long night, the substitute turns the game on its head. With the Clarets committed upfield pushing for the winner, a quick counter finds Sacko bearing down on goal. His powerful low right-foot shot is through the legs of Pope and in the net.

I know I didn't want extra time but I hadn't envisaged the deadlock being broken in favour of our visitors. Still there's ten minutes left to save the day, and we are given that opportunity on 89 minutes as a shirt tug on Kevin Long results in a penalty award. No mistake from Burnley substitute Chris Wood, and its 1-1. There's six minutes added time at the end but a late night now must be on the cards.

Not so apparently as on 90+4 minutes a pull on a Leeds shirt in the Burnley box by James Tarkowski gives the referee the opportunity to level the penalty count. No mistake from the Leeds man, and with two minutes to go its 1-2. That must be curtains for us, but incredibly it's not! A foul just outside the penalty area provides an opportunity for another substitute, Robbie Brady, to try one of his specialities. It's not a good idea to give Brady that chance and he duly dispatches a sublime free kick home to level the scores again. Unbelievably we have had four goals in the last 16 minutes, two of them in the final three.

I said I didn't want extras but that's what we get. Thirty minutes of fairly innocuous football produces no more goals and it's down to a penalty shoot-out lottery. What a poor way to end this tie, made even poorer by the fact that Leeds put all five free shots past Pope, whilst Tarkowski's effort is saved by Andy Lonerghan. So, once again our cup run comes to an early end. Which is more than can be said for my day, boy will I sleep tonight.

A game that should have been won slips away, but in the grand scheme of things it's not too great a disaster. I'd much rather we take three points from visitors Huddersfield Town on Saturday in the Premier League fixture. Still, it would have been nice to go a bit further in the competition, but it was not to be. Leeds United return to Yorkshire with a Premier League scalp and will no doubt be well pleased with their night's work.

Result – Burnley (Wood 89 pen, Brady 90+6) 2 – 2 (Sacko 80, 90+4 Hernandez pen) Leeds United. Score After Extra Time 2-2, Leeds United win 5-3 on Penalties.

Burnley Team

Pope, Bardsley, Tarkowski, Long, Taylor, Gudmundsson, Hendrick (Cork 90), Westwood (Defour 120), Arfield (Brady 72), Vokes (Wood 72), Barnes

Subs Not Used – Legzdins, Lowton, Mee

Leeds United Team

Lonerghan, Ayling, Shaughnessy, Berardi, Borthwick-Jackson (Sacko 60), Klich, Vieira, Roofe (Alioski 104), Grot (Lasogga 85), Dallas, Cibicki (Hernandez 79)

Subs Not Used – Wiedwald, Gomes, Phillips

Attendance – 11,799

Thursday 21st September is a sad day for Lancashire Dotcom Walkers, and particularly the Burnley Contingent, as we say goodbye to one of our stalwarts. Teresa Preedy's funeral is scheduled for today. Teresa, who has accompanied husband Dave twice weekly on most walks since July 2012, sadly passed away after an illness bravely borne. She was a courageous woman and the epitome of positivity and kindness. A real star who will be sadly missed by all who knew her. A huge turnout for her send-off is assured.

Game 6 - Saturday 16th September 15.00 – Burnley v Huddersfield Town

Home games against Huddersfield are always enjoyable for me as it means a chance to meet up with a contact from my now long forgotten working past. When you retire its often not the work you miss but some of the people. One such person is an old pal Rob Waterworth, a good guy with a sharp Yorkshire sense of humour, and an ardent Terriers fan. Rob, since their Wembley Championship play-off final triumph in May 2017, has been in his own words 'living the dream'. A good start to life in the Premier League sees the Town come to our town sitting in sixth place, currently one place above us in the league on goal difference. Let's hope he's living less of a dream as he wends his way homewards to darkest Yorkshire after 5.00 pm.

Having arranged to meet him at 2.00 pm at the Talbot Hotel, and advising him to cautiously cover up his Huddersfield Town shirt as best he can, Rob is predictably running late. Not for the first time he has underestimated the amount of time to make a twenty something mile journey to Burnley on match day. Still, after a couple of hasty phone calls to direct him to a suitable parking spot, he arrives in time for a quick pint of Guiness (paid for as usual by yours truly) ahead of the game. Pints duly downed, and reminiscences of old colleagues exchanged, we head for the ground and bid farewell till the return fixture at the Kirklees Stadium.

Rob's parting shot was to express the hope that we see a good open attacking game. Unfortunately, that was not to be the case. Burnley returned to a 4-5-1 formation which has been quite successful of late, but on this occasion, they could make little impact on their dogged visitors. In a dour first half perhaps shaded by the Clarets, neither side managed to force a save from the respective goalkeepers. Defences were well on top, and the guile needed to craft a decent opening was sadly missing. Probably the best chance of the half fell to the Clarets when a well worked move down the left gave Chris Wood, stealing in between two defenders, a headed opportunity unfortunately glanced wide.

The second half produced more of the same, with the exception that perhaps our visitors gained the upper hand. There were a couple of fairly routine saves for the respective keepers, but the only moment of real note was sparked by Terriers substitute Rajiv van La Parra. Operating in a left-wing role, he raced onto a pass on the left-hand side of the penalty area. Matt Lowton across to cover pulled out of a risky challenge, but the pacy winger had already decided he was going down. A blatant dive when ironically, he could have got a shot away, left him embarrassingly yellow-carded by the referee. Sean Dyche was singularly unimpressed by the stunt and condemned the action vociferously as cheating in his after-match comments. It's probably as well it happened as he may well have struggled to find anything else to talk about!

'Man of the Match' went to Steven Defour for an energetic and purposeful display. Defour is a much more motivated player this season than last and is now established as a key member of the team. All-in-all a poor game with honours probably just about even. Another valuable result for both teams in their quest to keep the points tally rolling in their quest for survival. It wasn't a game that will linger long in the memory, but that's still only the one defeat in this fledgling Premier League season and we remain optimistic about our chances.

Result - Burnley 0 - 0 Huddersfield Town

Burnley Team

Pope, Lowton, Mee, Tarkowski, Ward, Arfield (Gudmundsson 77), Cork, Defour, Hendrick (Barnes 74), Brady, Wood

Subs Not Used - Legzdins, Bardsley, Long, Westwood, Vokes

Huddersfield Town Team

Lossi, Smith, Jorgensen, Schindler, Lowe, Mooy, Hogg (Billing 80), Kachunga (Hadergjonaj 89), Sabiri (van La Parra 63), Ince, Depoitre

Subs Not Used - Green, Malone, Whitehead, Hefele

Attendance - 20, 759

Season To Date – Played 6, Won 2, Drawn 3, Lost 1, Goals For 6, Goals Against 5, Points 9

League Position after Game 6 – 9th

A weekend visit from my daughter Stephanie and son-in-law to be Tom, left my head reeling from talk of wedding guests, wedding venues, flowers, table decorations et al. All this and not even a date set yet, but suggested as some time in 2019! I fear a long road ahead, time to keep my head down and pray for a lottery win!

The Huddersfield Town game completed the set of fixtures for September and a satisfactory return of points was achieved. Only three Premier League fixtures in the month, and we are unbeaten in those. A home victory over pointless, so far, Crystal Palace, followed by a magnificent away point at Liverpool, then the draw with Huddersfield yielded five points from the possible nine. It's early days yet but nine points from the first six games sets us up nicely to beat the forty-point survival target. Although it's probably best not to get too carried away yet, 'there's many a slip twixt cup and lip'.

No midweek Clarets action provides an opportunity to update those of you who like to follow the walking calendar. Tuesday's Dotcom walk was scheduled as a lovely walk from Dunsop Bridge in the Trough of Bowland. With Group leader Bob Clare sunning himself in Puerto Pollensa on yet another holiday, the opportunity to lead this one fell to a 'novice leader', relative newcomer Tom Rice. No, not the one that writes musicals with Andrew Lloyd Webber, that's Tim Rice. This one is of the Red persuasion. No, not a communist, a follower of Liverpool FC, but we'll forgive him that. If we can tolerate a Rover, a Scouser is no big deal.

Assembling on the car park at Dunsop Bridge I am informed quietly by Tom that he thinks the walk will pan out at about 8.5 miles. Now this is slightly longer than a normal Tuesday walk, and with some knowledge of the terrain I can't help but suspect that some might find the outing a little challenging. It's a fine day for a change but Tom does suggest that waterproof overtrousers might be considered, as some of the route will pass through waist high bracken, which may be wet. Being tough, and water-resistant Burnley Lads, we decide to ignore Tom's advice and just 'go for it'.

The first half of the walk is easy, leaving Dunsop Bridge heading up alongside the River Dunsop on mainly tarmacadam track. From experience I knew as we headed up Costy Clough that the next part would be interesting. At this point we have to cross what on a previous excursion had been what could best be described, as a raging torrent. On that occasion it had taken a great deal of assistance by the 'Sherpa' Waltons to enable the party to ford the stream. With a party approaching 20 in number, this time it could get difficult. Fortunately, the volume of water on this occasion was not so great and all crossed without a single drowning. Also, Tom's 'wet bracken' turned out to be in fact very dry bracken, having benefitted from the autumnal sunshine. So on in good spirits to Whitendale and hopefully soon a lunch stop.

However, it is decreed that lunch will be taken a little further on the route, so we start the stiff climb out of Whitendale en route to Brennand Farm. It's certainly a climb that sorts the men from the boys (and girls), but we are driven on by the thrilling prospect of lunch on a 'grassy knoll' as described by Major Tom. It's also noticeable that the underfoot conditions appear to be deteriorating as we hit some boggy ground on the way to Far Pasture. Nevertheless, lunch is reached and all is well. We are assured by our leader at this point that "its downhill all the way from here".

Never before have truer words been spoken! Fortified by lunch we attempt to pick our way across sodden fields downhill towards Brennand Farm. Thankfully my dainty footsteps are keeping me on relatively 'terra firma' as I skip over the increasingly marsh like terrain. Not so fellow Burnley man Mike McDevitt. Mike has opted, rather daringly I think for shorts on this walk. As it happens this turns out to be a wise choice as he puts one foot in a bog and sinks slowly to his knee in cloying smelly mud, flavoured by bovine animal droppings. For a moment it looks like he is trapped by the mud, and may require assistance. That's not a prospect I am relishing, but fortunately with a mighty heave he manages to extricate himself. Mike is now displaying a classic two-tone look, one leg brown (and smelly) to the knee whilst the other is speckled white.

He however is fortunate, as a quick look back reveals Ed 'Sherpa' Walton, not opting for shorts, now encased in the glutinous bog soup to thigh level on both legs. That is the cue for much mirth, and some pointed ribbing of leader Tom for his guidance. Not being one's to hide their feelings there are a cacophony of jibes aimed at our poor 'rookie leader'. With threats that he will be reported back to Gruppenfuhrer Bob, currently sipping Margaritas in the Balearics. Tom still smiling but looking increasingly concerned can do nought but grin and bear it.

On reaching the Brennand River, Sherpa Walton ends his ordeal by dropping down to the water side, debagging from his trousers, at the same time displaying a natty pair of M&S underpants, and washing the aforementioned odorous 'keks' in the river. Not a pretty sight but still observed and photographed by all Dotcomers present. I am awaiting reports of poisoned fish downstream as I write. Perhaps we should have heeded the suggestion of overtrousers after all!

From here on in its an uneventful stroll in pleasant sunshine back to Dunsop Bridge. The day is rounded off with foaming pints of ale in the Higher Buck at Waddington, by which time Ed's trousers have lost their excess moisture if not their excess odour. A great day out, and a walk that will take its place in Dotcom Walkers folklore. I hope Tom recovers from the barbs and takes up the leadership challenge again 'ere long.

Thursday's Burnley Contingent walk turned out a much tamer affair. Eight hardy souls left from the site of the former Bairdtex weaving mill at Hollin Hall, Trawden, for a lovely 6.75-mile stroll. Once again, the weather was kind and the sun shone as we made our way via the Pennine Bridleway, and Bronte Way to the Atom panopticon, our lunch stop. After lunch the route continued through Wycoller and back to Trawden for once again beer at the excellent Trawden Arms. Naylor's Gold Ale was the choice of the day and didn't disappoint.

OCTOBER

As a result of Everton's Europa Cup game on Thursday we are once again scheduled for a Sunday game this weekend. Everton manager Ronald Koeman must be entering this game under increasing pressure. His team, after a large cash injection to fund summer transfers, is at the moment seriously underperforming. Indeed, the Europa cup tie with unfavoured Cypriot side, Apollon Limassol, resulted in a disappointing 2-2 draw at Goodison Park. Despite their new signings they are still to gel as a team, and are seriously missing striker Romelu Lukaku sold to Manchester United in the last window. Ahead of the game they sit fifth bottom of the Premier League. Let's hope we can ratchet up the pressure a little more.

Game 7 - Sunday 1st October 14.15 – Everton v Burnley

Another bizarre kick-off time today, once again to accommodate our Lords and Masters, the TV companies. I decide to have a go at picking up a live stream on my Android Digi (Dodgy) box, but alas after much searching have to concede defeat. It looks like another afternoon of nerve shredding commentary by Radio Lancashire. Still it's good to hear the old familiar voice of our favourite Scouser, ex Claret David Eyres, who sits in as summariser for this one. He must feel a little divided about this game as he is well known to be a lifelong fan of the 'Toffees'. To be fair though he is not showing anything other than commitment to the Clarets cause today. Good man!

Everton, not surprisingly after no doubt presumably 'harsh words' this week, start the game in determined fashion. However, our defence, resolute as ever, repels the early pressure comfortably. As we hit the twenty-minute mark the game is swinging back on a more level keel. Then on 21 minutes a moment of sublime magic from the Clarets. A move consisting of 24 passes ends with Jeff Hendrick sidestepping a weak Everton challenge and side-footing home from 15 yards. Yet again, for the third time in four away games, we have a precious lead.

Expecting a reaction from our hosts that doesn't materialise, we gradually take control of the game from this point. Despite the usual deficit on possession statistics, we are comfortably running the game and looking the more likely scorers. A slow build up and lack of cohesion upfront by the Toffees is meat and drink for outstandingly well-organised rearguard. Half time is reached with consummate ease, but there's still a long way to go.

Surely, Everton can't be so tame in the second half as they were in the first? The teams emerge unchanged for the second period and normal service is soon resumed. Clearly their game plan is not suited to their personnel and changes are surely needed to affect an improvement. These duly come with the introduction of old 'warhorse' Wayne Rooney, and young 'whippersnapper' Tom Davies. The changes spark a bit more emergency from the Blues but we continue along in a relatively unperturbed fashion towards the end. The final 10 minutes see a build-up of pressure from the increasingly desperate hosts. This is accompanied by frivolous penalty claims lodged in an effort to pressurise the referee.

Thankfully he is having none of it and we come away with yet another thoroughly deserved away victory. Last season one from 19, this time two from the first four! We now have more away points from four fixtures than we amassed in the whole of last season. There is no doubt there is a growing belief in this bunch of players, and today's magnificent result takes us on to 12 points, and up to sixth place! Everton left the field to a resounding chorus of boos and further question marks over Koeman's future.

Result – Everton 0 – 1 (Hendrick 21) Burnley

Burnley Team

Pope, Lowton, Mee, Tarkowski, Ward, Arfield, Cork, Defour, Hendrick (Barnes 88), Brady, Wood

<u>Subs Not Used</u> – Lindegaard, Bardsley, Long, Westwood, Gudmundsson, Vokes

Everton Team

Pickford, Martina, Keane, Williams, Baines, Gueye, Schneiderlin (Rooney 63), Vlasic (Davies 69), Calvert-Lewin, Niasse (Ramirez 82), Sigurdsson

<u>Subs Not Used</u> – Stekelenberg, Holgate, Klaassen, Lookman

Attendance – 38,448

Season To Date – Played 7, Won 3, Drawn 3, Lost 1, Goals For 7, Goals Against 5, Points 12

League Position after Game 7 – 6th

What a magnificent result, the first win at Goodison since 1976, we are laying some bogeys this time around. A great way to go into yet another international weekend break. Far better to return to league action on a high, rather than depressed after a defeat. Confidence should be high for the home fixture with West Ham United, another team whom we are overdue a result against.

The Match of the Day team of Mark Chapman, Danny Murphy and Matthew Upson are full of praise for our performance, and we even manage to make the first game slot, albeit with only three to choose from. For the second time in the space of a few weeks James Tarkowski is singled out for a special feature. 'Tarky' is certainly making an impact after his long wait as understudy to Michael Keane, and his reputation is growing fast.

His plaudits are clearly well deserved, but I'm sure he would be the first to admit that our current success is not down to individuals but rather to the collective effort. Teamwork and organisation is the key to our achievement, and with everybody pulling in the same direction, we are proving that results can be attained without spending unimaginable sums of money. Ex Claret Michael Keane must surely at the moment be feeling that the other man's grass is not always greener as he struggles to adjust to his new surroundings. A good player and level-headed lad is 'Keano' and all will come right for him before long.

Game 8 - Saturday 14th October 15.00 – Burnley v West Ham United

Back refreshed from my week in sunny Madeira, and having escaped the tedium of watching England's stuttering World Cup qualifiers, I'm ready for this one. In recent seasons we haven't enjoyed much success against the Hammers. However, with the team's confidence high following the win at Everton, I am reasonably optimistic today. It's even warm enough for pre-match pints outside the Talbot without being kitted out in thermals! A good sign.

The Clarets unsurprisingly are unchanged following the Everton game, but as the team news comes through I note that West Ham will play their one-man wrecking ball, Andy Carroll, up front. Bit of a 'loose cannon' is Mr Carroll, dangerous on his day but flawed in temperament and always flirting with red card danger.

An even start to the game with both sides looking to get on the front foot, the Hammers no doubt buoyed by their victory here in the last home fixture of last season. Then on 19 minutes a bit of a disaster occurs for the Clarets. A long clearance from goalkeeper Joe Hart has me on the edge of my seat as it bisects our central defensive pair. Ben Mee fails to cut out the danger and the pacey Michail Antonio is through on goal. It looks to me that Nick Pope has managed to stop the shot but he has only taken the pace and direction off it and the striker carries on to round him and score. Not the sort of start we wanted.

It has to be said that at this stage of the game our visitors are not shy of a physical challenge, or a histrionic dive. Unfortunately, the aforementioned liability that is Andy Carroll is about to display his suicidal tendencies. On 25 minutes he challenges for a high ball and catches James Tarkowski with his 'trademark' elbow. Despite his, or perhaps because of his vehement protestations of innocence, referee Stuart Attwell has no option other than to yellow card him. Not content with that, our petulant friend repeats his performance within 99 seconds, this time Ben Mee being the recipient. What choice has Attwell now? It's a second yellow and the long walk back to the player's tunnel for Andy.

Well that couple of minutes of stupidity have definitely altered the course of the game. The Hammers game-plan is now completely out the window and they now have to face an hour of the game with a one-man disadvantage. This I suppose also alters our plan. We now are faced with the challenge of having to break down defensively minded opponents, who are still dangerous on the counter.

For the remainder of the half its plenty of possession from ourselves but little penetration. There are a number of shots but mainly from long range and too high to trouble the England keeper Hart. One possible chance as half time nears sees Chris Wood, moving onto a through ball, thwarted by Hart's dive at his feet. Is it a penalty? From my seat I'm not sure, but the referee and his assistant give Hart the benefit of the doubt awarding a corner instead. This comes to nought and we trail at the half-way mark 1-0.

It's clear that we need to change something for the second period. West Ham will continue to try and absorb the pressure, waste time and counter swiftly. Our formation whilst giving us plenty of possession is not threatening sufficiently and Wood is short of support. Sean Dyche addresses this at half time by switching back to 4-4-2 with Sam Vokes going up alongside Wood, and Johann Berg Gudmundsson (JBG) replacing Scott Arfield.

The early exchanges show little sign of change and the visitors are still looking dangerous on the break. However, as the game goes on and legs start to tire we are gaining the ascendancy. An extremely close call as the lively JBG fires in a cracking effort from distance. His shot is too good for Hart but unfortunately not good enough to beat the post, from which it rebounds to the grounded but grateful goalkeeper.

With time running out and the Hammers intent on wasting as much of it as possible, I am beginning to fear a blank return today. Then on 85 minutes a sublime moment. JBG, with two defenders for company, takes on his full back and heads for the by-line, his pinpoint right foot cross is perfect for the incoming Wood who makes no mistake with his header from the centre of goal. A mighty outpouring of relief and elation greets the goal. Thank God for that!

Unfortunately, today God's benevolence can't stretch to two and we have to settle for a point. Still that moves us on to 13 from eight games and the unbeaten run now stretches to six. Manchester City, 7-2 home victors today over Stoke City, are next up at the Etihad Stadium. Hopefully they won't find our lads such a soft touch!

Match of The Day TV replays later that night show that Hart's dive at the feet of Wood should in fact have incurred a penalty. Wood clearly reaches the ball ahead of Hart's diving challenge which then wipes him out. Well… Sean Dyche is a great believer that over the course of the season these decisions even themselves out. In that case referees you owe us one!

Result – Burnley (Wood 85) 1 – 1 (Antonio 19) West Ham United

Burnley Team

Pope, Lowton, Mee, Tarkowski, Ward (Barnes 81), Arfield (Gudmundsson 45), Cork, Defour, Hendrick (Vokes 45), Brady, Wood

Subs Not Used – Lindegaard, Taylor, Long, Westwood

West Ham United Team

Hart, Zabaleta, Fonte, Reid, Cresswell, Antonio, Lanzini (Masuaku 88), Kouyate, Arnautovic (Obiang 45), Carroll, Hernandez (Sakho 75)

<u>Subs Not Used</u> – Adrian, Ogbonna, Noble, Ayew

<u>Attendance</u> – 20,945

<u>Season To Date</u> – Played 8, Won 3, Drawn 4, Lost 1, Goals For 8, Goals Against 6, Points 13

<u>League Position after Game 8</u> – 7th

There is no rest for the wicked, or so they say. Having returned from Madeira on Friday night Sunday is taken up with preparing daughter Stephanie's (now exiled in Darlington) bedroom for a major refit. It's a race against time to clear her 28 years' worth of accumulated junk out of one small room and into an even smaller one, in order to give the bedroom fitters of GM Fitted Furniture (yes, they of the sponsored added time at Turf Moor) a sporting chance.

For some reason as we empty the drawers in the bottom of the bed, four Duvets emerge. Why four I hear you ask? The answer is no-one knows, the assumption is however that because the first one was hidden beneath the bed a second was purchased. The process of storage (hiding) and repurchasing has then continued. No wonder I am skint!

Following the transference of said junk from one room to another, bedroom wallpaper stripping then becomes the next job on the agenda. In the natural course of events this will be followed by, removal of carpet and underlay, repair of walls, cleaning of paintwork and re-painting, wallpaper selection and hanging, carpet selection and fitting, and finally new bed selection and installation. Then of course re-patriation of aforementioned junk to its newly decorated abode. Is it all worth it I hear you ask?

Needless to say, the commencement of all this enforced labour seriously curtails this week's walking activities and as the bedroom fitters are due Wednesday, this week's Tuesday Dotcom walk is an early casualty. GM's fitters make light work of their part of the bargain, but my workload is still in its infancy. It looks like Thursday's Burnley contingent walk will also have to be sacrificed. That's a shame as the plan is for the annual October walk from Settle to see the salmon leaping on the River Ribble at Stainforth Force.

Fortunately, as I offer to do the honourable thing and miss the walk, my wife God bless her, insists that I must go. I must confess the prospect of missing out on Bacon Baps at Elaine's Tea Rooms at Feizor had rather dampened my spirits. My reprieve from the domestic drudgery however soon has them restored, and on a mild Thursday morning we depart for Settle.

The forecast is for light rain coming in about 2.00 pm becoming heavier by 3.00. The first three mile stint is swiftly conquered and the pre-lunch stop at the tea rooms is, as usual, enjoyed by all and we carry on for the next three mile stretch to Little Stainforth and lunch by the river. The salmon once again don't disappoint as they pursue their upriver battle against the raging torrent. By now the promised light rain has arrived but undaunted we eat soggy sandwiches with a cheerful demeanour.

The last stretch down river back to Settle sees the rain's intensity increase as promised. By the time we reach the vehicles I now have the unusual sensation of water running down the inside of my trousers (I hope it was water). Back at the car an excellent suggestion by one of my colleagues. *"Why don't you zip off the trouser bottoms?"* Good idea, I am much more comfortable now as I only have a wet area from my crotch to my knees! A fellow walker, Maureen, who shall remain nameless to protect her anonymity, goes one better and debags completely to her underwear before putting on her perfectly dry waterproof trousers, which she had carried around in her bag throughout the deluge. This public debagging thing seems to be developing into a worrying fashion, with Ed 'Sherpa' Walton setting the trend on the recent outing at Dunsop Bridge. Other members of the party, being less adventurous, merely rolled up their trouser legs. Heaven knows what the residents of Stackhouse Lane must have made of it all.

Suitably re-attired we adjourned to the nearby Harts Head Hotel in Giggleswick for liquid refreshment. I opted for a pint of Blond Rogue from the Brew Monkey Beer Company of Skipton and it was first class! This establishment has been very tastefully refurbished, and with its excellent location and good choice of real ales, will certainly be re-visited in the near future.

Game 9 - Saturday 21st October 15.00 – Manchester City v Burnley

Well, they certainly don't come any tougher than this one! Our terrific away form, with wins at Chelsea and Everton, and draws at Tottenham Hotspur and Liverpool, was surely going to be in for a serious testing. City are in terrific form and already looking like Champions elect. So far, they had amassed 22 points from a possible 24, and were in unstoppable goal scoring form. Their last three home Premier League fixtures had yielded no less than 17 goals, with five coming against Liverpool, five more against Crystal Palace and all topped off with seven last week at home to Stoke City. A daunting prospect indeed!

However, Sean Dyche's teams fear no-one, they respect the opposition but are not overawed and will make the City slickers fight for everything they get. Once again, the Clarets are unchanged for this one. Our illustrious hosts on the other hand, have the luxury of ringing the changes from their expensively assembled squad of superstars.

A quiet start to the game sees the Clarets giving as good as they are getting. There's no sign of an early collapse as our excellently martialled defensive framework copes admirably with the threat of Kevin de Bruyne, Sergio Aguero, Leroy Sane, and David Silva et al. Indeed, it's Burnley who fashion the best early chance as Chris Wood battles his way through for his shot to be smothered by City keeper Ederson. Scott Arfield fails to put away the loose ball after being adjudged to have impeded the keeper. That's almost the last we see of Wood as rather worryingly the impressive new striker departs with what appears to be a hamstring injury. He is replaced by Ashley Barnes, our only striking substitute on the bench, due to the absence of the injured Sam Vokes.

However, a defining moment on 30 minutes as Nick Pope saves brilliantly from De Bruyne. Bernardo Silva is first to the loose ball but as he is pursued by Pope, he tumbles theatrically to the ground and referee Roger East points to the penalty spot. Later TV replays show that there is minimal contact by the keeper and the official is conned into the decision by Silva's dive. How irritating is that? Last week a much clearer case as Joe Hart brings down Chris Wood is not given. It really is astonishing how many of these 50/50 decisions go the way of the so-called 'bigger club'. Just when we need a bit of help from the referee we are once again denied. Needless to say, Aguero dispatches the spot kick and we are one down.

Clearly incensed at the unjust penalty decision, for a short spell we are in danger of losing our customary defensive calm, but fortunately our discipline is maintained, and we recover our shape. Half time arrives with no further damage to the score line and we are still in the game.

Indeed, it's an impressive start to the second period as we go looking for the equaliser. We are pushing City back but unfortunately without the guile to create a gilt-edged chance. Inevitably as the half wears on City regain their control and in the space of two minutes, as the match enters its latter stages, the game is effectively over for us.

Firstly, Nicolas Otamendi rises highest to power a header goalward from a corner. Despite Steven Defour's positioning on the post the ball eludes him and the lead is extended to two. There's worse to follow as Sane takes advantage of yet another defence splitting pass from De Bruyne to finish emphatically.

Thankfully there are no more goals and although it seems a contradiction in terms, we end the game with a creditable defeat! In the context of City's excellent form and demolition of much more fancied teams than ourselves, there is no dishonour in this result. A poor refereeing decision has in no way helped our cause, but a very brave performance with rookie keeper Pope once again impressive, leaves me feeling not too deflated. City extend their lead at the top of the division to five points as chief rivals Manchester United go down 2-1 to newly promoted Huddersfield Town. I bet that ruined Jose Moaninho's weekend!

Result – Manchester City (Aguero 30 pen, Otamendi 73, Sane 75) 3 – 0 Burnley

Burnley Team

Pope, Lowton, Mee, Tarkowski, Ward, Arfield, Cork, Defour (Westwood 84), Hendrick, (Gudmundsson 71) Brady, Wood (Barnes 20)

Subs Not Used – Lindegaard, Bardsley, Taylor, Long, Westwood

Manchester City Team

Ederson, Walker, Stones, Otamendi, Delph, Fernandinho (Y Toure 78), De Bruyne (Gundogan 80), Silva, Bernardo Silva, Aguero (Jesus 76), Sane

Subs Not Used – Bravo, Danilo, Mangala, Sterling

Attendance – 54,118

Season To Date – Played 9, Won 3, Drawn 4, Lost 2, Goals For 8, Goals Against 9, Points 13

League Position after Game 9 – 8th

It looks like an interesting week ahead for the Clarets! The managerial merry go-round kicked into gear on Tuesday 17th October as Leicester City dispensed with the services of Craig Shakespeare. A dour home draw with West Bromwich Albion was enough to convince the owners that after eight games, poor old Craig was not the man for them! Still, he did get twice as many as Frank de Boer at Crystal Palace. Almost immediately there is media speculation that Sean Dyche may be a target.

On Sunday 22nd Everton were humiliated in front of their home fans by Arsenal, dumping the Toffees into a relegation spot in the bottom three. After a summer spend in the region of £140m, this was clearly not what the owners had in mind. The following day Ronald Koeman was asked to pack his bags and another managerial vacancy opened up.

Also skating on thin ice is Slaven Bilic at West Ham United. Without the suspended Andy Carroll following his Turf Moor assaults, they lose heavily at home to newly promoted Brighton and the murmurings of discontent are audible from here. They're not exactly blowing bubbles at the Hammers right now, more like blowing raspberries. It looks distinctly possible that a third vacancy may well arise before the week is out.

Unsurprisingly, Sean Dyche is being mentioned as a possible candidate for all the available, and soon to be available jobs. And, why would he not be? His team, possibly the least expensively assembled outfit in the division, sit comfortably in the top half of the table. Eight points have been gleaned away from home at five of the country's top clubs and there is a real air of positivity about the club.

I can't honestly see Leicester City or West Ham United having much attraction for Sean despite their more generous operating budgets. However, Everton may well be a cause for concern if they are indeed looking in this direction. Some would argue that it would be nonsensical to jump ship from probably the safest manager's job in the Premier League, to join teams that fire managers at the drop of a hat. Yet, Sean Dyche would no doubt be able to negotiate himself a three-year contract at significantly higher remuneration than he currently enjoys. If indeed he only lasted a matter of months, he would be entitled to a massive compensation package and would no doubt be back in work as soon as he was available.

So, it could get a bit nervy for Burnley fans this week. Let's hope that Sean is keen to carry on with his development of our team and training facilities and establish the club as a truly Premier League outfit. I suppose one consideration may be that at any other club he may not enjoy the autonomy over all the many facets of the club which he currently enjoys here. Fingers crossed he will lead us out at Turf Moor on Monday 30th October for the home game against Newcastle United.

Game 10 - Monday 30th October 20.00 – Burnley v Newcastle United

Well it's Monday night so it must be time for football! We have Saturday lunch time football, Saturday teatime football, Sunday lunch time football, Sunday afternoon football, here at Burnley Tuesday midweek football, but not today! To appease our Lords and masters at Sky TV tonight we have Monday night football! What is more we even have a later start than usual, kicking off at 8.00pm. That's nearly my bedtime.

Still, it's a fine night and a surprisingly large crowd for an evening televised game. Chris Wood is an absentee for the Clarets, carrying an hamstring injury, and Ashley Barnes deputises, with Sam Vokes and Nahki Wells waiting in the wings on the substitutes bench. Johann Berg Gudmundsson (JBG) is preferred on the flank to Scott Arfield, but apart from that it's the usual eleven.

Our visitors Newcastle United have made a good start to life back in the Premier League and currently sit one point and one place above us in the table. A close fought encounter should be the order of the day (or night). Uncharacteristically we are attacking the Bee Hole end goal, or should I say Jimmy McIlroy stand goal, for the first period. I hope that is not going to prove a bad omen. There's no sign of that though as Jeff Hendrick flashes an early chance across the face of the goal.

After that early rush of blood the game settles into what is becoming a familiar pattern at Turf Moor. The not so fancied, i.e. teams outside the top six, are wary of last season's impressive home form and our ability to soak up pressure and counter attack. The opposition are invariably 'setting up' in a similar fashion to ourselves and looking to play us at our own game. It soon becomes clear that this is unlikely to be a high-scoring contest.

I remark to my fellow Claret John W that the game is beginning to resemble a chess match. Both sides are probing the defences, but always mindful of their own vulnerability they are keeping numbers back in midfield and defence. We are enjoying a lot of possession but are being kept, in the main, at distance. It's fascinating but frustrating to watch as both side's tactics continue to cancel each other out.

Half time is reached with the score unsurprisingly at 0-0, and I head off onto the concourse to purchase a cuppa to keep out the chill.

The second half continues in much the same vein, with both teams holding the upper hand for short spells but with not much to pick between them. As the game wears on its Burnley gaining the upper hand and then the defining moment of class. The Magpies lose possession and the impeccable Jack Cork is on to it in a flash. Driving into the box he unleashes a fierce shot that keeper Rob Elliott can only parry, the ball falling to JBG. The Icelander takes a quick look up and seeing Hendrick at the 'back stick' finds him with unerring accuracy and he has an easy job to fire home.

It was always looking like a game that would be decided by a single goal and this turns out to be the case. The Geordies stung into action by the goal start to take the game to us but we are dangerous on the counter. Nick Pope makes some telling stops and at the other end Elliott defies Ashley Barnes with a good save. Without too much anxiety we close the game out and the points are ours.

Some terrific individual performances in this game from Cork, Matt Lowton, James Tarkowski, and a tireless battling effort from Barnes. However, once again the success was not down to individuals but more to a tremendous team effort. We have a very solid set up now and only two defeats from the first ten league fixtures is confirmation of that. The result lifts us back to seventh position in the table, level on points with sixth placed Liverpool. Sixteen points from ten games is an impressive haul, theoretically only 24 more needed to avoid the drop. With just over a quarter of the season gone we are in good shape!

Result – Burnley (Hendrick 74) 1 – 0 Newcastle United

Burnley Team

Pope, Lowton, Mee, Tarkowski, Ward, Gudmundsson, Cork, Defour (Westwood 76), Hendrick, Brady, Barnes

Subs Not Used – Lindegaard, Bardsley, Long, Arfield, Vokes, Wells

Newcastle United Team

Elliott, Yedlin, Lascelles, Lejeune, Manquillo, Shelvey, Diame (Gayle 83), Ritchie (Murphy79) Perez (Hayden 76), Atsu, Joselu

<u>Subs Not Used</u> – Darlow, Clark, Gamez, Saivet

Attendance – 21,031

Season To Date – Played 10, Won 4, Drawn 4, Lost 2, Goals For 9, Goals Against 9, Points 16

League Position after Game 10 – 7th

This fixture coincided with Sean Dyche's fifth anniversary as Burnley FC Manager. What a five year spell, and what a transformation!!! From lowly Championship side to, dare we say it, almost an established Premier League team. Dyche has firmly embedded himself as one of the Clarets greats.

However, as a result of all this success not unsurprisingly he is linked with every Premier League managerial post that becomes vacant. Strong rumours persist that Everton are about to try and prise him away from us, and who could blame them. He must be an ambitious man, and he must know in his 'heart of hearts' that there is a limit to how far he can take us on our restricted budget. It is inevitable that at some point, sooner rather than later, he will be tempted to try his luck with a 'bigger fish'. Let us hope that day has not yet arrived, and that he would at least see out the full season before departing with Premier League status intact, and a job well done.

NOVEMBER

The dreaded bedroom decorating saga continues, but thanks to the paperhanging skills of my father-in-law Albert Airey, it is rapidly drawing to a close. By Wednesday 1st November the wall decoration is complete and thankfully I am released from duties in time to enjoy Thursday's Burnley Contingent amble.

This time a hastily arranged walk to be used as a recce for a later Tuesday Dotcom outing sees us heading for the wilds of Colne. For early November the weather is very pleasantly mild, in fact I have to apply sun tan cream to my thinning pate, described by similarly afflicted Dotcomer Don Beal, as a 'solar panel for a sex machine'! A route circulated on Wednesday evening as being 5.3 miles, has by Thursday morning stretched to 6.28 miles, at the request of the 'Sherpa' Waltons, and Button the dog. It's a typical East Lancashire November slog through ankle deep mud, a feature that will probably last till next May! The highlight of the walk, some would say, were the magnificent views from the high ground on Blacko Hill Side overlooking the Foulridge reservoirs.

However, for me these were surpassed by the magnificent dive achieved by Ian Mckay, full length forward into the cloying mud. His rapid descent, at least every bit as dramatic as Bernardo Silva's penalty theatricals at the Etihad, served merely as a warm-up exercise. The indomitable Mckay, still with his left foot entangled in the collapsed fencing which had brought about his demise, promptly repeated the performance, this time with a back flip. Caked in mud, now both back and front, our hero carried on in true bulldog spirit claiming as a renowned local amateur footballer in his day, "*I am used to it.*" Needless to say the 5.3 mile, stretched to 6.28

miles, clocked in at 6.8 miles! The Walton's maintain their impeccable powers of distance inaccuracy once again. Still, a pint of Moorhouse's Blonde Witch in the Crown Hotel, Colne, ended another splendid day as we look forward to next week's planned trip to Stocks reservoir.

An interesting little aside here and an opportunity to dispel the myth, popular amongst my walking buddies, that writing books is a 'lucrative' business. Firstly, writing a book of this type is, by virtue of its diary style, quite a protracted and time-consuming business. However, this is quite often the easiest part of the process of turning original idea into tangible reward.

As an unknown author without a literary agent, and not being an ex-Premier League/International footballer, it is unlikely a publishing company will wish to get involved. This means that the author inevitably has to proceed down the self-publishing route. This in my case involves creating the book in an acceptable format, then finding a reliable and knowledgeable person to proof read the document. Then there is the matter of cover creation, sourcing suitable photographs and writing a brief summary of the book content for marketing purposes. Fortunately, I have been able to call on the assistance of extremely capable and talented people to assist, free of charge, to these ends.

Then comes the really hard part, marketing and selling the book! The first point of sale is obviously in this case through Amazon's website, which hopefully will generate sales over a prolonged period. The next port of call is to badger friends, relations, work colleagues and anybody else who comes into contact, to purchase the book. At this point one has to be prepared for the usual derogatory comments such as, *"it will come in handy for propping up the bed, or I'll put a hole through it and hang it in the lavatory."* This sales approach however is often quite successful as friends etc are usually quite supportive.

Finally, and without doubt the most frustrating approach is to contact local book retailers and try to get them to retail some copies. One would imagine that this would be quite an attractive proposition for small book shops and indeed the Burnley FC club shop. Unfortunately, not so! In many cases enquiries do not even merit a reply. How rude is that? Surely a quick email to decline the offer would not be a major inconvenience. Having bashed my head against this particular brick wall for some time, I decided on a final throw of the dice.

What better place to retail a few copies than in the local store of a major national supermarket chain who feature books with a local flavour. On approaching the management of said company I was politely and courteously informed that they in fact do not source the local books which they themselves sell. This is in fact done by a third party whom they very kindly put me in touch with. A quick email exchange with the 'middle-man' soon confirmed that this line of sale was in fact a dead-end. The 'middle-man' requires to purchase the books from the publisher (in this case me), at a whacking 65% discount! If the author (me again) takes into account the printing and transport costs, this would then effectively mean selling every book at a loss.

So, as you can see, an author's lot is not a happy one (or is that a policeman's?) with this in mind I urge all you readers out there to write glowing reviews of the book and treat all your family and friends to copies for Christmas.

One organisation whom I must give full credit to for their help in promoting the books is the splendid 'Up the Clarets' website. Editor Tony Scholes (ClaretTony), never fails to give the books a full-length feature on the site, and the messageboard is an invaluable tool for making people aware of their existence. Cheers Tony!

Anyway, that's got that little whinge out of the way, back to the more important matters at hand. It's back on the road for the Clarets with a long away trip to kick-off November's fixtures, another testing away fixture on the south coast at Southampton.

Game 11 - Saturday 4th November 15.00 – Southampton v Burnley

Here we go again, five away fixtures completed and with the exception of the Manchester City game, all excellent performances with thoroughly merited points. Could we maintain the incredible away run at once again a difficult ground for us? The answer, a resounding YES!

A long trip to the south coast ahead of yet another international break, but good news with the welcome return of Chris Wood from injury. The unlucky Ashley Barnes drops to the bench to accommodate him, but that's the only change from Monday's victory over Newcastle United. Our opponents Southampton, under yet another new manager, have not made the best of starts to the season and lie three places below us in 10th place with three points less.

Ex Claret Charlie Austin, usually a thorn in our side, we are glad to see only making the substitutes bench. Strange that, as the Saints are hardly prolific scorers and Austin certainly knows where the net is.

It's a predictable start as our hosts enjoy the lion's share of possession whilst we maintain our shape and look to keep it tight. Wood is ploughing a lonely furrow up front, but is proving a willing worker. A first half of Southampton pressure, punctuated once again by some fine saves from goalkeeper Nick Pope, sees the sides go in all square at half-time.

The second period continues in the same vein, but as our hosts get increasingly frustrated they look to be running out of ideas. Sean Dyche sensing the game may be there for the taking decides on a change of strategy. On 65 minutes he replaces the tiring Wood and Jeff Hendrick with two out and out strikers in Ashley Barnes and Sam Vokes. Southampton also make a change, bringing on Austin for the largely ineffective Marco Gabbiadini in an effort to beef up their attack.

Dyche's substitutions certainly do the trick as the Clarets, growing in confidence start to take the game to their opponents. On 81 minutes the switch pays off as Johann Berg Gudmundsson swings over an excellent cross from the right flank. Barnes draws the giant centre back Virgil van Dijk to the near post and coming in behind him is Vokes. Sam outjumps his marker Maya Yoshida and from around the penalty spot powers a tremendous header across goalkeeper Fraser Forster and into the corner of the net. How sweet must that have been for Sam, a Southampton lad being watched by many friends and family.

It's equally as sweet for me as it's the cue to pour an extremely large gin & tonic and settle back to fret out the remaining few minutes. Not so sweet for my pal John W who is up a ladder painting. The shock of the goal causes a temporary off-balance and almost a nasty ceiling incident!

We ride out the closing stages without too many scares and once again we are returning from our travels with maximum points. A team last season that could only manage seven points from 19 away fixtures, have this time accumulated 11 points already from a mere six games. How can that happen? You tell me! The Clarets maintain their upward trajectory and after the weekend fixtures lie seventh, or if you prefer joint fifth, level on points with Arsenal and Liverpool. We are in Dreamland!

Result – Southampton 0 – 1 (Vokes 81) Burnley

Burnley Team

Pope, Lowton, Mee, Tarkowski, Ward, Gudmundsson, Cork, Defour, Hendrick (Barnes 65), Brady, Wood (Vokes 65)

<u>Subs Not Used</u> – Lindegaard, Bardsley, Long, Westwood, Arfield

Southampton Team

Forster, Cedric, van Dijk, Yoshida, Bertrand, Boufal (Ward-Prowse 90), Davis, Tadic (Long 76), Romeu, Redmond, Gabbiadini (Austin 65)

<u>Subs Not Used</u> – McCarthy, Hoedt, McQueen, Hojberg

Attendance – 30,491

Season To Date – Played 11, Won 5, Drawn 4, Lost 2, Goals For 10, Goals Against 9, Points 19

League Position after Game 11 – 7th

Following this game, I thought I'd just out of interest, take a look where we were at the corresponding stage last season. In fact, from 11 games we then had 14 points, five fewer, and sat a respectable 9th in the table. However, our position at that point was slightly skewed due to the imbalance of home games to away fixtures completed. Owing to the early season switch in 2016 of the Liverpool fixture, we had played seven at home, and only four away, which had yielded only one point, surprisingly at Manchester United. I can only conclude that this season's position looks infinitely healthier.

Once again, it's a blank week for football coming up as it is yet another international break (yawn). Our Irish contingent of Stephen Ward, Kevin Long, Jeff Hendrick and Robbie Brady, but minus the injured Jon Walters, depart for two crucial World Cup play-off matches with Denmark. Chris Wood likewise makes the marathon journey to represent New Zealand against Peru in their valiant effort to qualify for the final stages. For Johann Berg Gudmundsson a more relaxed break as Iceland, already qualified, play a couple of friendly fixtures. It's a similar situation for Steven Defour linking up with Belgium. Sam Vokes joins up with Wales, also for friendlies, but there will be no place in the finals for the Welsh Dragon this time.

With Michael Keane departed, and Tom Heaton injured, there is no England representative this time for the Clarets in the two prestige friendlies against Germany and Brazil. However, as multiple players, mainly from the 'big six' clubs suddenly develop mysterious injuries and pull out of the squad, there is a major boost for one Claret, Jack Cork. On Wednesday 8th November, Jack gets a richly deserved call to join up with the depleted England squad. 'Corky', who has played every minute of Burnley's Premier League campaign so far, has represented England previously at levels up to Under 21, and his call up now hopefully completes the set.

Good news for Jack, although not named in the starting XI against Germany on Friday 10th November, he does at least get to grace the 'hallowed turf'. He manages an 86th minute substitute's appearance to complete a very good week for a very talented and popular member of our team. Well done Jack!

Not such good news however for our players involved in World Cup qualifier play-offs. Globetrotting Kiwi Chris Wood sees his hopes of glory extinguished as New Zealand, not unexpectedly, perish at the hands of Peru. More surprising is the capitulation of the Republic of Ireland's effort. Supposedly in pole position after a hard fought 0-0 draw in Denmark they come apart at the seams back in Dublin. Leading with an early goal all seems set fair before the wheels come off big time and they are trounced on home soil 1-5. Let's hope our boys are not too deflated when they return this coming weekend to the serious business of Premier League point collection.

Tuesday 14th November is the date for the eagerly awaited and vigorously contested annual Dotcom Walkers Quiz. The venue this time will be The Three Fishes at Mitton, and thrown in courtesy of the generosity of Bob Clare and 'Satnav' Dave, is a free lunch. Bob and Dave have been instrumental in devising a series of walks from pubs for the Ribble Valley Inns chain. Rather than take payment for their services the pair suggest that the pubs periodically provide the Dotcomers with a free lunch. Once again it will be a walker's favourite, Nigel Haworth's famous Lancashire Hotpot with spiced red cabbage, followed by a small dessert.

However, before we can sample these delights there is the small matter of the Tuesday walk, which I suppose is the primary reason for us being there. This time it's a short and sometimes muddy circular from Mitton to Edisford Bridge. With 23 walkers, boosted to 30+ by the walking wounded, it's a bumper turnout. Testimony to the power of a free lunch!

Once again, our 'Bamber Gascoigne' is the unfortunately named Chris McCann (no relation), who is quick to point out that this year there will be no music round in the quiz. It's a cunning ploy as he is well aware of the vast musical knowledge of the Burnley contingent. The real reason is that he now has no laptop computer, having last time emptied a pint of beer into his space age technology. Once the teams had been selected, two from Burnley and six from the Rest of The World, battle commenced. In a very close fought encounter - with accusations of cheating rife - I have to say that my particular foursome fared very well. The team consisting of ex teachers Dave Preedy, John Weir, Andy Burton (drafted in from Yorkshire) and myself (former textile worker, renowned author and broadcaster) finishing a creditable second, pipped by one point by a Rest of The World squad.

Once again, I have to say that in my opinion the questions were rather biased. There were lots of questions about the rest of the world and none about Burnley! How fair is that?

Game 12 - Saturday 18th November 15.00 – Burnley v Swansea City

Team news filters through as we consume pre-match pints at the Talbot Hotel, or should I say I consume the 'nectar of the gods'. My colleagues John and Judy W are involved in some sort of self-punishment ritual that debars them from drinking alcohol. This lunacy has been afflicting them now for the best part of two months. Today they are joined by my other veteran Clarets soul mate John G, who usually a staunch supporter of the brewing trade, opts for a pint of Lime and Soda!!! I suppose I can accept his lapse in that he is about to shortly depart for a three-week expedition of the ale houses of Tenerife and wants to be in prime condition on arrival. The other two though, I have serious fears for their sanity.

The only change for the Clarets is the absence from both team and squad of striker Chris Wood, no doubt still suffering a backlash from his 'time-travelling' adventure to darkest Peru. In for him comes Ashley Barnes, who you just know will never let you down.

Our visitors are currently enjoying a dire run of form and sit next to bottom of the table. Let's hope that run continues today, as we are due a result against them having lost all our four previous meetings with them in the Premier League. Two pints of Moorhouse's Premiership bitter duly despatched, along with the J2O and Soda drinkers, we depart for the Turf. It seems an age since we were here, and it is in fact almost three weeks since we defeated Newcastle United here at the end of October. The crowd looks a bit thinner than in recent weeks, largely down to the sparsely populated 'away end' where the travel distance and poor form of our visitors has taken its toll.

I'm expecting the Swans, in view of their parlous position to be pretty defensively minded, but their team selection suggests they are perhaps not going to sit too deep. They have plenty of pace in the team particularly former loanee Nathan Dyer, and newly capped England striker Tammy Abraham. The game starts with them on the front foot but it's not long before the tide is turning. As we get into our stride we are starting to create chances at regular intervals and our visitors are relying heavily on their keeper Lukasz Fabianski. A bit of an enigma is this guy, I always felt he was a rather 'dodgy keeper', but he seems to save his best performances for us.

On 29 minutes we have the lead that our dominance certainly deserves. The move is started as Jack Cork, ironically signed this summer from the Swans, wins the ball in midfield. His driving run towards the penalty area results in a perfect ball to Barnes who instantly lays it off to Robbie Brady on the left wing. His pinpoint cross is met first time by the head of Cork continuing his run into the box and there's nothing Fabianski can do to stop it.

With our tails up, and our opponent's head's down, it feels like only a matter of time before we score again. It is! On 40 minutes Steven Defour wins a tussle in midfield and feeds Jeff Hendrick. Hendrick's incisive pass is inch-perfect for Barnes lurking about 25 yards to the left of goal. Ashley takes one touch to control it then lashes a fearsome drive in off the near post for a classic strike. They have been two brilliantly constructed and executed goals, worthy of winning any game.

Two up at half time and seemingly coasting it's a happy Turf Moor crowd who tuck into their Pies and Bovril. I'm expecting a bit of a backlash from our opponents in the second half. No doubt with ears stinging from a half time volley from beleaguered manager Paul Clement, that is what they attempt. Wilfried Bony is brought on to give some much-needed muscular support to the young Abraham, and to be fair they improve on a wretched first half performance. However, it's not enough to seriously trouble one of the best defensive units in the Premier League. With rookie keeper Nick Pope growing in stature with every game, we are indeed a difficult team to break down. Our opponent's efforts continue to founder on our defensive rock, whilst we carry a significant threat on the counter.

A disallowed 'goal' from James Tarkowski is the nearest we get to adding to our total but it's a relatively comfortable afternoon. I can't recollect Pope having a single save to make all afternoon, apart from the routine collection of crosses. Indeed, his first real action comes in the fifth minute of added time as he stops a Bony header, which in truth was straight at him. A 'Man of the Match' award to Ashley Barnes is thoroughly deserved, as he once again demonstrates what an underrated footballer, at least outside of Burnley, he is!

So, another three points added to the total, taking us impressively on to 22 from 12 fixtures. A third successive Premier League victory, the best run in the top division since 1975. We sit one point behind fourth placed Tottenham Hotspur, and level on points with Arsenal and Liverpool. Heady days are these at Turf Moor, what a great time to be a Claret!

Result - Burnley (Cork 29, Barnes 40) 2 - 0 Swansea City

Burnley Team

Pope, Lowton, Mee, Tarkowski, Ward, Gudmundsson, Cork, Defour, Hendrick (Vokes 80), Brady, Barnes

<u>Subs Not Used</u> – Lindegaard, Taylor, Long, Westwood, Arfield, Wells

Swansea City Team

Fabianski, Naughton, Fernandez, Mawson, Olsson, Fer (Sung-yueng 70), Clucas, Sanches, Dyer, Abraham (Narsingh 82), Ayew (Bony 45)

<u>Subs Not Used</u> – Carroll, Nordfeldt, van der Hoorn, Routledge

Attendance – 18,895

Season To Date – Played 12, Won 6, Drawn 4, Lost 2, Goals For 12, Goals Against 9, Points 22

League Position after Game 12 – 7th

Game 13 - Sunday 26th November 14.00 – Burnley v Arsenal

This is a difficult match to review in light of what I have just witnessed. Game 13 is a very appropriate number for this fixture. Ahead of the game I mused on the fact that on both occasions the sides met last season, the games were won by Arsenal by virtue of highly dubious added time goals. Surely this time anything controversial would be in our favour, or so I thought.

Hoping for a cold and wet Lancashire day to deter our southern visitors I was not disappointed as I went about my chores on the morning of the game. As I left for Turf Moor bang on cue came some rain to add to their discomfort. This had clearly had the desired effect as early team news showed no Mesut Ozil in the Arsenal squad. Probably took one look at the weather and decided to stay in bed. Nevertheless, a very strong Gunners squad took the field against yet again an unchanged Clarets XI.

I was anticipating a game characterised by sparse possession for ourselves and a lot of chasing as our visitors stroked it around. The first five minutes probably reflected that but as time ticked on we started to impose ourselves. A highly impressive first half performance saw the Clarets giving as good as they got, and on occasions, more. Playing some attractive football there was no shortage of crosses into the Arsenal box and some decent spells of pressure. Johann Berg Gudmundsson (JBG) was closest to scoring with a rasping right-footer that cannoned off Petr Cech's left hand goalpost. Cech also was at full stretch to save a Robbie Brady free kick and Jeff Hendrick header.

Some woeful decisions by the officials, a feature of games between 'minnows' and the 'elite', unsurprisingly saw two bookings for the Clarets yet none for Arsenal. Steven Defour was yellow carded for having words with the assistant referee, whilst Alexis Sanchez complained against every decision that didn't go his way, generally behaving like a four-year old, yet didn't incur the official's wrath. Once again, an example of one law for the rich and a different one for the poor. Similarly, Robbie Brady's sliding challenge was adjudicated a 'cardable' offence, whereas the same tackle by a Gunner went unpenalized and seen as 'taking the ball'.

No goals at half time but a very entertaining game with the Clarets turning in perhaps their best home performance of the season so far. The first half statistics showed Burnley with

45% possession, and four shots with one on target. Our esteemed visitors had 55%, eight shots but none troubling keeper Nick Pope.

The second half started with Arsenal in much more determined mood, pushing us back deeper towards our goal. However, the magnificently marshalled rearguard coped relatively comfortably with everything thrown at it. Once again James Tarkowski and Ben Mee were at the heart of everything, with full backs Steven Ward and Matt Lowton also performing at their peak.

The pattern of Arsenal pressing and Burnley countering on the break continued throughout the half. As usual it was edge of the seat viewing but the clock ticked inexorably on. Entering the final 10 minutes I couldn't help feeling that we had very much deserved a point from a very hard-fought encounter with a top six team. Ninety minutes were up, and the fourth official indicated a measly two minutes added time. A precious point must be ours, just keep the ball away from our goal and run the clock down.

But no, tragedy strikes! A ball into the box from the right is headed back across goal, going for it are Tarkowski and Aaron Ramsey who theatrically hits the deck! The referee has the chance he has been waiting for all afternoon and wastes no time pointing to the penalty spot. Sanchez who minutes earlier had looked on the verge of tears after yet another tantrum, despatches the penalty and with almost the last kick of the game we are sunk!

How cruel was that? 18,000 Clarets can hardly believe what they've seen. Worse than that it's now happened three consecutive times against this opposition. I am speechless and so are many more. The game can sure kick you in the teeth sometimes.

Was it a penalty? From where I sat I couldn't say, there were so many bodies between the incident and me. I suppose I'll have to wait for tonight's TV coverage for a definite picture. I sincerely hope we haven't been robbed of our point by an act of simulation, we shall see.

Our three-game winning sequence therefore comes to an end, but we stay in seventh position. Two away games coming up this week; Wednesday night brings a mammoth trek to Bournemouth, followed by Saturday's visit to Leicester City. Hopefully our impressive away form continues, and we can repair today's damage.

Result – Burnley 0 – 1 (Sanchez 90+2) Arsenal

Burnley Team

Pope, Lowton, Mee, Tarkowski, Ward, Gudmundsson, Cork, Defour (Wood 78), Hendrick, Brady, Barnes

<u>Subs Not Used</u> – Lindegaard, Bardsley, Long, Westwood, Arfield, Vokes

Arsenal Team

Cech, Koscielny, Mustafi, Monreal, Bellerin, Ramsey, Xhaka, Kolasinac, Iwobi (Wilshere 67), Sanchez, Lacazette (Wellbeck 79)

<u>Subs Not Used</u> – Ospina, Mertesacker, Coquelin, Maitland-Niles, Giroud

Attendance – 21,722

Season To Date – Played 13, Won 6, Drawn 4, Lost 3, Goals For 12, Goals Against 10, Points 22

League Position after Game 13 – 7th

Tuesday 28th November has me out on a Dotcom walk in hostile territory, skirting the environs of Blackburn. Starting from the Hare & Hounds pub in Abbey Village the plan is to walk the Reelers Trail, one of the walks in the Witton Weavers Way collection. The walk is advertised as 7.5 miles, but due to waterlogged conditions and 'seas of mud', walk leader Nigel Hext has amended the route and thinks it may come out short of that distance.

The funny thing with Nigel's walks is that something usually goes amiss. Three times this year he has proposed to lead a walk on Waddington Fell and on each occasion the weather has intervened to cause a cancellation. This time the weather though bitterly cold is not unkind, but the wet and slippery conditions do claim a casualty. Crossing a stile some way into the walk, Helen of the Preston mob takes a heavy tumble that inflicts some probable ligament damage. That's a bit of a problem as we are a good way from the nearest road to affect a rescue. There's nothing for it but for her to limp on painfully till we reach civilisation.

This considerably slows our progress but after a particularly difficult stretch parallel to the M65 we are able to summon assistance by taxi to return her to the pub. No further incidents occur and at the appointed time we are back at the hostelry to sample the well-priced soup and sandwich combo. Pints of Moorhouse's White Witch complete another fine day out. Helen is able to see the funny side of it but I bet she'll be sore in the morning.

Game 14 - Wednesday 29th November 19.45 - Bournemouth v Burnley

After Sunday's late stunner against Arsenal I suppose the conundrum on many fans minds was how would the team react? Would that result knock the stuffing out of them, or would it strengthen their resolve? A bit of a daft question really when considering a Sean Dyche team. Bournemouth away gave the Clarets an early opportunity to banish the Sunday blues.

However, it wasn't going to be an easy fixture, the Cherries after a poor start to the season, had of late hit a good run of form to lift them up the table. Add to that the fact that the game also coincided with ex Claret's boss, now Bournemouth manager, Eddie Howe's 40th birthday, it had all the hallmarks of a testing evening. Not so for this ruthlessly efficient, supremely fit, well organised and highly motivated outfit; this was just the opportunity to get back on track!

Missing from the starting line-up was Matt Lowton who sustained a knock in the Arsenal game, and in his place came Phil Bardsley who got the opportunity of a rare outing. From the off our heroes showed their intent forcing three corners in the first five minutes. Chris Wood, back in the side at the expense of the unfortunate Ashley Barnes, was already proving a significant handful for the home defence and it wasn't long before he hit the top of the bar with a header. Obviously, this effort was meant as a 'sighter' and his next contribution was to bring a fine save from home custodian Asmir Begovic.

Little or nothing was being seen of Bournemouth as an attacking force as the Clarets ramped up the first half pressure. The next opportunity fell to Jeff Hendrick as Wood teed him up, but a brilliant block by Bournemouth defender Steve Cook saved the day. With the relentless pressure being applied a goal had to be coming, and it duly arrived on 37 minutes.

Robbie Brady's flicked pass found Jack Cork advancing on the Cherries goal, 'Corky' returned the favour and Brady's cross cum shot came off the hapless Cook to fall straight into the path of Wood. Needing no second invitation, our Kiwi striker stroked it home from close range. A goal to go in to half time with a richly deserved lead. Indeed, on another day Wood could have had a first half hat-trick, but let's not be greedy!

The second half started with more of the same as the impressive Clarets maintained their grip on the game. That hold on the game looked unassailable on 65 minutes as Brady doubled the advantage. Johann Berg Gudmundsson coming in from the right flank fed Robbie just outside the box, taking it on his left, then switching it to his right, he let fly from the edge of the area curling the shot just inside the post. Magnificent!

Birthday boy Eddie had started to ring the changes earlier as Harry Arter and Marc Pugh, were replaced by Lewis Cook and Jermain Defoe respectively. The goal prompted the final change with Ryan Fraser replacing the disappointingly expensive Jordon Ibe. The changes perhaps did the trick as they pulled a goal back. Defoe's shot from the right of goal was palmed out by Nick Pope but only as far as Josh King who fired home. That might have made for a nervy ending, but not on this occasion, once again the team proved its undoubted defensive solidity and the points were ours.

This win, coupled with Tottenham Hotspur's defeat at Leicester City the previous evening, lifted the Clarets up to an unimaginable sixth in the table. Fourteen points had now been gained from a possible 21 on our travels making a complete mockery of last season's away day blues. Four wins, two draws and a solitary defeat at runaway leaders Manchester City, make for pretty impressive reading. Four wins from the last five games and the points tally rolls on to 25 with still five games to play to the half way stage. What a time to be a Burnley fan! Let's enjoy this incredible season while it lasts.

Result - Bournemouth (King 79) 1 - 2 (Wood 37, Brady 65) Burnley

Burnley Team

Pope, Bardsley, Mee, Tarkowski, Ward, Gudmundsson, Cork, Defour (Westwood 75), Hendrick (Barnes 86), Brady, Wood (Vokes 90)

Subs Not Used - Lindegaard, Taylor, Long, Arfield,

Bournemouth Team

Begovic, Francis, S Cook, Ake, Daniels, Ibe (Fraser 69), Surman, Arter (L Cook 58), Pugh (Defoe 64), King, Wilson

Subs Not Used - Boruc, Gosling, Afobe, A Smith

Attendance - 10,302

Season To Date - Played 14, Won 7, Drawn 4, Lost 3, Goals For 14, Goals Against 11, Points 25

League Position after Game 14 - 6th

It's the last day in November and for me a bit of a change. No Thursday walking but a trip on the train to York with wife Julie for a pre-Christmas meet up with daughter Stephanie. It's a convenient way to get there although perhaps not the quickest, certainly not on this occasion as our direct train to York decides it will have to terminate at Leeds! A slight delay as we change trains, so slight that I am sure some of the less mobile passengers are left at Leeds, means we arrive in York 10 minutes late. It's a bit easier for Stephanie as her east coast main line train covers the distance from home in Darlington to York in about 30 minutes.

After a lovely (if expensive) lunch, the girls hit the shops whilst I head for the National Railway Museum (free entry) keeping my wallet safely in my pocket. There's a lovely atmosphere in York at this time of year and the Christmas Market is in full swing. To add to the festive spirit, it even decides to snow! Still, a good day out and Stephanie at least did her best for the local economy by attempting to empty the shops.

DECEMBER

A busy month of football coming up as we face seven more stiff challenges ahead of the New Year. First on the agenda are Leicester City at the King Power Stadium, and after Wednesday's superb performance we go there full of confidence. The Foxes, after a shaky start which cost manager Craig Shakespeare his job, are recovering well under new boss Claude Puel. Today will be a difficult fixture with our hosts also confident after a midweek home victory over Tottenham Hotspur, but then again, every game in this league is a 'toughie'.

Game 15 - Saturday 2nd December 15.00 – Leicester City v Burnley

The team line-up is the same as midweek as once again Matt Lowton misses out, Phil Bardsley deputising. A strong looking Leicester City attack with no less than Riyad Mahrez, Jamie Vardy and Demarai Gray, looks certain to give our defence a stiff test.

As at Bournemouth it's a quick-fire start from the Clarets but then on six minutes we are uncharacteristically rocked back on our heels. As a fairly innocuous Mahrez cross from the right eludes the central defenders, Nick Pope can only palm the ball into the path of the onrushing Gray who squeezes it home before colliding with the post. A poor goal to concede and most un-Burnley like. However, undaunted the Clarets come storming back, and there are corners and shots aplenty. Yet again away from home we are exuding a confidence not seen on our previous Premier League adventures.

Just as it seems we are going to get back into the game disaster strikes! Influential play-maker Robbie Brady is seriously injured in a collision with Leicester City centre back Harry Maguire. Played in by Johann Berg Gudmundsson and Jeff Hendrick, Brady had looked set to shoot but only succeeded in connecting with Maguire. Both players are injured but Brady comes off much the worse. After a lengthy stoppage he is stretchered off with his leg heavily strapped and receiving oxygen.

Prior to this the Clarets had dominated play, despite the early goal, and fired in no less than seven shots. Scott Arfield replaced the injured Brady and unsurprisingly some of the sting went out of our play. Despite it being all Burnley in the first half we trail at the interval to the solitary goal.

Unfortunately, the disruption to the team meant a more even second half. Arfield, not a player ever lacking in effort and commitment, unfortunately has not the same ability as Brady to unlock a defence. Whilst still attempting to press our hosts as much as possible they are able to affect a greater attacking influence themselves now.

As the game progresses there are no further goals but with time running out its time for a gamble. Off comes the tiring Chris Wood and on come Ashley Barnes and Sam Vokes as we go two up top. This ambitious move clearly opens up the game even further and Leicester are able to create chances of their own, all thankfully not taken. We similarly manage to conjure up a couple of late openings but sadly they come to nought. A thoroughly entertaining game but on this occasion, no points.

Result – Leicester City (Gray 6) 1 – 0 Burnley

Burnley Team

Pope, Bardsley, Mee, Tarkowski, Ward, Gudmundsson, Cork, Defour (Barnes 66), Hendrick (Barnes 86), Brady (Arfield 31), Wood (Vokes 74)

<u>Subs Not Used</u> – Lindegaard, Taylor, Long, Westwood,

Leicester City Team

Schmeichel, Simpson, Morgan, Maguire, Chilwell, Albrighton, Ndidi, Iborra, Mahrez, Vardy, Gray (Okazaki 88)

<u>Subs Not Used</u> – Hamer, Fuchs, Dragovic, King, Iheanacho, Ulloa

Attendance – 30,714

Season To Date – Played 15, Won 7, Drawn 4, Lost 4, Goals For 14, Goals Against 12, Points 25

League Position after Game 15 – 7th

Well! What an eventful week that was. Firstly, the trauma of the undeserved late defeat to Arsenal. This was then followed by the exhilarating and comprehensive away victory at Bournemouth. Then the disappointment of the away defeat at Leicester. Nobody can say that supporting Burnley FC is ever a boring experience.

By far the worst thing coming out of the Leicester game is not the loss of three points, but rather the potential serious injury sustained by Robbie Brady. His form in recent weeks has been outstanding and the injury follows a Man of the Match performance at Bournemouth. By Monday evening there is still no firm news as to what the nature and severity of the injury is, but noises coming from the club are not hopeful.

What a damn shame! This mishap could be a season defining moment in our fortunes as Brady is probably the one player that we would find most difficult to replace. He is much more to us than an out-and out winger. He is at the centre of most of our creative play and is also a highly effective dead-ball specialist. Their wouldn't appear to be anybody currently in the squad with the same skill-set and it is perhaps fortunate that the transfer window will re-open in just a month's time.

However, it is by no means certain that we will pursue that route. The injury may prompt a change in formation which Dyche seems less averse to now we have a stronger squad. Summer recruits Charlie Taylor and Nahki Wells are both fit and looking to force their way into the team, also returning to full fitness is Jon Walters. Whilst none of these players would be seen as a like-for-like replacement as the saying goes, 'there is more than one way of skinning a cat'. I guess it's now a case of wait and see and hopefully the injury will prove to be not as serious as at first feared.

Sadly, on December 6th the club released the news that Robbie Brady had in fact suffered a patellar tendon tear and would be out for a substantial recovery period. Without doubt this means Brady has played his last game of the 2017/18 season, and I'm sure all Clarets fans wish him well and a speedy, and full recovery.

With the points tally after 15 games standing already at 25, and with a projected safety target of 40 seemingly easily reachable, some fans were optimistically casting their eyes at other prizes. Some had notions of qualification for Europe, maybe not the Champions League but at least the Europa League. Others had the temerity to suggest that a day out at

Wembley and an FA Cup Final might be beckoning. Monday December 4th saw the draw for the Third Round Proper (why did they always used to call it Proper?) of the cup, and with it the disappearance of some of those lofty notions.

Who did we draw? Well, out of the 64 clubs remaining at this stage, which still contained some of the 'minnows' that make the competition so interesting, we get runaway Premier League leaders Manchester City! And away at the Etihad to boot! Now, it may well be that as City chase glory in the League and the Champions League that the FA Cup may feature low on their list of priorities. It may be that they will use this competition to field a so-called 'weakened team'. However, such is the depth of their expensively assembled squad that if they change the whole starting eleven they can still probably fill every position in the team with players of international calibre.

For myself, my priority target is still the 40 points required for safety, anything else is just 'icing on the cake'. Plus, I suppose it's less embarrassing to exit the FA Cup away to Manchester City than at home to Lincoln City!

Game 16 - Saturday 9th December 15.00 – Burnley v Watford

It's a bitterly cold day in Burnley, after sub-zero overnight temperatures the day's high is expected to be no more than 2°C. As Julie completes the transformation of the house into Santa's Grotto, I consider my apparel options for the day. A difficult one this as I need to be sufficiently thermally insulated to stand a couple of hours of physical inactivity at a freezing Turf Moor. The other side of the coin is that I need to be able to shed layers rapidly as I hit the densely populated, super-heated atmosphere of the bar of the Talbot Hotel for pre-match drinks.

Suitably attired I'm on my way and not at all surprised that as I approach the pub on the coldest day of the season so far, my colleagues, joined on this occasion by Ed 'Sherpa' Walton', have taken up position OUTSIDE the pub. Still I mustn't complain as waiting on the 'picnic bench' is a foaming pint, suitably chilled, of Moorhouse's Premiership Bitter. At that moment, to complete the wintry scene, it starts to snow. Fortunately, at this point the Sherpa's phone starts to ring and within seconds he disappears into the seething mass of humanity that is the pub. Within seconds he re-appears with the good news that husband and wife combo, Mike and Lesley McDevitt are established in the 'snug' and seats are available. Thankfully we take up the offer and decamp into the heat in time to see lowly West Ham United complete their defeat of high-flying Chelsea.

Although we don't have long to tarry in the pub, this time to me sums up all that is best about Saturday afternoon football. It's a chance to meet up with pals in the convivial atmosphere of like-minded people. An opportunity to quaff a couple of pints, look forward to the football, and talk nonsense. All too soon that time is up, and we head rapidly to Turf Moor before we miss all the goals!

I must confess to being a little apprehensive before this fixture due to a sudden spate of injuries. Matt Lowton misses out for the third consecutive game, Robbie Brady is now confirmed as a long-term casualty, and today the bad news that Mr Consistency, Ben Mee, is also unavailable having had stiches inserted in a leg wound. Phil Bardsley continues at right back, Scott Arfield comes in for Brady, and there is a rare start for Kevin Long in central defence. In Mee's absence, Jack Cork is handed the captain's armband, a thoroughly deserved honour indeed. This game marks the first return to Turf Moor for former Clarets striker Andre Gray following his summer move south to the Hornets. Gray is a player who sharply divided opinions amongst Burnley fans, but I have to say that his departure does not seem to have adversely affected us. Today however, he will get no early chance to show us what we are missing as he starts on the substitutes bench.

Not surprisingly in view of the changes it's a somewhat sluggish and hesitant start, characterised by a few under-hit and misplaced passes. Our visitors who currently sit one place below us in the table certainly look up for it. Let's hope these particular Hornets don't possess a nasty sting.

Gradually though we are coming more into the game and once again with our Iceman, Johann Berg Gudmundsson (JBG), in good form we are starting to test the visiting keeper Huerelho Gomes. Gomes is one of a number of keepers who can be described as unpredictable, but as with Swansea's Fabianski, is one who usually saves his best displays for games against us.

Steven Defour and JBG are obviously being charged with assuming free-kick responsibilities in the absence of Brady, and the latter brings an excellent save from Gomes from one such opportunity. This is followed by another fine stop to deny Chris Wood. We are asserting ourselves now and looking for that break to give us the lead. By my reckoning Nick Pope is not called on to make his first save until the 37th minute, which he handles in routine fashion. Then on 39 minutes we are handed a significant advantage as Watford's Marvin Zeegelaar rashly goes into a two-footed challenge on

Defour. Our Belgian maestro is left crumpled on the Turf as referee Lee Probert reaches for the red card.

Fortunately, after treatment Defour is able to resume and now with a one-man advantage we go looking for the vital first goal. It duly arrives on the stroke of half time as Cork wins the ball in midfield and feeds JBG on the right flank. The winger then plays a low square ball across the edge of the penalty area that is dummied by Jeff Hendrick and collected by Arfield. The oft maligned Scotty immediately rounds full back Daryl Janmaat and slots a perfect shot past Gomes for a 1-0 lead. The goal is swiftly followed by loud claims for a penalty as an Arfield flick-on is apparently handled by a defender, but referee Probert is having none of it. Half time and a valuable one goal advantage!

One goal up and a man advantage should signal the opportunity for a more relaxed second half than normal, but we know from past experience this is often not the case. The visitors re-group during the interval and re-emerge in determined fashion. Once again, our rearguard, this time much changed in terms of personnel, maintains its miserly efficiency. Looking to seal the victory around the hour mark we introduce Ashley Barnes to bolster the attack.

The arrival of 'Basher' usually sparks some controversy and this time is no exception. Assistant referee Simon Beck, for reasons best known to himself, manages to chalk off two 'goals' with dubious offside decisions given against Barnes. Had either of these incorrect decisions not been made we could have comfortably closed out the game with a two-goal advantage. As it was, despite the introduction of Andre Gray, and one or two attempted 'dives' to sway the officials, our goal remained largely unthreatened. Indeed, the nearest to a goal came again from a stinging JBG shot well saved by Gomes's parry which just eluded the oncoming Wood.

Then that was it, game over! Time to head home for another Saturday evening of smugly studying the Premier League table and dreaming of Europe! Today, fielding a defence with arguably three players starting who would not normally be considered first choices, we were just as impregnable as ever. Testimony once again to the effectiveness of the 'system' and its application by the players.

It really is fantasy land for us Clarets at the moment. We have reached 28 points and still are three games short of the halfway point. Who would have dared think that at the start? Stoke City are next up on Tuesday evening at the Turf as the games come thick and fast. Could we pass the thirty-point mark? I wouldn't bet against it.

Result – Burnley (Arfield 45) 1 – 0 Watford

Burnley Team

Pope, Bardsley, Long, Tarkowski, Ward, Gudmundsson, Cork, Defour (Westwood 90+4), Hendrick (Barnes 60), Arfield, Wood

<u>Subs Not Used</u> – Lindegaard, Taylor, Ulvestad, Wells, Vokes

Watford Team

Gomes, Janmaat, Mariappa, Kabasele, Zeegelaar, Doucoure, Cleverley, Carillo (Gray 79), Pereyra (Holebas 44), Deeney, Richarlison

<u>Subs Not Used</u> – Karnezis, Prodl, Watson, Success, Capoue

Attendance – 19,479

Season To Date – Played 16, Won 8, Drawn 4, Lost 4, Goals For 15, Goals Against 12, Points 28

League Position after Game 16 – 7th

Aside from the football it's a big week coming up on the social front as the festive pace gathers. Tuesday 12th December is the Dotcom Walkers Annual Xmas lunch and Awards ceremony at the Corporation Arms near Longridge. Always a good feed at the Corporation, even though I may have to take out a bank loan to pay for it. This will be followed by the Burnley Contingent Annual Christmas Bash on Thursday 14th. The plan this year is a short bus trip to Colne (bus passes at the ready) followed by a six-miler taking in Laneshawbridge, Wycoller and finishing in Trawden. A three-course lunch will then be taken at the Trawden Arms, accompanied by copious quantities of real ale. The day will end with a bus ride, complete with bursting bladders, back to civilisation in Burnley. Apologies in advance to any poor unsuspecting bus commuters. What better way to celebrate the festive season!

You may recall some pages back that I had a mini rant about the difficulties of finding marketing avenues and book retailers. Not coming out of this in a good light I have to say is the Burnley FC club shop. Despite several attempts to persuade them to stock Volume 3, and indeed Volume 2 they - for reasons best known to themselves - refuse to do so. I think that's a pretty poor show particularly as they are retailing other books of a similar nature.

Anyway, I won't bore you with that particular 'beef' but would at this stage like to give credit where credit is due.

My grateful thanks I must extend firstly to Tony Scholes editor of the 'Up the Clarets' website. In response to my request for him to give the book a 'festive plug' he produced an excellent article on the website featuring my effort. Similarly, fellow author Dave Thomas, who has always been very supportive and helpful, has promoted the book through his Facebook and Twitter pages. A special mention also to Steve of Burnley Memorabilia in Burnley Market Hall. Without quibble he has offered to retail a few copies in the pre-Christmas period and this offer has grown to represent a not inconsiderable number of books. The efforts of these people, and the consequent sales boost, have convinced me that it is worthwhile to commit this, the fourth volume, to print. So dear reader, if you don't like the book, you know who to blame!

Game 17 - Tuesday 12th December 19.45 – Burnley v Stoke City

Following close on the heels of the Watford encounter is another home game, this time with Stoke City, who are currently not enjoying the best of runs. Saturday saw them defeated 5-1 at Tottenham Hotspur and manager Mark Hughes is coming under increasing pressure.

For me it's a quick change at home after the Dotcom walkers 'bash' in Longridge. A gentle six-mile stroll in lovely cold, crisp wintry conditions followed by the usual excellent fare at the pub, made for another great day out. The much coveted 'Moll of the Year' award went for the second time to Sandra Livesey and that went some way to making up for her fall earlier in the day in the slippery conditions. Incidentally, you may recall Helen of the Preston Mob's fall some pages back on the walk from Abbey Village. Poor Helen's injury turned out to be more serious than at first thought. Her subsequent visit to hospital revealed a double ankle fracture which has required a metal plate and several pins. She now faces six weeks in plaster, followed by a further 4 weeks in a protective boot. Some Christmas present that! We wish her a speedy recovery and look forward to seeing her on some more jaunts in 2018.

Now the omens are not good for this match, allow me to explain why. One of my long time Claret buddies is currently enjoying a winter break in the Tenerife sunshine. I have been handed his season ticket to allow somebody else the use of the seat whilst he soaks up the beer. On this occasion, as with last Saturday's against Watford, the ticket is in the possession of Geoff 'The Jinx' Ashworth, who some of you may know from his days as a former Barden school PE Teacher. From previous experiences it has been found that Geoff's appearances at Turf Moor usually coincide with disaster! Hence, he has acquired over the years the reputation of being a jinx.

You might argue that Saturday's 1-0 victory over Watford dispels his unlucky reputation. Not so, the fact is that Geoff, very much a pie aficionado, contrived to miss Saturday's goal whilst on a procurement mission for the said item. Clear proof that his absence had a beneficial effect on Scott Arfield's moment of magic. This was confirmed by his second half performance whereby he remained in his seat, despite suggestions that he might want another pie or a visit to the loo, and our subsequent failure to score again. In fact, I do believe he may have been largely responsible for the two offside decisions, wrongly given by the Assistant Referee, which cost us the safety net of a second goal. Foolishly I have left him in possession of the ticket for this evening's encounter. I hope I don't live to rue the day.

After a very pleasant if cold day, the weather decides to do it's worst just in time for the game. Shortly after 6.00pm the heavens open, with a swirling wind and a temperature just above freezing, it's a foul night for football. The team news confirms no changes from Saturday, Ben Mee and Matt Lowton, though both thought to be close to fitness, both fail to make the squad.

With 'The Jinx' in position, and the usual crop of giants facing us as is often the case with Stoke City, my mate John W remarks that he has a bad feeling about this one. I concur but tell him I have a bad feeling about them all. A discussion follows in which we both agree we haven't had a good feeling since 1973!

As the game gets underway its soon apparent that this is not going to be a game for the football 'purists'. The wind is swirling around, one minute holding the ball up, the next driving it merrily on its way. The Potters with the beanpole striker Peter Crouch up front are looking to utilise his height advantage from the off. After a couple of early scares though James Tarkowski and Kevin Long are beginning to get to grips with him. At the other end there's precious little to write about as an isolated Chris Wood is being ably marshalled by Ryan Shawcross and the impressive Kurt Zouma. Despite repeated pleas from several spectators, and even offers to buy him a pie, 'The Jinx' remains steadfastly in his seat. More bad news on 41 minutes as Stephen Ward sustains what appears to be a knee injury and can't continue. In his place comes Charlie Taylor, signed in the summer from Leeds, who has had to bide his time patiently. Half time arrives with the score still 0-0, and its hard to think of any memorable incidents.

I decide to head down onto the concourse to avoid the swirling rain and purchase a cup of coffee to raise the body temperature. Its not a good idea, as the entire population of the James Hargreaves Upper stand have had the same one. It's a veritable human log-jam down there and its apparent that I won't be getting coffee this side of the second half.

Back up for the re-start and the weather conditions if anything have worsened. On the pitch its more of the same, two teams trying to knock hell out of the ball, but with little creativity. One moment of magic or a mistake is going to decide this one. Then an injury blow for the visitors as Zouma is on the deck and unable to continue. That's a big loss for Stoke as he has been in commanding form. In what is becoming a regular move on 71 minutes Ashley Barnes replaces Jeff Hendrick, to add a bit more punch up front.

Suddenly with the loss of Zouma, the Potters defence doesn't look quite so impregnable. Perhaps sensing the victory Sean Dyche makes the last throw of the dice as he introduces Sam Vokes for the tiring Wood. Almost immediately we are posing a more potent threat getting the ball up quickly to our battling duo of substitutes. Time though is running out, and I must confess that I'll be glad to get out of the cold and wet when it ends. Then as so often happens Ashley Barnes comes up trumps! Jack Cork plays a ball up to 'Basher' who chests it off to Scott Arfield in the inside right channel. Scotty returns the favour and Ashley hits a cannonball shot from 12 yards to leave the net rippling. Cue absolute delight for the half-frozen Clarets fans, a mighty roar and smiles like the Cheshire Cat. A goal in the 89th minute, surely that must be the winner!

There's four minutes added but these are eaten up safely and unbelievably we have won again!

And what of Geoff 'The Jinx' Ashworth? He has consigned the title to the dustbin, and gone from jinx to 'Super Hero' in one night. The club should provide him with free pies for life.

Result – Burnley (Barnes 89) 1 – 0 Stoke City

Burnley Team

Pope, Bardsley, Long, Tarkowski, Ward (Taylor 41), Gudmundsson, Cork, Defour, Hendrick (Barnes 71), Arfield, Wood (Vokes 82)

Subs Not Used – Lindegaard, Westwood, Ulvestad, Wells

Stoke City Team

Butland, Cameron, Shawcross, Zouma (Wimmer 66), Pieters, Fletcher, Allen, Diouf, Shaqiri (Chopo-Moting 84), Crouch, Sobhi

Subs Not Used – Grant, Afellay, Adam, Edwards, Berahino

Attendance – 19,909

Season To Date – Played 17, Won 9, Drawn 4, Lost 4, Goals For 16, Goals Against 12, Points 31

League Position after Game 17 – 6th

A second consecutive 1-0 victory and briefly up to FOURTH in the table, albeit only for 24 hours as two of our rivals playing catch up on the Wednesday night record victories to go above us. However, their advantage is on goal difference only, so I think we'll say we are equal fourth.

With only 16 goals scored from 17 fixtures we could hardly be described as prolific. However, with only 12 goals conceded we certainly could be described as miserly. In fact, in nine home games we have been breeched only three times. In a total of four defeats in the season to-date, we have lost by more than one goal on only one occasion, that being at runaway leaders Manchester City I think makes it excusable.

Without doubt the bedrock of our success is our immaculate defence. This is even more remarkable when you consider we have been without our England goalkeeper for most of these matches. It's even more incredible when you think that of the back five (goalkeeper + back four) that finished the game on Tuesday, only James Tarkowski would be classed as first choice. Even 'Tarka' wasn't a regular until the summer departure of Michael Keane. The continuing frugality despite the enforced changes is testimony to the growing depth and quality of the squad. But of course, the key to successful defending is not just the guys at the back, it is a team effort and the 'pressing' of the opposition by the forwards and midfield is a key factor in the success.

Who would have thought it 31 points, and not even Christmas and the half way point? There are still two fixtures before that milestone is reached starting with Brighton & Hove Albion away this coming Saturday. There are no easy games in this league, and although the Seagulls are currently enjoying a bit of a slump, we will need to be at our very best to return with anything. We'll be ready though, bring them on! With our current points tally even I'm beginning to think beyond survival. Europe here we come!

Thursday 14th and the annual Xmas bash is upon us. After a Wednesday of bitterly cold temperatures and torrential downpours, and the forecast for today not much better, we set off for the bus somewhat apprehensive. It's a while since I've been on a Burnley and Pendle Transdev 'Mainline' bus. In fact, it's even longer than envisaged as the intended M3 bus to Trawden is running late, instead we clamber aboard the M4 Keighley bound bus to alight at Colne Cricket Club.

In my absence from bus travelling it transpires all sorts of exciting new developments have been introduced. First to catch my attention is the free WiFi, amazing I am able to keep up with Day 1 of the Third Ashes Test from Perth as we trundle along. Next, I notice an onboard display that tells me not only which service I am currently travelling on but also what the next stop will be. How useful is that! However, this information feed goes further, there is even a recorded voice message that relays the stop information and on some occasions even adds little comments like;

"Next stop is Casterton Avenue, a short walk to Burnley General Hospital."

As we travel along my colleagues and myself find ourselves listening more intently to the pronouncements. It soon becomes apparent that there is more than one recorded voice joining in the party. Firstly, there is what sounds like a delightful young lady providing interesting snippets of information and even wishing us a *"Merry Christmas"*. Then there is a rather more brusque, dictatorial fellow who favours a more direct approach, *"Get off at Lomeshaye!"*

After some time listening to these contrasting styles we postulate a theory that the particular voice is dependent on the locality of the bus at that moment in time. That is, in the more rural areas with the more expensive housing we get the lovely young lady, whilst in the urbanised industrial areas it is the aggressive bruiser! This of course may be a total load of b*****ks, but just have a listen out yourselves as you ride the mainline.

Anyway, bus fun over with we settle into a foreshortened five-mile walk led by Ed 'Sherpa' Walton, who has now been given the moniker of Captain Mainwaring by walker John W. For the moment the Captain is taking it in good humour, but if I were John W I'd be wary of a backlash. Thankfully the weather is kinder on this occasion and by 1.30 we reach the Trawden Arms slightly dampened and muddied but raring to go.

An excellent three course lunch, several pints of foaming real ale, and a bloody good time enjoyed by a healthy turnout of 29 from the Burnley Contingent. The highlight of the proceedings was the Lyrical Pen Pictures of several contingent members, penned by the prolific John W. These were well known pieces of music with the words adapted to fit the character of the unfortunate subject. Meant to both amuse and offend, they certainly hit their targets. The 'choir', led by John W, performed the ditties in an atmosphere akin to Community Singing at Wembley Stadium, much to the amusement of locals and barstaff. The tribute to exiled former walkers Jim and Anne Kendra, now resident in Australia, set to the tune of Waltzing Matilda, was particularly poignant. So much so that it was repeated, and video recorded to be subsequently posted on Facebook for our old amigos to enjoy. Maybe a little tear and thoughts of home there for Jim and Anne.

Bellies full, clothes dried out, and spirits lifted it was time for the more sensible members to head for the 16.41 Transdev M3 back to Burnley. For the less sensible members, McDevitt's and Gibson's et al, time for a longer session at the pub and a taxi ride home. A great start to the Christmas festivities and many thanks to the Trawden Arms, a brilliant venue. When you're next in that area pay them a visit, you won't be disappointed!

Game 18 - Saturday 16th December 15.00 – Brighton & Hove Albion v Burnley

Some good news on the injury front as Ben Mee returns to the starting line-up and Matt Lowton makes the substitutes bench. Kevin Long is somewhat unfortunate to lose his place after two excellent stand-in performances, but with games coming thick and fast his chance will no doubt come again soon. Not so good news is that Steven Ward fails to make it and may be out for some weeks. Charlie Taylor makes his first full Premier League start after a long and patient wait.

As mentioned earlier Brighton are not enjoying the best of form at the moment having taken only two points from the last six fixtures. Goal scoring seems to be their big problem having netted only once in the last five outings, and that a penalty converted by Glenn Murray. With their misfiring forwards and our rock-solid defence, this one has all the makings of a low scoring contest.

To be honest in the first half we are not as they say, 'at the races'. We're pretty much under the cosh and there's little to be seen of our attacking intent. The Seagulls are pressing forward at every opportunity and are unfortunate not to lead as a shot from Pascal Knockaert beats Nick Pope but hits the post. Another close call as a header from a corner looks a certain goal before Phil Bardsley saves the day with a tremendous headed clearance off the goal line.

Then a controversial moment as Murray and James Tarkowski tangle for a ball with the striker inside the penalty area but heading away from goal. Down tumbles Murray and after some hesitation the referee awards a penalty. A look of incredulity from Tarka, at what appears a very harsh decision. TV replays confirm that Murray had entwined his leg through those of Tarkowski and 'won' the penalty decision. Still, not to worry as Murray strides confidently up to take the kick, and fires high over the crossbar into Row Q. Justice is done!

Later in the half the pair tangle again as Tarkowski, clearly incensed by Murray's antics over the penalty, gives him a sly dig in the ribs with his elbow. The referee on this occasion clearly sees the incident but fortunately takes no action. Just a bit of a worry here that the football authorities may review the match footage and take retrospective action against our man. Half time arrives, and we somewhat fortunately go in all square.

Thankfully an improved second half performance sees us perhaps unfortunate not to take all the points. Whether our hosts ran out of steam, or whether we, having weathered the storm, decided to 'go for it' is debatable.

Ashley Barnes, returning to his old club, was introduced into the fray on 68 minutes, this time at the expense of Steven Defour. As is often the case, it didn't take Ashley long to make an impact as his first action saw him yellow carded for an assault on home keeper Matt Ryan.

A close call for the home side as Johann Berg Gudmundsson played a ball into the box and Jeff Hendrick moved it on sideways to Scott Arfield. Scotty first shot is saved by the keeper's legs and then he is up quickly to parry the second attempt. The ball drops to Chris Wood who fires home but is flagged offside. Another fine chance to steal the points goes begging as Barnes puts Wood in the clear with an intelligent through ball. Now one on one with the keeper, Wood can only hit Ryan with his attempted chip and the chance is gone.

There's still time for a theatrical dive by Brighton substitute Izquierdo as he throws himself into the penalty area at Ben Mee's challenge. No action here from the referee for what is a blatant attempt to cheat. Perhaps if the Tarkowski incident is retrospectively reviewed then this should also definitely be.

There are no more real threats at either end, though as we enter the last few minutes Brighton throw caution to the wind. Once again, our defence is solid and another away point is in the bag. These are indeed changed days when I feel slightly miffed that we are coming home from an away game with a solitary point instead of all three. That is truly an indication of how far out team has developed. We need to wait until the Sunday fixtures are completed before we can see where we are in the table. However, with Tottenham Hotspur losing heavily at Manchester City, we will be no lower than sixth!

Result – Brighton & Hove Albion 0 – 0 Burnley

Burnley Team

Pope, Bardsley, Mee, Tarkowski, Taylor, Gudmundsson, Cork, Defour (Barnes 68), Hendrick, Arfield, Wood (Vokes 81)

Subs Not Used – Lindegaard, Lowton, Long, Westwood, Wells

Brighton & Hove Albion Team

Ryan, Bruno, Duffy, Dunk, Bong, Knockaert (Izquierdo 85), Stephens, Propper, March, Murray (Hemmed 63), Gross (Brown 73)

Subs Not Used – Krul, Goldson, Kayal, Schelotto

Attendance – 29,921

Season To Date – Played 18, Won 9, Drawn 5, Lost 4, Goals For 16, Goals Against 12, Points 32

League Position after Game 18 – 6th

As expected we are dealt a serious blow ahead of the Christmas fixtures as James Tarkowski's elbow to the ribs of Glenn Murray earns him a three-match ban for violent conduct. A bit extreme to label it 'violent' it could have been described more as 'playful'. Sean Dyche is not best pleased and cites provocation as a mitigating factor but alas to no avail. 'Tarks' will miss the forthcoming home game against Tottenham Hotspur, followed by the two away games at Manchester United, and Huddersfield. Probably more painful for the player is the fractured hand he sustained in the running battle with Murray. This injury, although he played the full 90 minutes has required surgery, and the insertion of a metal plate and pins. Ironically that would probably have ruled him out of the fixtures in any case.

So, it's a quick return for Kevin Long in central defence and what a prospect he faces in the next two games. On Saturday he will face Spurs Harry Kane, and that followed on Tuesday by a tussle with Romelu Lukaku - two of the top strikers in the Premier League, it doesn't come any harder than that. Come on Kev lad, show them what you're made of!

Better news on the injury front is the return to full fitness of forward Jon Walters, and midfielder Dean Marney. Both will be available if called upon for the hectic holiday period fixtures.

Game 19 - Saturday 23rd December 17.30 – Burnley v Tottenham Hotspur

A Christmas appetiser against old adversaries Tottenham Hotspur marks the half way point in what so far has been for us an incredible season. Going into the game we sit sixth in the Premier League, one point and one place above today's opponents. If somebody had suggested to me back in August that this would be the case, I would have suggested he had lost his marbles! But, the table doesn't lie, and we are where we are on merit. I think a testing time coming up now as injuries and a string of difficult looking fixtures are upon us.

Again, it's one of those unloved kick-off times as the game is moved from it's traditional spot of 3.00pm to 5.30pm to accommodate TV viewers. Apart from the absence of the suspended James Tarkowski, we are again without the long term injured Robbie Brady. Stephen Ward is again ruled out so it's a second full start for Charlie Taylor at full back.

It's a strange Saturday afternoon for me, as fans all over the country head to their respective grounds for the traditional 3.00pm kick-offs, I find myself watching 'Harry Potter and the Philosophers's Stone'. Perhaps some of Harry's magic will rub off on us today.

I'm at the ground in good time and the weather for a change is surprisingly mild. The pitch looks immaculate and the stadium is at full capacity, can the Clarets once more rise to the occasion?

Ahead of the game an interestingly named chap called 'Peppered Steak Pie' posted a topic on the 'Up the Clarets' messageboard entitled, 'Guess the time……Penalty'. Clearly a man of the same opinion as myself regarding dodgy decisions given against us in fixtures against the 'Big Six'. Somewhat prophetically as it turned out, he suggested one may be conceded as a result of *"possibly the slightest bodily contact leaving Dele Alli 'entitled' to go down"*.

It doesn't take long for the controversy to begin. On four minutes the talented but obnoxious Alli can count himself very fortunate to be still on the pitch. Losing the ball in centre midfield he launches himself at Charlie Taylor in a desperate attempt to regain possession. The impact leaves Taylor in a crumpled heap, and our cocky 'friend' with a look of surprised innocence. Unsurprisingly referee Oliver decides a yellow card is sufficient. I bet if the challenge had been the other way around, i.e. Taylor on Alli, the card would have been red! Sean Dyche rather more diplomatically puts it;

"It's a real tough one. He's out of control, he's never going to get the ball. By the modern rules, he got lucky with it".

"It's the old favourite – an orange card"!

There is no disputing that Alli is a very talented player, however there is 'dark edge' to his game that is in danger of spoiling his reputation. It doesn't take long before our 'villain' shows another unpleasant feature of his game, i.e. the tendency to hit the deck at the slightest hint of contact. In the seventh minute he has the ball in the penalty area to the right of the goal. Rapidly running out of pitch, Kevin Long rather naively instead of standing off him, sticks out a leg. No further invitation required, he hits the turf like a wounded pheasant. No hesitation from Mr Oliver, he can't point to the penalty spot quick enough. Peppered Steak Pie has it bang on! Harry Kane despatches the 'gift' convincingly sending Nick Pope the wrong way.

What looked like a difficult fixture from the start now has become a major challenge. Unfortunately, on this occasion it's one we are nowhere near up to. The rest of the first half consists of Spurs making chances with consummate ease. Fortunately thanks to good goalkeeping and profligate finishing no further damage to the score line is sustained. The ease with which a very impressive team are able to carve out openings is extremely worrying. Our normally resolute defence is at times shambolic as the opposition go through it like the proverbial 'hot knife through butter'. Has the loss of key players through injury and suspension finally come home to roost? Or is that our visitors with players like Kane and Christian Eriksen, who both retain the ball so well, are too good for us?

Chris Wood is ploughing a lonely furrow up front and the term feeding off scraps is certainly applicable here. Too often when we have the luxury of possession in advanced positions the ball is ending up being channelled back to Pope for a hopeful punt upfield. Our five-man midfield is being completely overrun by technically and physically superior opposition.

Worse is to come. On a rare foray upfield, Wood manages to wrestle control of the ball and feed Steven Defour to the left of the penalty area. Defour's low cross is cut out at the near post by keeper Hugo Lloris as Wood attempts to apply the finishing touch. The pair collide, and our expensive striker comes out of the impact the worse for wear. A brave attempt to play on ends after a few minutes and he limps off to be replaced by Ashley Barnes.

Half time arrives with the score somehow still just at 1-0. There doesn't seem much hope of a comeback, but where there's life there's hope!

The second half continues in much the same vein, a lot of huff and puff from us but to little effect, whilst our visitors continue to create decent opportunities. The referee is giving us nothing and we are not helped by our inability to retain possession and frequent mistakes. From one such error the game is effectively over on 69 minutes. The ball given away in midfield is played straight through our central defence to the lethal Kane who one-on-one with Pope was never going to miss.

Time for the referee's affliction of partial blindness to persist as he turns down a couple of penalty appeals for fouls on Barnes. The condition lifts sufficiently for him to chalk off a 'goal' from substitute Sam Vokes, presumably for a push on Lloris.

Then on 79 minutes Harry Kane's night is complete. Winning the ball in a sprawling challenge he feeds Ben Davies to his left. Picking himself up he heads straight for goal, the ball finds its way to him via the despicable Alli, and in a flash its nestling in the net. I have to say that Kane has produced a superb display of the striker's art. What a contrast his selfless and hard running performance is to that of the petulant Alli.

Thankfully our visitors have had enough after that one and the game fizzles out to finish 0-3. Not the ideal start to Christmas, but to be fair it was a game that was always going to require us to be at our best. Tonight, we were far from that. Still not to worry its only Manchester United at Old Trafford on Tuesday!

The only good thing coming out of the evening was Harry Kane's hat-trick earned me a bagful of points in my quest for Fantasy Football League riches!

Result – Burnley 0 – 3 (Kane 7, 69,79) Tottenham Hotspur

Burnley Team

Pope, Bardsley, Mee, Long, Taylor, Gudmundsson, Cork, Defour, Hendrick (Vokes 71), Arfield (Wells 86), Wood (Barnes 35)

Subs Not Used – Lindegaard, Lowton, Walters, Westwood

Tottenham Hotspur Team

Lloris, Aurier, Sanchez, Vertonghen, Davies, Sissoko, Dier (Lamela 83) Eriksen, Son Heung-min (Dembele 78), Alli (Llorente 87), Kane

Subs Not Used – Vorm, Trippier, Rose, Foyth

Attendance – 21,650

Season To Date – Played 19, Won 9, Drawn 5, Lost 5, Goals For 16, Goals Against 15, Points 32

League Position after Game 19 – 7th

So, that's the half way point in the season reached. Thirty-two points amassed and seventh in the table, I think I can say we'll settle for that. The half term grade has to be an A* for manager, players and fans. Little old Burnley this time not only punching above their weight, but also slaying giants! It will be difficult to match that points haul in the second half of the campaign. With this team though who would back against it?

Game 20 - Tuesday 26th December 15.00 – Manchester United v Burnley

Following our mauling at the hands of Harry Kane on Saturday, it was reassuring to see him reprise his impressive hat-trick feat in the Boxing day lunchtime kick-off against Southampton. This time the rampant Spurs ran in five against the ragged Saints as they enjoy a golden spell of form. It's good to know we weren't the only Christmas Turkeys!

In an attempt to escape the grip of Christmas 'cabin fever', and taking advantage of a rare cessation of rain, we decide on a family trip to Towneley Park ahead of the kick-off at Old Trafford. Once again, I'm more than a little apprehensive about this fixture. United sit second in the table although some way adrift of runaway leaders Manchester City.

Chris Wood fails fails to make the squad following his injury sustained on Saturday and Ashley Barnes takes his place. The Reds name an impressively expensive line-up with a formidable looking forward trio of Marcus Rashford, Zlatan Ibrahimovich and Romelu Lukaku. Our old friend Jose 'Moaninho' must be really fancying his chances in this one.

A short stroll to the Stables restaurant, and a cappuccino duly despatched, we set off for a slightly longer amble to take the air. As we leave Thanet Lee Wood, off goes the often dreaded 'goal alert' on my phone. It can't be surely, they've only just kicked off. My wife Julie, ever the optimist, proffers the view that we will be already a goal down. I tell her not to be so negative, but as I reach for my phone, I fear the worst. Quelle surprise! As I hesitantly look at the alert I am amazed to read:

'Manchester United 0 – 1 Burnley (Barnes 3)'

What a start, and how glad I am to see that it's none other than 'Basher', Moaninho's nemesis, who has notched! Great! Only 87 minutes, plus the ubiquitous 'added time' to survive. I feel my mood instantly lifted and continue the rest of the route 'walking on air'. On arrival back at the car I can't wait to switch on the radio, and in doing so I am further stunned by the announcement that the score is now 2-0! I have missed the second goal alert, but who cares. Half time arrives safely, and we have a precious two goal lead. It's a bit like that feeling I had when we led 3-0 at Chelsea in the season's opener. Delight and disbelief at the score tinged with the dread of what is to come in the next 45 minutes.

Jose, 'The Special One', has obviously seen enough and promptly removes Marcos Rojo and Ibrahimovich, replacing them for the second period with Henrik Mkhitaryan and Jesse Lingard respectively. The expected one-way traffic towards our goal is not long in coming, as United no doubt with their ears stinging from the half time chat, come at us with a vengeance. I'm now back at home and unable to bear the stress of a Radio Lancashire commentary, I'm following the action on the BBC's Final Score. On 53 minutes comes that familiar sinking feeling as Lingard scores to put our hosts back in the game.

Ironic that as only minutes earlier the striker had missed an easier chance as his close range shot hit Nick Pope in the face and bounced up to hit the bar. Just a one goal lead now and still 37 minutes to play. It's going to be a long second half. However, despite a barrage of home attacks, we are restricting the number of clear cut chances very effectively. The Clarets defence has once again discovered its composure and resilience. As the seemingly endless half finally draws towards its close, the inevitable added time of five minutes is announced.

Surely, we can safely navigate our way through just five more minutes. Then with that same air of inevitability, with one minute of added time gone, Lingard scores again taking advantage of a loose ball from a free kick to rifle home. Surely, we can't lose the game now, can we? With the Old Trafford crowd roaring their heroes on to glory it's a nerve wracking few minutes, but we survive intact.

So, a game where we hoped a two-goal lead at half time would bring us three more precious points, eventually yields just one. But how can we complain about that? We certainly would have settled for that before the game started. It's just that having lead for so long, we feel a little cheated to just come away with a draw. Changed days these for we Clarets when we leave Old Trafford with a draw and feel slightly disappointed!

Watching the action later that evening on Match of The Day (MOTD) I relive the joy of Barnes's opener, a bit of a scrappy affair as he reacts quickest to a loose ball in the United box. Then next I marvel at the sumptuously struck free kick by

Defour that doubles the lead. The Daily Mail gives the statistics as, Shot Distance: 28 yards, Speed of Shot: 48.5 mph, but raw stats can't describe the beauty of the strike. A right foot shot clearing the defensive wall then arcing and dipping into the top corner. Unstoppable even for a keeper of David De Gea's ability.

The second half I find not so entertaining although I have to admit that both Lingard's goals are well taken efforts. Sean Dyche is unhappy that the fee kick given for a foul by Sam Vokes is a tad harsh, arguing that the United player turned into Vokes and he had nowhere to go. I later learn that Vokesy is doubly unfortunate in that he has also had a goal disallowed for offside. There seems to be some doubt as to whether this was in fact the case. MOTD however declined to show the incident, no real surprise there!

The general consensus in the media seems to be that Burnley have been superb in the first half, and dogged in the second. Moaninho, with characteristic bad grace is unable to crack a smile. He prefers instead to claim that the £300m spent in the last 18 months is insufficient to challenge rivals Manchester City. I wonder what Sean Dyche could do with £300m? I'd warrant a damn sight more than that. Dyche, needless to say, is wearing a big smile and looking forward to the next encounter, Huddersfield Town away on Saturday. With only two defeats in 10 away fixtures we now fear nobody on the road, but at the same time we underestimate nobody either.

Result – Manchester United (Lingard 53, 90+1) 2 – 2 (Barnes 3, Defour 36) Burnley

Burnley Team

Pope, Bardsley, Mee, Long, Taylor, Gudmundsson, Cork, Defour (Vokes67), Hendrick, Arfield, Barnes (Walters 81)

<u>Subs Not Used</u> – Lindegaard, Lowton, Marney, Westwood, Wells

Manchester United Team

De Gea, Young, Jones, Rojo (Mkhitaryan 46), Shaw, Pogba, Matic. Mata, Ibrahimovich (Lingard 46), Lukaku, Rashford

<u>Subs Not Used</u> – Romero, Blind, Lindelof, Herrera, Tuanzebe

Attendance – 75,046

Season To Date – Played 20, Won 9, Drawn 6, Lost 5, Goals For 18, Goals Against 17, Points 33

League Position after Game 20 – 7th

The last game of a hectic December coming up now, with key players still out injured and the transfer window about to re-open, January could be a very interesting month.

Game 21 - Saturday 30th December 15.00 – Huddersfield Town v Burnley

These days I don't get to many away fixtures, this is one I would very much have liked to have attended. An ex work associate and pal Rob Waterworth is a massive Huddersfield Town supporter. He always makes his way to Burnley when the teams meet, and we enjoy a pint or two ahead of the game. Back in September, he as usual, invited me to join him at the reciprocal fixture for pre-match pints in The White Rose. Now free beer from a Yorkshireman is not something that should be missed!

Unfortunately, I was under the impression that the return game was not till late in the season, that is until I saw on the Up the Clarets website that all tickets for this game were sold out! Bugger, missed out on that one, and it looks like another afternoon of torture with Radio Lancashire.

I have a certain admiration for Huddersfield Town, they are much like ourselves in that they are a town club with a proud tradition, passionate fans, and thoroughly deserving of their chance at the big time. Having said that, I'd still like us to wipe the floor with them today, and then restore my affection for them later.

After Tuesday's magnificent draw at Old Trafford, unsurprisingly Sean Dyche names an unchanged side again with the same 18 players on duty. It's the last game of James Tarkowski's suspension, and Chris Wood is believed to be near full fitness. Just as well as the games are still coming thick and fast, and we will be back in action again on Monday for a home game with in-form Liverpool.

Two players who will be looking to impress today are Scott Arfield and Nahki Wells, both ex 'Terriers' returning to their old stomping ground. Arfield starts but Wells will have to hope for an opportunity coming off the bench.

Its a comfortable enough start for the Clarets, who these days fear nobody on their travels. As the first half progresses we ae getting into our stride and dominating play. Ashley Barnes is proving a handful up front and is being ably supported by Johann Berg Gudmundsson (JBG).

Gudmundsson is close to opening the scoring as his surging run ends with his shot fizzing past the post. Similarly, Steven Defour, breaking forward, lets fly and his effort also narrowly goes wide of the post. There's precious little being seen of our hosts as an attacking force, as we go into the half time break at 0-0, but well on top.

More of the same at the start of the second half, and our friends from Radio Lancashire reckon the cigars should be out by now for the Clarets. Then an incident that is becoming an increasingly frequent source of annoyance. As Burnley counter attack Jack Cork's pass somewhat fortuitously finds Arfield, who plays in Jeff Hendrick. Hendrick's control is perfect, and he takes the ball around the Town keeper Lossl, who promptly takes his trailing leg and down he goes. The empty net is beckoning but our man is sprawled on the deck. The commentators are adamant it's a penalty, the pundits on Final Score reckon it's a 'stonewall penalty', but the referee who has a good view doesn't give it! If it's not a penalty it must surely be a booking for a 'dive' or simulation, to give it it's posh title. No, no yellow card. How can that be?

Once again, we are on the wrong end of a contentious decision, is it bad luck or don't the Premier League like to see the humble Clarets challenging the big six? Match of the Day give the incident the full analysis and to a man agree we are robbed. My mate Rob, who after the game was convinced it wasn't a penalty, texts me to concede that after seeing it again, it was. Even Huddersfield Town manager David Wagner admits it should have been given. Still it would have been a rare novelty if it had, we haven't been awarded one all season!

Buoyed by their good fortune over the penalty incident the Terriers enjoy their best spell of the game, but without causing too much alarm. Wells gets his opportunity to put one over his old mates as he gets a final nine minutes of action. What is more he almost does so as his toe-poked finish from a Sam Vokes knockdown almost wins the game at the death. However, it's not to be and we have to settle for an away point that probably should have been three.

The match statistics confirm a dominant performance, 11 shots to 3, 4 on target to 1 and it's another point towards safety. The teams immediately below us, Leicester City and Everton, both lose 2-1 away from home and the gap behind us widens to seven points.

Result – Huddersfield Town 0 – 0 Burnley

Burnley Team

Pope, Bardsley, Mee, Long, Taylor, Gudmundsson, Cork, Defour, Hendrick (Vokes 73), Arfield, Barnes (Wells 81)

Subs Not Used – Lindegaard, Lowton, Marney, Westwood, Walters

Huddersfield Town Team

Lossl, Hadergjonaj (Smith 45), Jorgensen, Schindler, Malone, Mooy, Hogg, Quaner (Williams 82), Ince (Lolley 55), van La Parra, Depoitre

Subs Not Used – Coleman, Cranie, Hefele, Mounie

Attendance – 24,095

Season To Date – Played 21, Won 9, Drawn 7, Lost 5, Goals For 18, Goals Against 17, Points 34

League Position after Game 21 – 7th

December has been a mammoth month of football, and I think its fair to say has seen us destroy the myth that we have been enjoying a fluke run. Seven games in the month have seen us record, two wins, three draws and two defeats, whilst maintaining our seventh place in the table. Highly satisfactory and with a bit more 'rub of the green' it would have been even better. Bring on 2018!

A 'Leninesque' Sean Dyche casts a wary eye over visitors on the approach to Burnley. Sadly, the mural and building no longer exist.

Not many managers get a pub named after them, and free beer for life!

The Football club catering team get the European message, it's now "More than just pies".

The author pictured outside the gates of David Moyes's mansion. Needless to say, he wasn't invited in!

Lancashire Dotcom Walkers official badge – all suggestions for a suitable motto welcome.

'Give it a kick! A 'carbuncle' on the face of the landscape a fallen (like the team) sign on the entry to Belmont. The author obliges watched by a smiling Steve Glover (PNE fan), who wants to be next.

Strangling Blackburn John. The deluded Rovers fan gets the full treatment, that'll teach him to come out in that scarf.

Confused at Staups Mill! Burnley Contingent Walkers looking for direction, but all looking in different directions!

The author poses for his photo for Charles Buchan's Football Monthly.

Spot the ball. A sloping pitch and Keith appeals, for what?

I think we may be a bit too old for the Academy. The author and Blackburn John show there's no hard feelings outside Brockhall.

Mission accomplished. Trig point at Simon's Seat.

Burnley Contingent walk debrief at the Pendle Inn, Barley.

Fancy this job. Man abseils on wind turbine to get a better view of the Turf Moor action. I hope he's got good eyesight, it's on Winter Hill!

Man takes picture of man taking picture atop Pendle Hill.

Why so happy chaps? Don't they know we're about to enter 'The Valley of Desolation'.

The jewel in Burnley's crown – Towneley Hall.

Burnley's beacon – Pendle Hill. In the words of John W, you can't be lost if you can see Pendle.

My daughter's wedding venue, the Charles Bathurst Inn, Arkengarthdale

JANUARY 2018

The first game of the New Year poses a bit of a selection dilemma for Sean Dyche. Should he re-instate James Tarkowski, now free of suspension, or retain Kevin Long at the heart of the defence? Long has enjoyed two fine games at Manchester United and Huddersfield Town, after a more difficult time against Tottenham Hotspur. Dyche is not a man to tamper with something that is working well, and my gut feeling is that Kevin will get the nod. Another very testing fixture coming up against Liverpool, who are excellent going forward, but not so sure at the back. A lively start to 2018 looks likely to be on the cards.

Game 22 - Monday 1st January 15.00 – Burnley v Liverpool

A new year dawns in Burnley, but to the casual observer its no different to the old one. Yes, its cold, wet and miserable. Now in the good old days I would be rising from my bed around lunchtime, with a monster hangover and looking forward to some relief by means of the 'hair of the dog'. Not today though I am up and alert by 9.00 a.m., and what is more so are my fellow Clarets John W, and John G. I text them to wish them Happy New Year and point out how uncharacteristic it is for us to be so 'chipper' at this early hour. John G's response is, *"Still feel crap though"*. Now that's more like it, a man who has fully embraced the New Year celebrations. With arrangements made to reconvene for pre-match pints at the Talbot, all is set fair.

As I launch in to my first pint of Golden Pippin, the usual tipple of Moorhouse's Premiership having 'gone off', team news comes through. James Tarkowski regains his place at the expense of the unfortunate Kevin Long, but that's the only change for the Clarets. Liverpool are without the injured Mohammed Salah, and I am truly thankful for that. The Egyptian is having a terrific first season with the Reds and scoring goals for fun. Also missing is Brazilian playmaker Philippe Coutinho, who I can only assume is not being risked ahead of a January transfer to Barcelona. Surprisingly, also omitted but on the bench, is fellow striker Roberto Firmino, a victim of Jurgen Klopp's rotation policy.

The early exchanges see Burnley, attacking the Cricket Field end goal in torrential rain, and against a stiff wind, mostly on the defensive. The recalled-after-injury Adam Lallana is pulling the strings for the Scousers and looking to create openings for Sadio Mane and Dominic Solanke. With Ben Mee and Tarkowski in dominant form the Clarets are resisting comfortably and as the half wears on, coming more into it as an attacking force.

It's goalless at half time in what is proving to be a fairly even contest. I'm hopeful that with the wind at our backs in the second half we can find the momentum to claim a victory. The game restarts and after the first quarter hour its still pretty much even-stevens. But then a bolt from the blue; Mane, who up to this point had been anonymous, controls a ball played in from the right wing. From his position, edge of the penalty area but central, he swivels and fires an unstoppable left-footer high into the net giving keeper Nick Pope no chance.

A bit harsh on the Clarets that one, but nothing for it but to get on with it. Now chasing the game, the usual substitutions are made as Sam Vokes replaces Jeff Hendrick, and Nahki Wells gets about the last 10 minutes replacing Scott Arfield. There are chances at both ends Pope saving well on a couple of occasions from Trent Alexander-Arnold, whilst Simon Mignolet does well to keep out a Vokes header. Then as time is running out a Charlie Taylor cross is headed on by Vokes and headed home by Johann Berg Gudmundsson from close range.

Fantastic, an equaliser on 87 minutes! Surely in my opinion, a thoroughly deserved point poached at the end. However, as is often the case, a very late goal robs us of our share of the spoils. In the fourth minute of added time a softly conceded free kick is poorly defended allowing Ragnar Klavan to steal in and nod home from almost on the goal line. In doing so becoming the first Estonian to score in a Premier League fixture.

What a tragic end to what had been not a classic match but a hard-fought encounter in terrible conditions. Personally, I didn't think there was much to pick between the teams, but once again the game is decided by 'fine margins'. Nothing for it but to go home and 'kick the cat'. Before any animal lovers get upset, can I just point out I don't have a cat. It'll have to be the wife instead!

Result – Burnley (Gudmundsson 87) 1 – 2 (Mane 61, Klavan 90+4) Liverpool

Burnley Team

Pope, Bardsley, Mee, Tarkowski, Taylor, Gudmundsson, Cork, Defour, Hendrick (Vokes 71), Arfield (Wells 86), Barnes

<u>Subs Not Used</u> – Lindegaard, Lowton, Long, Westwood, Walters

Liverpool Team

Mignolet, Alexander-Arnold, Lovren, Klavan, Gomez, Mane (Firmino 72), Can, Wijnaldum, Lallana (Milner 86), Oxlade-Chamberlain (Matip 90+6), Solanke

<u>Subs Not Used</u> – Karius, Robertson, Ings, Woodburn

Attendance – 21,756

Season To Date – Played 22, Won 9, Drawn 7, Lost 6, Goals For 19, Goals Against 19, Points 34

League Position after Game 22 – 7th

With the coming of the New Year comes also the bi-annual transfer window torture! Yes, all the speculation, disappointment and occasional elation that is associated with Burnley FC's transfer dealing is about to rear its head once more. True to form by the 2nd January names are once again beginning to appear in the press. First to surface are rumours of a move for Celtic centre back, Jozo Simunovic, and Everton winger Aaron Lennon. Both are players in positions where we could be looking to strengthen, but the reports could just be a rehash of last summer's speculation.

A more bizarre suggestion is that we may be interested in Theo Walcott from Arsenal. I really can't see that as a realistic proposition considering the sort of wages he must be receiving currently. Some are suggesting that with the World Cup finals to be played this summer the player needs to be playing regular football. The inference is that he would get that opportunity at Burnley. I'm not so sure about that, Sean Dyche is well known to favour letting newcomers 'bed in' before they become regulars. I'm also not sure that Walcott is our type of player, we prefer workhorses to race horses.

Similarly, another name mentioned is Johnathan Viera currently at Spanish La Liga club Las Palmas. Can you see a lad currently enjoying the year-round sunshine of the Canary Islands swapping that for the freezing monsoon conditions of a Burnley winter?

In fact, mention of the weather brings me to the first Burnley Contingent Thursday walk of 2018. What a start to the walking year. Once again, a walk master minded by the 'Wandering Weirs', starting from Todmorden Leisure Centre and taking in Lumbutts and Mankinholes. Now that has to be a north country walk! Can you see villages in the Home Counties having such evocative and sexy names?

What a gentle reintroduction to our Thursday walks after the Christmas excesses. The walk billed as 7.1 miles, but actually measuring 8.4 miles on the day, was said to have no major climbs. Can anybody imagine a walk in the Todmorden area without major climbs? If the ascents weren't major, they were certainly continuous. To add to the fun the walk started in light rain, progressed to heavy rain and finished with a descent from Todmorden Golf Club in a wind assisted torrential downpour. Fourteen hardy souls survived the elements, despite being advised by the leader to have lunch in the shelter of a wood. This would have been a great idea had the trees been in leaf, but a deciduous wood in January?

Suitably soaked, and dripping from head to toe, we effected a quick change out of the sodden gear and re-grouped at the Rifle Volunteer in Burnley. Revived by post walk pints, and the news that James Tarkowski had committed to a new contract with Burnley FC taking him through to June 2022, a good end to a good day.

That was good news on the Tarkowski front, already after just a half season of Premier League football, the player was being linked with possible interest from Manchester City and Arsenal. With just a season and a half left on his existing contract it was important to get him committed longer term. Whilst this won't stop envious glances from the 'Big Six' it will mean that his transfer value to ourselves is protected, and there will be no cheap sales of a player coming out of contract.

A good week for myself on the Transfer Terrorism Fantasy Football league run by the lads and lasses at Burnley M&S. After a difficult few weeks my tactical nous, and shrewd operation of the transfer market has seen me move into second place in the table. 'Dyche's Dream Team' are now in hot pursuit of leaders 'Taking my ball home!' Now lying just 14 points off top spot, I am starting to smell the serious money. A break this weekend though from the fantasy action as the Premier League gives way to FA Cup action. That's perhaps not a bad thing as I plan my next strategy.

The Clarets cup action will be a daunting task at unbeaten Premier League leaders Manchester City. With a number of injuries, and players showing signs of fatigue after the hectic December schedule, major team changes are envisaged for this game. For both teams the competition will be very much a second priority, particularly for City who are chasing trophies on four fronts. However, the depth of our hosts playing squad will ensure that even with multiple changes, they will field a formidable line-up.

FA Cup Round 3 - Saturday 6th January 15.00 – Manchester City v Burnley

The team news would indicate that whilst both teams make four changes they are still taking the competition seriously. Scott Arfield with a tight hamstring is replaced by Sam Vokes, whilst James Tarkowski's injured hand is given a week's break to further recover. Phil Bardsley and Steven Defour take a well-earned rest, their places being filled by Matt Lowton and Ashley Westwood respectively. City take the opportunity to rest some defenders and the currently unplayable Kevin De Bruyne. However, a team that still boasts attacking players of the calibre of David Silva, Sergio Aguero, Leroy Sane and Raheem Sterling, can hardly be described as weak.

From the off we are being pushed back by our hosts, but they are lacking their usual penetration against our formidably organised defence. Indeed, we come closest to scoring early on as Ben Mee's header from a corner, needlessly conceded by Claudio Bravo, just eludes Ashley Barnes's attempt to get a finishing touch. We are growing in confidence as the game plan appears to be working perfectly and then on 25 minutes, the perfect boost! Nick Pope's kick is flicked on by Sam Vokes, City defender John Stones is nearest to it but makes a terrible hash of a clearance. His attempt is sliced high and into the path of Barnes who heads it into his path, advances towards goal, then unleashes a terrific right-footer beating Bravo 'all ends up' at his near post. Good old Ashley a goal at Old Trafford recently and now this one at the Etihad.

Buoyed by our lead and having something even more valuable to defend, we make it through to the break, a goal to the good against our surprisingly lacklustre opponents. It's a strangely quiet Etihad stadium, well from the 45,000 shocked home fans, but there's plenty of noise coming from the 7,600 Clarets!

Don't you just wish sometimes that there was no half time break. It disturbs the flow and gives the team who are underperforming the opportunity to address their shortcomings. This was certainly one of those occasions, although there was no hint of it till just short of the hour.

As Barnes is penalised for a challenge, the Clarets are slow to take up their defensive positions as Westwood consults the referee. City take the opportunity to take a crafty 'quick one' freeing Aguero to shoot past Pope unmarked. Sean Dyche and Ian Woan are understandably incensed that the official has allowed the kick to be taken with Westwood nowhere near 10 yards from the ball. A touchline dispute erupts between the pair and City coach, Pep Guardiola. The mayhem and confusion does nothing to aid our concentration and within a couple of minutes we concede again. Ilkay Gundogan with a sublime back heel from the edge of the penalty area finds Aguero, again all alone and he makes no mistake.

How quickly the game can turn, particularly against what is currently probably one of the world's leading club sides. The game has changed totally now, and we are well and truly up against the wall. On 71 minutes it's all over as a contest as another flowing move ends with Sane rolling home goal number three. Then to rub it in De Bruyne is introduced from the bench for a 15-minute cameo performance. With a trademark killer pass he frees Sane who rounds Pope, who for some reason best known to himself has decided to join the outfield players. Unselfishly the young striker pulls the ball back to substitute Bernardo Silva who easily fires into an empty net.

Thankfully that's the end of the scoring. Unfortunately, it's also the end of our interest in the FA Cup for another season. What started so promisingly has ended somewhat disastrously, but against a team as good as this it was always a possibility. There's no need to dwell on it, it was a diversion from the main event, so we'll hopefully learn from it and move on!

Result - Manchester City (Aguero 56, 58, Sane 71, Bernardo Silva 82) 4 – 1 (Barnes 25)) Burnley

Burnley Team

Pope, Lowton, Mee, Long, Taylor, Gudmundsson (Walters 75), Cork (Wells 69), Westwood, Hendrick, Vokes, Barnes

<u>Subs Not Used</u> - Lindegaard, Bardsley, Marney, Ulvestad, Defour

Manchester City Team

Bravo, Danilo, Stones, Otamendi, Zinchenko (Walker 72), Gundogan (De Bruyne 76), Fernandinho, Silva, Sterling, Aguero (Bernardo Silva 79), Sane

<u>Subs Not Used</u> – Ederson, Mangala, Diaz, Toure

Attendance – 53,356

On Tuesday January 9th there's some early transfer window activity at the Turf. Coming in is 22-year-old winger, Georges-Kevin Nkoudou, from Tottenham Hotspur on a loan till the end of the season. The player is described as left sided and a pacy dribbler, and those are certainly assets missing from the squad. Hopefully he may turn out to be just what we needed to cover for the injured Robbie Brady. Although he has relatively little first team experience at Spurs, he should be hungry to play and hopefully quick to adapt to his new surroundings.

It's a case of one in and one out as the club announce on the same day the departure of Luke Hendrie. Hendrie, a young Development Squad player, has spent most of his time with the Clarets out on loan. The first half of this season has been spent at Bradford City, but he has been recalled and now leaves for League One pacesetters Shrewsbury Town on a permanent 18 month contract.

The same day sees an interesting restart to the Dotcom Walkers season. The programme kicked off with a morning visit to Bowland & Pennine Mountain Rescue based at Garstang. A very informative morning was spent learning about the team's operations and structure. I'm sure all present now realise what an extremely valuable service is provided by a thoroughly dedicated and highly trained team of men and women, all on a purely voluntary basis.

One slight concern was the extremely low temperature encountered in their headquarters, a unit on the Creamery Industrial estate. Having been informed by their excellent speaker Ian Maddison of the dangers of Hypothermia, I couldn't help but feel after a couple of hours they were trying to give us a practical demonstration!

The visit was followed by a hastily eaten lunch and a short four mile walk in the surrounding environs. It's fair to say that the temperature was slightly higher outside the building than in it! However, we came away much wiser and infinitely more knowledgeable about this fine group of people.

As the transfer window hots up the speculation mounts. The latest rumour is that a bid has been placed for young Nottingham Forest centre back Joe Worrall. An offer of £8m plus two players, one on a permanent transfer and one on loan is muted. Whether this has any substance at this stage is anyone's guess.

Rumours also surface of interest in our own Scott Arfield from West Ham, with a figure of £2m mentioned as the fee. Whilst this looks like a derisory amount for an established Premier League midfielder, the fact that he is out of contract in the summer may lend some credence to the story. The 'Up the Clarets' website is quick to publish an article on Thursday 11th claiming that a contract offer has been made by Burnley FC to retain the player. We shall see.

On the same day reports are circulating of a loan bid from Sunderland for Jon Walters. The striker/midfielder, just recovered from injury, seems to be currently well down the pecking order at Turf Moor. With the Clarets out of both cup competitions game time here would appear to be at a premium and a move may suit both club and player in the short term.

This Thursday's Burnley contingent walk was once again led by the 'Wandering Weirs'. Thankfully this week the weather was much kinder than last time's outing from Todmorden. In fact so much so that at one point walkers were even able to dispose of gloves and hats for a short spell. An excellent circuit from Chatburn taking in Worston, Little Mearley Hall and Downham was thoroughly enjoyed by 14 hearty souls and Button the dog. Billed as a 7.4 miler it not unsurprisingly overran (yet again) to 8.0, but we can live with that.

Game 23 – Saturday 13th January 15.00 – Crystal Palace v Burnley

Although I always try to be positive where the Clarets are concerned, I must confess that ahead of this game I am not confident. Whether it's because of our poor run of results of late, or a feeling that Crystal Palace are a much better team than their lowly points return would suggest, I'm not sure. For sure Palace's revival under Roy Hodgson has been impressive. After a horrendous start to the season, seven defeats in their first seven fixtures, they are now sitting much more comfortably in the table.

Unfortunately, on this occasion my lack of confidence was well justified. We go into the game showing three changes from last week's FA Cup diversion. Back into the starting line-up come Phil Bardsley, James Tarkowski and Steven Defour. Our hosts are without several key players including Jeffrey Schlupp, Andros Townsend, Chelsea loanee Ruben Loftus-Cheek and Mamadhou Sakho. However, they are still able to field a strong team including the dangerous Wilfried Zaha, man mountain Christian Benteke and Bakary Sako.

From the start we are clearly struggling, the defence usually so assured is today looking jittery as the Eagles attack with pace and power. We are struggling to get a toe-hold in the game and things get worse as we go behind on 21 minutes. Following good build up play between Zaha and Benteke, Sako is allowed to attack the box unchallenged as the defence backs off. Needing no second invitation as he nears the goal from the left side he fires a low shot that eludes Bardsley and Tarkowski and appears to loop up off Nick Pope to land high in the net.

At this point an interesting statistic emerges. It would seem that in 48 Premier League games where we have gone behind in Sean Dyche's tenure, we have failed to come back and win any, recording 40 losses and eight draws. We are not very good when we go behind, and that unenviable record is about to extend to 49 games.

My fellow Clarets buddies, John W and John G, along with myself, have taken to having WhatsApp messaging interchanges during these games. Today I must say that the tone of the chat, initially abusive, was rapidly degenerating. Seemingly bereft of attacking ideas and coming under constant pressure we are looking to reach the sanctuary of half-time without further damage.

Thankfully we make it with still just the one goal deficit. Our poor run of results, six games without a win (counting the cup defeat) looks like continuing. Are our injuries to key players, Tom Heaton, Stephen Ward, Robbie Brady and Chris Wood now starting to impact. That's a lot of major players to lose from a team that in the earlier stages of the season was brimming with confidence, playing well and getting great results.

Into the second period and some signs of improvement as Palace perhaps take their foot off the gas and we start to assert ourselves a little. New man Georges-Kevin Nkoudou, is quickly summoned to the fray replacing the disappointing Jeff Hendrick. Ashley Barnes goes upfront with Sam Vokes and with the new man showing some nice touches we are certainly looking livelier. The best chance falls to Barnes but he is unable to convert and the game ends tamely with us going down again to a single goal defeat.

Although it's only the third away defeat in 12 fixtures, there is for me a bit of a feeling that the season is petering out after our fine first half. Some players notably Jack Cork, and Jeff Hendrick are looking somewhat jaded and that is always the problem when operating with a small squad. Definitely the team needs to find some new impetus, and with still plenty of time left in the transfer window, perhaps that will come through new acquisitions.

We have had a tough run of fixtures through December and early January which hasn't been helpful, but not to worry its only Manchester United up next!

Result – Crystal Palace (Sako 21) 1 – 0 Burnley

Burnley Team

Pope, Bardsley, Mee, Tarkowski, Taylor, Gudmundsson (Wells 85), Cork, Defour, Hendrick (Nkoudou 63), Vokes, Barnes

<u>Subs Not Used</u> – Lindegaard, Lowton, Long, Westwood, Walters

Crystal Palace Team

Hennessey, Fosu-Mensah, Kelly, Tomkins, van Aanholt, Zaha, Milivojevic, Riedewald, McArthur, Benteke, Sako

<u>Subs Not Used</u> – Speroni, Cabaye, Chung-yong, Souare, Kaikai, Delaney, Wan-Bissaka

Attendance – 24,696

Season To Date – Played 23, Won 9, Drawn 7, Lost 7, Goals For 19, Goals Against 20, Points 34

League Position after Game 23 – 7th

No midweek soccer action for the Clarets this week but plenty of walking action for myself. On Tuesday it's a short walk from Colne to accommodate lunch at the Crown Hotel and sample the delights of the 'Pensioners Special' menu. The Dotcomers have used this venue in the past and it has been very popular with the greedy but cheap members, of which I class myself. Let's hope it lives up to expectations. We certainly can't complain at the price, £5.90 for two courses!

However, before we can enjoy the reward we have to put in the miles. I'm a little hesitant as to whether I should attend this walk as I have been struck down with the Dreaded Lurgi. I've almost lost my voice and am feeling decidedly throaty. What is more the weather forecast is bloody awful, snow, sleet and rain. A circuit starting from the Boundary Mill store and taking in Slipper Hill, Blacko Hill Side and The Cross Gaits Inn (Free Beer Tomorrow), led by Ed 'Sherpa' Walton didn't disappoint. It had all the forecast elements in plentiful supply with hail stones and driving wind thrown in for good measure. If that wasn't enough it also had the 'Sherpa's' favourite, MUD in Californian mudslide proportions. Dotcom leader Bob Clare was of the opinion that it may well have been the worst weather conditions we have endured on a Tuesday, and then at the death, the sun shone!

Surprisingly 26 walkers survived the elements and were joined at the Crown by two sick-bay non-combatants, Jim (Skipper of the Yard) and Geoff (Just one more) Ashworth, who couldn't resist the allure of a cheap lunch. Not sure how that worked for Jim though, he had to make the round trip from Preston to get it! It must have cost him more in petrol. But what splendid fare, I opted for the Pie of the Day, to be followed by 'Dessert of the Day'. The pie turned out to be Plate Meat & Onion, accompanied by Chips, Peas, Cabbage, Carrots and Gravy. The dessert chosen was Strawberry Cheesecake with Ice Cream. What can I say? Superb 'proper' grub, in ample portions and all for £5.90. Washed down with a pint of Moorhouses's Pride of Pendle, my throat was almost cured. Although now my voice is making me sound as hard as Ray Winstone but without that awful southern twang.

If we thought Tuesday's walk was muddy, the 'Sherpa' excelled himself on Thursday. Obviously impressed with his mud divining skills he managed to find an even more glorious 'Mudfest' for the Burnley Contingent walk. This time it was a walk from Spring Wood Car park, Whalley. Due to the once again threatened abysmal weather conditions, a high-level route to the 'Nick of Pendle' and a lower level route if conditions unsuitable, were proposed. On assembly the weather seemed unseasonably kind, no wind and watery sunshine meant the Nick was a goer.

All went well with atmospheric conditions, well at least till lunchtime, however underfoot was a different matter. Most of the early part of the walk consisted of squelching across fields saturated with water, interspersed with frequent patches of liquidised earth. Our leader, clearly in his element, ploughed through it all with gusto, completely oblivious to the rumblings of discontent among his troops. On reaching the Nick and with the sun still shining, the 'Sherpa' or Captain Mainwaring as he has now been christened by John W, decreed it was lunch. A hasty (not tasty) snack was taken seated on sodden ground and with freezing hands, at which point the weather decided to take a turn for the worse.

Hastily packing up the lunchboxes, the precipitation commenced. Clearly now above the snow line that's what we got. At the same time the paths became increasingly difficult to locate whilst the bogs became easier to find. After much tramping about and cursing, the relative sanctuary of Wiswell was attained. Not far to go now but far enough for the heavens to open for the last mile or so, and ensure we are well and truly saturated at the finish. My voice by now has gone from Ray Winstone to Sean Dyche, and I don't eat earthworms! (Google it). Pints of White Rat (Huddersfield Brewery) at the Pendle Witch, Sabden, then home for a hot bath! That was lovely, we must do it again someday, but not too soon, please.

Tuesday 16th January saw the first goal to be awarded by the Video Assistant Referee (VAR) in a major competition in England. The VAR overruled an offside decision in the Leicester City v Fleetwood 3rd Round FA Cup Replay, to allow the goal to stand. In this case the correct decision. However, on the following night the VAR was again called into action during the Chelsea v Norwich City replay and on this occasion incorrect calls were made.

I have to say that at the moment I am not in favour of VAR. I fear that the referral to the VAR will inevitably disrupt the flow of the game and lead to a very stop/start contest. I can see it's place in Cricket where the game is at a much more leisurely pace, and even in Rugby where there are frequent stoppages. However, football is a game that needs to flow to maintain the excitement. The worst games are always those heavily punctuated by fouls and stoppages by the referee's whistle. For sure errors are made by the officials especially as the game today is played at a frenetic pace. But often TV pundits, analysing the action from several angles with multiple cameras, cannot agree. At the risk of being labelled a Luddite, I for one would prefer to stay as we are and let the match referee make the call.

Game 24 – Saturday 20th January 15.00 – Burnley v Manchester United

This was never going to be the ideal fixture to arrest a depressing run of results. No wins in the league since December 12th, and a fixture against the second placed team, who are currently enjoying a long unbeaten run, didn't bode well. We've had a hard run of home fixtures of late with Tottenham Hotspur, Liverpool and now Manchester United since that last victory. Suffice it to say I didn't realistically view this game with much pre-match optimism.

With Chris Wood and Stephen Ward still unavailable but with Scott Arfield able to return we go with one change from last week. Sam Vokes drops to the bench to accommodate the return of Arfield. A truly awful morning's weather precedes the kick off, continuous sleet and a forecast of heavy snow before the game has me donning the thermals and waterproofs. Typically, as I park the car and head for the pre-match pints it fines up and a weak sun fitfully appears. Still it's cold and the extra layers are much appreciated. I doubt the daytime temperature has risen above 6^{0}C in the last week accompanied by zero temperatures at night. Still it is Burnley in January and that's about right.

There's no sign of Everton winger Aaron Lennon for whom we are rumoured to have agreed a fee and personal terms, perhaps it will be Monday before he signs on. A good crowd in fine voice for this one, and the snow-capped hills are looking magnificent from my seat in the James Hargreaves Upper. United hold the upper hand in the early stages but there somewhat cagey approach is causing no major concerns. Big money signings, Paul Pogba, Romelu Lukaku and Anthony Martial certainly look the part but we are not overawed. As is often the case we are growing into the game as the half develops and coming more of an attacking threat also without unduly troubling the United custodian, David De Gea.

Without any major alarms at either end half-time is reached with the score goalless and I'm a little more confident that we may get something from the game. That confidence unfortunately is misplaced as the Reds take the lead shortly after the break. Lukaku's strength and persistence carries him through a couple of challenges and he picks out Martial on the left side of the penalty area with a lovely pass. Martial controls, takes one pace forward and lashes an unstoppable effort in off the underside of the crossbar. Bugger!

United teams of old would probably have taken that as the cue to take the game by the scruff of the neck and go on to win in style. However, this lot, under the influence of Jose Mourinho, are a much more cautious outfit. This gives the Clarets the opportunity to have a go back at the Reds and we push them back for concerted spells. The visitors are content to play on the counter and eat up time as professionally as possible.

If there is a slight criticism of our approach it is that it lacks flexibility. We, as previously stated, have yet to come back to win when trailing in a Premier League game under Sean Dyche. Despite our valiant and wholehearted efforts, we are making little impression on the defence and its surely time to try a different tack. On the bench is the latest acquisition, Georges-Kevin Nkoudou and he's itching for his chance.

However, the time ticks on and he's still itching! There's a comic moment as Jesse Lingard (aptly named in the circumstances) goes down after a challenge. As if fatally stricken he rolls over and over and off the pitch, only to be rolled back like a piece of carpet by Mourinho, who for once goes up in my estimation! Finally, on 81 minutes a double substitution as Vokes and Nkoudou replace Jeff Hendrick and Arfield. It's a lively little cameo from the loanee Frenchman which only begs the question as to why he wasn't introduced earlier.

As our attacking threat intensifies Johann Berg Gudmundsson (JBG) almost repeats Steven Defour's party piece from Old Trafford. His shot from a free kick 20 yards out clears the wall, curls, and then agonisingly hits the bar. There are a couple of close calls at either end as Martial's shot is well saved by Nick Pope, and JBG's driven low cross just evades the lunging James Tarkowski. On 89 minutes Nahki Wells replaces Ashley Barnes. Why? At this late stage what possible contribution can he make? The answer is none, and yet again we concede the points.

Once again, a bloody shame, a game where we gave as good as we got but came away with nought. One piece of devastating finishing was the difference between the sides and this is the one quality that United's vast financial resources are able to provide. In statistical terms there was nothing between the sides. Possession Burnley 48%, United 52%, attempts on goal, us 13, them 12, attempts on target two each. Once again just a one goal margin, but once more against rather than for us. We need a break to get out of this run and with a free weekend next, and the possibility of new recruits, hopefully it is coming soon.

Result – Burnley 0 – 1 (Martial 54) Manchester United

Burnley Team

Pope, Bardsley, Mee, Tarkowski, Taylor, Gudmundsson, Cork, Defour, Hendrick (Vokes 81), Arfield (Nkoudou 81), Barnes (Wells 89)

Subs Not Used – Lindegaard, Lowton, Long, Westwood

Manchester United Team

De Gea, Valencia, Jones, Smalling, Young, Mata (Fellaini 72), Pogba, Lingard (Rashford 80), Matic, Martial (Herrera 90+4), Lukaku

Subs Not Used – Romero, Rojo, Shaw, McTominay

Attendance – 21,841

Season To Date – Played 24, Won 9, Drawn 7, Lost 8, Goals For 19, Goals Against 21, Points 34

League Position after Game 24 – 8th

One thing I hadn't realised till after the game was the fact that Mourinho's carpet rolling of Lingard was not as I at first thought an effort to get him to 'man up'. No, it was more an attempt to get him back on the field to ensure the game was stopped to allow treatment, rather than it carry on whilst he was off the pitch. So, I'll take my credit for Moaninho's actions back and once again view him as the sly, underhand manipulator, that I always knew he was.

The closure of the transfer window edges closer and with it come even more bizarre rumours of ins and outs at Turf Moor. By Monday evening 22nd January there's still no sign of Aaron Lennon over the Turf threshold, although he has reportedly had a medical. The best one yet is the reported interest of mighty money-bags Chelsea in our own Ashley Barnes. Now I've always thought of Ashley as a poor man's Diego Costa but I think this link is stretching the imagination a bit too far! Further rumours are linking Sam Vokes with a move back to his home town of Southampton, again highly unlikely. However, the cream of the crop is an alleged £20m bid by Burnley for Glasgow Celtic's highly rated young striker Moussa Dembele. If that happens I'll eat hay with a donkey!

Hooray! Tuesday 23rd sees the arrival from Merseyside of the long-awaited Mr Lennon, and with him hopefully some new attacking options. Better still on the same day comes the news that Sean Dyche has signed a contract at Turf Moor taking him through to the summer of 2022. I'm sure most fans will agree that this is a deal more important than any other that could be forthcoming. Of course, in this day and age in many cases contracts count for nothing, but Mr Dyche is a man of integrity and this shows his total commitment to the Clarets cause.

Also, on Tuesday it's the first of the bi-weekly opportunities for another muddy squelch around the paddy fields of Lancashire. This time the start point is the Gamecock at Great Harwood where our reward at the end will be a hot carvery lunch. Once again, the weather forecast is atrocious, and you'd have to be a bit mad to go out in it. Nevertheless, eighteen hardy, and slightly mad souls assemble for the privilege. I'm greeted on the car park by Manchester United fan Paul Taylor who of course can't wait to see me. We embrace warmly to show there is no lingering animosity after Saturday's fixture and a photo of the smiling pair is taken for posterity.

There follows a quick briefing, or perhaps not so quick, from leader for the day Nigel Hext. Like all ex school teachers Nigel can't half go on a bit! The upshot is that we have the option of a short walk (4 miles), to avoid the worst of the weather, or the full walk of 7.5 miles. The first part of the walk is a celebration of the opening to the public of the Martholme viaduct. What! I hear you say. Yes, the Martholme viaduct, part of the long defunct railway branch line linking Burnley to Blackburn via Padiham and Great Harwood, is now open to walkers. Well I say it is but it's only open at one end! You can walk across the viaduct but the other end is gated and locked so you have to retrace your steps. Still who could miss such an important opportunity.

The first short loop of the walk completed we arrive back at the Gamecock, but as it's far too early for lunch, and the weather is still kind, we press on with the longer loop. You can imagine what comes next. We follow the River Calder down and into Whalley taking in the much more impressive, all 48 arches of it, Whalley railway viaduct. As we start the climb up through Spring Wood the promised rain arrives. By the time we have passed Whalley Golf course and the track to Read Hall it's persistent. The good old Lancashire weather ensures we are well and truly soaked on arrival back at the pub, and of course the quoted mileage has grown from 7.5 to a measured 8.2. Still, for the second week running our spirits are revived by an ample and very reasonably priced meat feast. The Gamecock, another on the highly recommended pub list.

If we thought Tuesday was bad, for the third time in two weeks the 'Sherpa' Waltons excelled with another muddy marathon on Thursday. This time Ed 'Sherpa' Walton, I think stung by recent criticisms, ceded leadership to wife Gwen. Our 'Sherpess', if there is such a thing, devised a circular route from Higham via Newchurch, Barley, Roughlee and Noggarth.

Although she confessed that she hadn't reconnoitred the route, in fact had just drawn a line on a map, she promised 7.2 miles of mud free perambulation. Ha-ha, a physical impossibility in the winter wetlands of the Pendle environs. Within 50 yards of the start we are sinking in ankle deep brown stuff and almost wishing that we had not been so hard on 'Captain Mainwaring', i.e. 'Sherpa' Ed last week. What an uncanny ability this pair have for mud-divining, if only they could market the stuff, they'd be millionaires.

Still, putting a brave face on it, we ploughed on (literally) in surprisingly pleasant weather to lunch at Roughlee. Deviating slightly from Gwen's course to take in the statue of Alice Nutter, she of Lancashire Witches fame, we started the return leg. In a repeat of Tuesday, the weather once again turned against us. After a further 3-4 miles of cloying mud and heavy rain we reached the sanctuary of the cars. Nothing for it but to head for the Sparrow Hawk at Fence and debrief over some Reedley Hallows Brewery, Filly Close Blonde. As expected Gwen's mileage estimate of 7.2 once again proved completely fictitious as we recorded another 8.5.

Next week the Waltons will be absent, skiing in Switzerland, and the Weirs will be returning from the hopefully successful conquest of Newcastle United. The McDevitts will have started their long break in New Zealand so a smaller but more select band will take on the challenge of the Tolkien Trail from Hurst Green. I am already praying for some fine weather ahead of this one.

As there's no game this weekend due to our early exit from the FA Cup, time for a little rant I think. Anybody out there fed up of being asked to write reviews? It seems that every time you buy something, go on holiday, or use a service some body wants you to tell them all about it. If I spent my time filling in every request I wouldn't have time to buy anything, go on holiday or use any services! This week alone I have been asked to review my experience with LateRooms, BT, Staysure and Homeserve. The NHS are also in on the act, asking me how likely I would be to recommend the GP Practice to a relative or friend! Now come on! Nothing wrong with my GP, but my recommendation to a relative or friend would be to stay away from the place at all costs. No wonder the NHS is under so much stress if people keep recommending their friends and relatives to go and check out the offer! If Frank Skinner ever offers me a guest spot on Room 101, I know what's going in there first!

The season has hit a bit of a lull. The early excitement following the win at Chelsea, and the subsequent excellent away results has lately gone a bit flat. The poor run of results, if not performances, since mid-December has taken some of the gloss off, and we need to reignite the passion. Let's hope starting at St James Park on Wednesday.

Meanwhile on Monday 29th January, and with just two days of the transfer window left open, Sean Dyche dampens fans expectations. In his press conference ahead of Wednesday's game at Newcastle he says that any further signings this window are unlikely. At the same time, he reveals injuries to James Tarkowski and Steven Defour. Well if the doom mongers were unhappy before they are apoplectic now!

Best just to stay calm for the moment and see what develops. That's easier said than done though as transfer speculation approaches fever pitch!

Wednesday 31st January, transfer deadline day! Its safe to say it came and went with precious little to report. There was much speculation concerning Nottingham Forest's young centre back Joe Worrall, and reportedly three bids rejected. Ultimately, it was suggested that the acceptable price was £20m and that, quite rightly, was the end of that.

Leaving the club, on loan till the end of the season, was defender Tom Anderson. Recently recalled from a loan at Port Vale, and now on his way to Doncaster, a step up for the lad. Several exotic sounding names are being linked, but as always with little or no substance. So, by early evening its time to forget all that nonsense and concentrate on the job at hand.

Game 25 – Wednesday 31st January 19.45 – Newcastle United v Burnley

My daughter Stephanie and future son-in-law Tom, currently resident in the North east are attending this one. They have tickets provided by a client of Tom's family business which unfortunately puts them in the stand with the massed ranks of Geordies. It's a relatively short run from their home in Darlington but Stephanie is a little apprehensive about the natives' reaction to her Lancashire accent. I tell her not to worry, it's a while since the North Easterners of Hartlepool hung a monkey, believing it to be a shipwrecked French sailor! I do however instruct her not to jinx the Clarets but am wary that as she has inherited some of her mother's genetic material, that is just what she may do.

As expected neither James Tarkowski or Steven Defour feature in this one. Indeed, it's rumoured that 'Tarks' groin strain may keep him out for three weeks. Worse still though is the news that Defour faces an operation on his knee and that will render him unavailable for at least two months, and most likely the rest of the season. The squad and defence in particular is looking decidedly paper thin. Kevin Long once again returns in central defence to partner Ben Mee, but what happens if one of these gets injured is anyone's guess. Replacing Defour is Ashley Westwood, and the transfer window signings, Georges-Kevin Nkoudou (GKN) and Aaron Lennon are both on the substitutes bench.

Our hosts the Magpies are well and truly embroiled in the relegation battle that currently involves at least half the league. Their form of late isn't great and they are without a home win since October. I don't like the sound of that! Manager Rafael Benitez is openly critical of their failure to bring in more players, but they will tonight field Chelsea loanee Robert Kenedy Nunes Nascimento, or Kenedy for short. This looks like a game we can win with the right approach. Conversely it looks like a game Newcastle United must win.

The first half is a bit of a sorry tale for the Clarets as we are clearly second best. Stephanie is relaying texts predicting impending doom, the radio commentators are trying to put a positive spin on it, but the overall impression is not good. Kenedy makes his presence felt with a shot that Nick Pope is able to turn onto a post. Phil Bardsley then brings down the Brazilian in the box but fortunately Jose Luis Sanmartin Mato, Joselu for short, can only hit a tame penalty which is saved by Pope.

At the other end Cork is impeded in the box by a player rolling into him and sending him crashing. A penalty surely? Don't you believe it, we haven't had one in the previous 24 games and this referee is not going to end that run now. Following this incident Ashley Barnes has the ball in the net but is adjudged to have pushed the defender. Kenedy is proving a handful down the 'Toon' left side and poor old Bardsley is struggling to cope with him.

Somehow half time is reached with the score 0-0. The half time report from the Weirs ensconced in the 'gods' at St James's Park is brief and to the point; *"That was truly awful"*. Stephanie is slightly wordier; *"Two words, scrappy and worrying"*.

I fear a long 45 minutes ahead and the early exchanges do nothing to dispel those fears. In an attempt to inject a bit more attacking threat, Aaron Lennon is introduced on 60 minutes, replacing Scott Arfield. His initial contribution 'nutmegging' an opponent gives rise to a faint glimmer of hope. However, this is promptly extinguished as the Magpies take the lead on 65 minutes Jamaal Lascelles heading in from a corner.

This again is the signal for Burnley to decide to take the initiative and on 70 minutes Sam Vokes replaces Westwood as we go to 4-4-2. Why oh why do we only start to play when we go a goal behind. A bit more adventure from the start may well have proved more fruitful against a side low on confidence. Gradually the momentum of the game changes as we start to push forward, and the hosts look to hold on to what they have. On 83 minutes the last throw of the dice as GKN replaces Johann Berg Gudmundsson, and on 85 minutes we are level. Hallelujah!

Following a spell of concerted pressure Vokes heads goalwards from Kevin Long's flick on, the hapless Toon keeper Karl Darlow in attempting to push it over the bar only succeeds in pushing it into the top of the goal. We think Sam's goal, but it goes in the record books as a Darlow own goal. Who cares? Not me, perhaps Sam, but not me. As we enter the last five minutes and stoppage time there's only going to be one winner now, and it's not the black and white stripeys. Unfortunately, we are unable to repeat the trick and settle for a precious if at times unlikely point.

Once again, a seriously injury weakened team has got a result. Leicester City lose at Everton and incredibly the Clarets without a win in 2018, climb a place back to 7th in the Premier League. Stephanie, safe from her mingling with the Geordies, is still however unimpressed. But then again, what does she know. Time for a stiff Whisky and off to bed a happy man. Up the Clarets!

Result – Newcastle United (Lascelles 65) 1 – 1 (Darlow o.g 85) Burnley

Burnley Team

Pope, Bardsley, Mee, Long, Taylor, Gudmundsson (Nkoudou 83), Cork, Westwood (Vokes 70), Hendrick, Arfield (Lennon 60), Barnes

Subs Not Used – Lindegaard, Lowton, Ulvestad, Wells

Newcastle United Team

Darlow, Yedlin, Lascelles, Clark, Dummett, Atsu (Murphy 64), Diame, Merino, Kenedy (Ritchie 72) Perez (Gayle 85), Joselu

Subs Not Used – Hayden, Shelvey, Manquillo, Woodman

Attendance – 50,174

Season To Date – Played 25, Won 9, Drawn 8, Lost 8, Goals For 20, Goals Against 22, Points 35

League Position after Game 25 – 7th

FEBRUARY

January, a month that seemed to last forever has finally gone, and with it the chance to add further players to what is currently an injury ravaged squad. Regular players unavailable at the moment are, Tom Heaton, Stephen Ward, James Tarkowski, Steven Defour, Chris Wood, Robbie Brady, and I'll throw in Jon Walters and Dean Marney. If I have omitted any, my apologies.

The January window did yield two new recruits, first Georges-Kevin Nkoudou (GKN) on loan, and Aaron Lennon on a permanent deal from Everton. It's fair to say that both will add some much-needed pace and flair to our attacking options. The big worry now though is the centre back positions. We enter the final third of the season with only two recognised specialists for those positions. An injury or suspension now to one or the other of this pair could prove extremely awkward.

Were we right to resist the ludicrous fees being quoted for possible replacements? Of course, only time will tell, but Sean Dyche is happy to go with what we have, and we must trust his judgement.

Just when we all thought the transfer activity was done for the season, Friday 2nd of February throws up another surprise as we learn that Frederik Ulvestad has left the club. Very much a fringe player these days having never really being able to command a place, albeit having been an unused substitute in the last game, he has joined Swedish club Djurgardens IF on a three-year deal. Apparently, the transfer window in Sweden is still open and so he has been able to complete the move. Hopefully, the switch can restart the midfielder's career, but it leaves another empty seat on the Burnley bench. Who will step up and fill it? We'll soon find out as we are back in action this coming Saturday, at home to none other than Champions elect Manchester City.

As I think I mentioned in the previous chapter, this week's Thursday walk would be without the leadership of the 'Sherpa' Waltons and the 'Wandering Weirs'. This enables us to take a more leisurely approach and we opt for the Tolkien Trail starting at Hurst Green. The walk is billed in the literature as 5.5 miles, but on plotting the route on OS Maps it shows 6.4 miles. Oh well, it's a nice enough day for a change and 11 enthusiastic walkers, led by the recovering Geoff Ashworth (Leader from the Back) set off in sunny conditions. Only one minor hiccough as Bob Walsh arrives at the car park to find he has come without his boots. No worries ever prepared Mr Ashworth has a spare pair which surprisingly will fit. I have to warn Bob that he will probably need to get his feet fumigated at the end of the walk, but he is undeterred.

Needless to say, within the first quarter mile we have encountered heavy mud and Geoff's spare pair are now well and truly coated. Nevertheless, it's a thoroughly enjoyable ramble, without any missed turns and a lunch taken sat in the sun on Cromwell's Bridge. Once again, the mileage forecast is adrift as we record 7.4 miles for the trip, but the extra mile only adds to the pleasure of the pint of Lancaster Blonde in the Bayley Arms, Hurst Green.

Game 26 – Saturday 3rd February 12.30 – Burnley v Manchester City

This was a game that completely defined Burnley FC. A fixture against the soon to be crowned Champions, beaten only once this season and looking for their 23rd victory from 26 games, should have been in boxing terms a 'no-contest'. For long periods of the action that is exactly what it felt like. Manchester City all accurate pass and move, one-touch football, are one of the most expensively assembled squads in world football, and in a word, CLASS.

The forward threat of players of the stature of Sergio Aguero, Kevin De Bruyne, Raheem Sterling and Bernardo Silva, at times threatened to bury us. Indeed, had they been less profligate with their chances, they may well have done so. However, Burnley are not a team that lies down and dies. We rode our luck, kept it tight, battled for everything and never stopped believing.

With Sean Dyche's squad severely injury ravaged, this was probably not the ideal game to make changes. However, changes there were, in both personnel and formation. The Clarets opted for a 4-4-2 formation with Sam Vokes coming in. Jeff Hendrick dropped back into a more central midfield role replacing Ashley Westwood, and Aaron Lennon signed in the January window, made a home debut in place of Scott Arfield.

It wasn't long into the game before a rash of knocks to Burnley players had me seriously concerned. Within the first 10 minutes Ashley Barnes, Phil

Bardsley, Nick Pope and Sam Vokes, had required treatment from the physio. Thankfully, all were able to continue.

For the rest of the first half City dominated as they calmly stroked the ball around with supreme confidence. Good saves from Pope, and good defending kept them at bay, until on 22 minutes an unstoppable effort from distance by full back Danilo Luiz da Silva opened the scoring.

Undaunted the Clarets kept pegging away, pressing high up the pitch and constantly harrying the man in possession. Vokes was making his aerial presence felt and winning his fair share of aerial duels. A close call for City as Ben Mee fired in a shot from a left-wing cross which was saved at full stretch by Ederson Santana de Moraes.

Half time 0-1 and I, and the rest of the crowd around me are hoping that we can keep the score down second half and not suffer a demoralising defeat. The interval brought a significant change for the Clarets, Matt Lowton replacing the presumably injured Bardsley for the second period.

What Pep Guardiola said at half time certainly galvanised City into action, and for a 20-minute spell we were under severe pressure as they attacked in waves. A continuation of fine defending, good saves and extremely wasteful finishing, including two glaring misses by Sterling kept us in the game.

Inspired by our good fortune and with Lennon, switched to the right flank, teaming up impressively with Lowton, we began to come into the game and pose more of a threat. Sterling was hooked from the fray and given the opportunity to rue his misses from the bench. The Clarets fans sensing there may just be something in it for us upped the volume.

The team responded magnificently, a fine move saw Lennon's powerful shot bring the save of the game from Ederson, as he tipped it onto the post. The growing belief was tangible and on 82 minutes the old ground erupted. Following a raid down the left flank the ball was recycled via Jack Cork to Lowton deep on the right side. His immaculate cross eluded all the City defence and was met by the onrushing Johann Berg Gudmundsson. His magnificent cushioned half-volley rocketed into the back of the net despite another gallant effort by Ederson.

Ecstasy for the Clarets, but all we could think of was 10 minutes to survive and take a magnificent point. Cue more resolute defending and then a huge sigh of relief and joy as the referee blows the final whistle. As I made my way out of the ground somebody remarked that it felt like we had won, and that is exactly what it did!

Truly a Turf Moor day to live long in the memory. Glowing words of praise from City boss Pep Guardiola who described us as the 'most British of teams'.

"Of course we are frustrated in terms of the result but the performance was outstanding against a Burnley side who are the most British of teams in terms of long balls and the way they play.

"But football is about goals. We needed to score the second, third and fourth when we had the chance. When you arrive at the last 15 minutes at Burnley 1-0, this is what can happen. I'm sad for my players because we played so well.

"What they have done this season, Burnley, is amazing. We controlled the game, but when we arrived at the last 10 minutes 1-0, there is danger."

Another precious point and we remain in seventh place. A very difficult run of home fixtures is now out of the way having faced Tottenham, Liverpool, Manchester United and Manchester City. It doesn't come any harder than that.

There was a major contribution from Matt Lowton forging an impressive partnership on the right with Lennon. However, once again it was a magnificent team performance all-round the pitch. Special mentions also for Charlie Taylor and Kevin Long who will not face more difficult opponents and emerged with great credit.

Manchester City were a tremendous team and will shortly be crowned worthy Champions. But for me, in the words of Sean Dyche; "I am the proudest man in Proudsville."

UP THE CLARETS!

Result – Burnley (Gudmundsson 82) 1 – 1 (Danilo 22) Manchester City

Burnley Team

Pope, Bardsley (Lowton 45), Mee, Long, Taylor, Gudmundsson, Cork, Hendrick, Lennon, Barnes, Vokes

Subs Not Used – Lindegaard, O'Neill, Westwood, Wells, Nkoudou, Arfield

Manchester City Team

Ederson, Walker, Kompany, Otamendi, Danilo, Bernardo Silva, De Bruyne, Gundogan, Fernandinho, Sterling (Diaz 74), Aguero

Subs Not Used – Bravo, Y Toure, Laporte, Zinchenko, Adarabioyo

Attendance – 21,658

Season To Date – Played 26, Won 9, Drawn 9, Lost 8, Goals For 21, Goals Against 23, Points 36

League Position after Game 26 – 7th

Strangely for this game Guardiola only selected six substitutes claiming he didn't have enough players to name a full complement. I think Pep is trying to make some sort of point but let's be serious! If Burnley with probably the smallest budget and squad in the league can do it, I'm sure that City with all their resources could have found another bench-warmer.

After a week in which I had been subjected to Mauricio Pochettino's views on players diving, more politely referred to as 'simulation' to 'win' penalty decisions, I was looking forward to some outdoor pursuits to get some fresh air and take in the views. Mr Pochettino, the Argentinian born coach of Tottenham Hotspur is of the opinion that it is perfectly fair that players 'cheat' in order to gain an unfair advantage. In fact, he feels that in his native Argentina this is a skill that is praiseworthy. Unfortunately, his views on the subject seem to be shared by many other 'knowledgeable' people in the game.

Heaven help us! If this is what it has come to it's no wonder that many fans are becoming rather disillusioned with the game at the highest level.

Anyway, Pochettino may have his views but the Lancashire Dotcom Walkers certainly didn't have theirs. Tuesday's walk starting from Denham Quarry car park, Brindle, should have afforded some spectacular sights from the nearby Trig point. However, having left Burnley in light snow, it got progressively worse as we travelled West. I am informed, (reliably or perhaps not), that from this point the whole of Lancashire, The County Palatine, can be seen. Not so today! When 27 weather hardened veterans had made the high ground the visibility had decreased to the point where we could just about see our feet!

Undeterred we ploughed on with our ramble, along snowy tracks, cross fields more akin to paddies, until we reached the relative sanctuary of the Leeds/Liverpool canal. Not the best day for views perhaps but still a good opportunity to catch up with some football chat about other North West teams.

Still, not to worry Thursday's Burnley Contingent walk, an old favourite from Settle via Feizor and Little Stainforth will provide some excellent views of the Dales and Pen-y Gent. Wednesday was a glorious cold, clear and sunny day. What happened Thursday? I could have written the script, overcast, damp for the early part then followed by incessant rain for the remainder. Once again, the highlight was the Bacon butty stop at Elaine's Tearooms, Feizor. The best idea would probably have been to terminate the walk at that point. Still had we done so we would have missed the Burnley Contingent's version of their winter sport, mud skiing. Plenty of fallers on this outing, the most spectacular early effort being Jan Gibson's, only to be pipped for the Gold medal by Ian Mckay, who limped back to base camp with the aid of a walking pole. Yours truly almost came a cropper on the stretch back to Settle along the river Ribble. However, my lightning quick reflexes allowed me to bounce back from the ground with minimal contact.

No scenic views again on this outing as the cloud cover and mist completely obscured visibility. Another mention here though for the excellent after walk refreshment at the Hart's Head Hotel, Giggleswick. A great choice of real ales, a roaring log fire, tastefully decorated surroundings and obliging staff. The Burnley Contingent walkers can thoroughly recommend this pub. Drink of the day was Tirril Brewery, Ullswater Blonde, a cracker!

Time, I think now for another little rant. Is anybody out there getting as fed up as me with would be scam phone calls. As part of my BT telephone package I have an add-on, BT Call Protect. This attempts to filter out nuisance calls before they reach me and also gives me the facility to blacklist 'dodgy' numbers. I have adopted a policy of not answering any unknown numbers, instead referring them first to an app called 'Who-called-me'. This app allows you to see how many people have searched on a particular number and grades them as Neutral, Harassing and Dangerous. There is also the opportunity to leave comments to advise other enquirers of the nature of the calls. Having ascertained the type of call I can then go back to my BT account and blacklist the 'scammers'. Well I reckon this week alone I have blacklisted at least one number per day and now have a personal banned list of 21. How many of these bloody clowns are there out there? I'm sure many people must now be frightened to pick up the phone. It's about time some action was taken by the authorities to track these people and stop their operations. Rant over, back to the football.

Game 27 – Saturday 10th February 15.00 – Swansea City v Burnley

As the Clarets headed South West my wife and I were travelling in the complete opposite direction. We are on a mission to reconnoitre a potential wedding venue for daughter Stephanie in deepest Arkengarthdale. **Where!** I hear you say. Well, the place in question is the Charles Bathurst Inn, better known as the CB Inn, and is situated in North Yorkshire approximately three miles from Reeth (Google it).

After studying the map, and consulting the RAC route planner, the favoured route in terms of distance would appear to be via Colne, by-passing Skipton then taking the B6160 through Threshfield, Kilnsey, Kettlewell, and Buckden towards Aysgarth. The route then takes us through Leyburn and on in to Reeth. In this case we have a slight diversion to rendezvous with Stephanie and future son-in-law Tom in Richmond for the obligatory coffee and cake stop.

Carefully monitoring weather forecasts in the days leading up to the trip I have to confess to being a little apprehensive. The week has been a real rag-bag of weather with torrential rain, snow and the occasional sunny spell. Saturday doesn't look promising and having travelled this road once before I am aware it's not the best in bad weather. Saturday morning dawns in Burnley with heavy rain confirming my fears. Suffice it to say that the weather and road conditions didn't disappoint, throwing the whole lot at us, rain in the early stages followed by sleet and snow at Buckden to eventually fine up at Richmond.

As we leave Richmond just after 3.00 p.m. I desperately ty to catch some football action on the car radio. I do manage to get some barely audible coverage of Premier League matches on Radio Five Live who are covering Everton v Crystal Palace but giving updates on the other games. I am relieved to hear that after 30 mins there is no score in any of the 3.00 p.m. kick off games, so it's onto the CB Inn and hopefully some better coverage.

Thwarted again, there's no mobile phone signal in this part of the world, so no text updates from the 'Wandering Weirs' who have made the long trip down to South Wales. The Inn has WiFi but I am (reliably as it turns out) informed that it doesn't work very well in the excellent room that we have been allocated. However, there is a TV and by now Final Score is about to start on BBC. Saved! Well hardly, the CB Inn is a magnificent place but if I have one little quibble it has to be that the TV signal is exceptionally poor! I suppose it goes with the remoteness of the location. Anyway, I do manage to glean that after 78 minutes the score is still 0-0 but the best chances have been squandered by the Clarets.

With that it's off to the bar where I am again reliably informed that the WiFi is very good. How true! As I order my first pint of Deuchars IPA, my phone informs me via the BBC Sports App Goal Alert function that on 81 minutes, Swansea have gone ahead through some very exotically named foreign gentleman. Bang on cue a WhatsApp message from the Weirs, *"Swans score"*. Bloody Hell, or words to that effect, that's not what I wanted to hear. Once again, the Clarets are contriving to mar what promises to be a lovely weekend for us. Nothing for it but to pray that the phone will vibrate in my pocket signalling another late equaliser, but alas its not to be. Crestfallen and with the arrival in the bar of Tom's parents,

Stu and Sue, who are joining us for the night, I have no alternative but to have a second pint of IPA, which of course I let Stu pay for.

Can I just say now that after the initial disappointment of the result, the evening thanks to the intervention of good food, ample drink, and most important of all great company, was a roaring success. I can heartily recommend the CB Inn to all of you as a fantastic pub in a superb setting. There's no decision yet as to whether Stephanie will choose this place as her wedding venue, but I am sure my wife and I will visit again. After a lovely walk from Reeth on the Sunday, which necessitated a little detour due to the high level of the River Swale covering the stepping stones, we returned home via a slightly different journey. This time I opted for the better roads afforded by a route through Leyburn, Hawes, Horton-in-Ribblesdale and Settle. A bit longer in mileage, but in the difficult weather conditions, a less stressful drive.

So, what went wrong with the Clarets as they failed to win for the 10th consecutive game? Apparently, according to all reports, the game was as drab and dreary as the south Wales weather. Swansea, still deeply embroiled in the relegation battle but enjoying a significant revival under new boss Carlos Carvahal, were expected to pose a real threat. Recent home victories over Liverpool and Arsenal should have seen them brimming with confidence. However, it was the Clarets who started the game on the front foot. Indeed, 'ClaretTony' in his report for the *Up the Clarets* website, felt Burnley keeper Nick Pope could have sat with the substitutes on the bench for the first half and it would have made little difference. Tony's summary of first half events read that we were the more likely looking of two very average sides.

The second half saw little change and the best two opportunities fell to Johann Berg Gudmundsson whose shot was tipped over by the Swans keeper, and an Ashley Barnes effort fired just wide. With time running out, Swansea replaced former Claret loanee Nathan Dyer with Tammy Abraham, a move which proved a game-changer. Suddenly we started to come under pressure defensively and Pope had his first save of the match to make. However, just as the point looked to be almost in the bag, he could do nothing about Ki Sung-yueng's effort and we were behind with little time to play. The usual desperate 'huff and puff' stuff ensued but no real chances arrived and once again the long trip had proved fruitless.

The long winless run continues, now stretching back into mid-December and up to 10 Premier League games. Unbelievably we still lie seventh in the table, but that position is now coming seriously under threat due to our lack of recent points. Our drift needs to be arrested quickly if we are not to see our magnificent early season efforts massively eroded. The injury situation is a major contributory factor and the sooner we can get some players back the better. Stephen Ward looks close to fitness now and made the substitutes bench at the Liberty stadium, but there's still no sign of Chris Wood. A blank weekend coming up for us so hopefully the break will allow some much-needed recovery time.

Result – Swansea City (Sung-yeung 81) 1 – 0 Burnley

Burnley Team

Pope, Lowton, Mee, Long, Taylor, Gudmundsson (Nkoudou 85), Cork, Hendrick, Lennon (Arfield 74), Barnes, Vokes (Wells 81)

Subs Not Used – Lindegaard, Ward, O'Neill, Westwood

Swansea City Team

Fabianski, Naughton, Van der Hoorn, Fernandez, Mawson, Olsson (A Ayew 59), Dyer (Abraham 74), Carroll, Sung-yeung, J Ayew (King 90), Clucas

Subs Not Used – Nordfeldt, Bartley, Routledge, Narsingh

Attendance – 20,176

Season To Date – Played 27, Won 9, Drawn 9, Lost 9, Goals For 21, Goals Against 24, Points 36

League Position after Game 27 – 7th

It's another FA Cup weekend and consequently a blank one for us, our interest in the competition having ended almost as soon as it began with the defeat at Manchester City. Similarly, it's a blank week for Dotcom walking due to it being school half-term week. What has that got to do with walking I hear you say? Well, for those of you unfamiliar with previous diaries, suffice it to say that we are led by former schoolteachers for whom old habits die hard!

That means for the 'Wandering Weirs' and myself the opportunity to do the same walk twice in a week. The planned Burnley Contingent walk is an old favourite starting from Heptonstall and taking in Hebden Bridge, the Rochdale canal, Staups Mill and Blackshaw Head. We are keen to 'recce' the walk ahead of the Thursday group as the Weirs report a problem with the footbridge at Colden Clough, which has been partially destroyed by a fallen tree. This may necessitate a detour, and we are also keen to find an alternative descent from Heptonstall to Hebden Bridge, which has been in the past rather precipitous!

Undeterred by a less than favourable weather forecast on Tuesday we make a prompt start. John W has forwarded me a Gpx file of the route which shows a proposed mileage of 5.6 miles, which both Jude W and myself consider a tad understated. Our early effort to find an alternative descent ends in failure as we contrive to end up on the same old track. Not to worry, we have spotted where we may have gone wrong, so we backtrack to prove the new route. Its extra mileage but its early in the walk so who cares. It's raining a bit but we find an improved descent, so we are reasonably happy.

Onto the Rochdale Canal now and heading back towards Todmorden. We are enjoying ourselves so much, even though the rain is now quite heavy, that we overshoot the exit point from the canal, adding further distance to our trek as we retrace our footsteps to bridge number 21. It's the start now of a stiff climb up Jumble Hole to the ruined Staups Mill. Still raining heavily, but well and truly clad in thermal gear to keep out the perishing cold, a degree of internal overheating now starts to take place. Getting clammier and clammier we continue our upward climb and approaching Blackshaw Head we are obviously now above the snow-line. Yes, there's a veritable blizzard going on and what is more, its lunchtime. We take lunch stood up sheltering behind the church wall with snow settling gently on our sandwiches.

At least the route is mainly downhill and flat from here, so refreshed and once again frozen, we press on. Down through the now snow filled fields we do our own impression of the Winter Olympics arriving at the aforementioned collapsed footbridge. There are no shortage of signs informing us of the closed footpath, but they are not very helpful at suggesting the alternative route. So, we decide to return to Jack Bridge and follow the footpaths back towards our goal. This is easier said than done, but after tramping through several fields, flirting with electric fences, we are finally where we want to be. That's more extra mileage but what's the alternative?

John W and myself decide to check out the fallen bridge over Colden Water and after two or three traverses declare it safe enough to be worth the risk, whilst at the same time renaming it 'The Bridge of Death'! Finally, we make the last couple of miles back along the Calderdale Way to Heptonstall, ironically now in sunshine. We have been soaked, sweated, frozen and as a result of the detours clocked up an additional three miles, the total coming in at 8.6. That should make for a fun day on Thursday.

Needless to say, Thursday dawned a completely different sort of day with wall to wall sunshine. A much more pleasant experience enjoyed by 12 of Burnley's finest and 'Button the Wonderdog'. With the improvements to the route and the decision to brave the 'Bridge of Death', we completed the trek in 6.5 miles on this occasion. 'Sherpa' Ed Walton, better known now as Captain Mainwaring, even performed the noble act of chaperoning two lady walkers who shall we say were somewhat fearful, across the accursed bridge. Back in good time, we hit the White Lion in Heptonstall, another pub well worth a visit. Beer of the day for me was Chinook from the Goose Eye Brewery, Keighley, and there were plenty of equally tempting offerings. A favourite walk that I'm sure will be re-visited ere long.

In the absence of any meaningful Saturday football again it's another trip to view a potential wedding venue. This time the destination is Kendal and the Castle Green Hotel. It's a much easier drive than last week's weather blighted trip up the B6160, and in good weather and light traffic we make the venue in 80 minutes. A very impressive building and with all the facilities, large function room, 90 plus bedrooms, a fitness club with swimming pool and plenty of local accommodation in Kendal.

It would appear to tick all the boxes, but my wife and I get the distinct impression that the 'happy couple' are much more enamoured by the rural charms of the CB Inn. A deciding factor for me would be the choice of, and price of the beer, but youngsters have some funny ideas. Anyway, although the big day is not planned till June 2019 at least things seem to be moving in a more definite direction regarding the venue. Hopefully within the next fortnight the venue and date will be set, then all I have to worry about is paying for it!

Tuesday 20th February sees the resumption of Tuesday Dotcom walks. This week for a pleasant change we are on home soil. We are allegedly scheduled for a 6.56 mile walk from Hurstwood, to be led by the Burnley Contingent's Dave Preedy (He's one of our own, he's one of our own, and so on ad nauseam). A bit worrying this since the 'Wandering Weirs', in a brief encounter with our friend Dave on Monday, revealed he was unaware of the start time and meeting point! Doesn't augur too well that.

However, Tuesday dawned bright and sunny and the walk, led mostly from the back by Dave P, was a resounding success. Thirty-one walkers, almost a small army, ensures that nobody is going to mess with us! The route From Hurstwood, via Worsthorne, Gorple Road, Cant Clough reservoir and Middle Pasture Farm, ran out to my reckoning at 7.8 miles. Lunch was taken in the weak but welcome sunshine at the Gorple Stones, and the scenery did us Burnley lads (and lasses) proud. There were also a number of opportunities to remind those less fortunate football fans that on the route they could see the ONLY PREMIER LEAGUE GROUND IN LANCASHIRE. The Burnley Contingent accompanied by some of the more alcoholic Preston brethren finished off with a stop at the Thornton Arms. Today's brew of choice, Timothy Taylor's Golden Best. Next week its back into hostile territory starting at Witton Park, Blackburn. I'd better get my body armour on for that one!

This week the 'Wandering Weirs' have proposed a longer than usual supposedly 9.5-mile Burnley Contingent ramble. This causes some concern for me regarding the fitness levels and staying power of the group. Having expressed my doubts to the WWs, John W assures me that the walk is on good tracks and won't feel anything like that. Interestingly, at the same time he seems to have categorised the group into three main types, the lame, the insane and the depressed. I can't help thinking that he has perhaps missed a category, i.e. the confused, which I believe could probably be applied to all of us.

We have in the past had incidents of wrong car park instructions, notably when one member who for anonymity's sake we'll call Geoff Ashworth, informed 'Postman Keith' to meet at Roughlee car park. He then picked me up and we headed for Barley car park. Unsurprisingly, at the appointed hour there was no sign of Keith at Barley. On quizzing Mr A as to what he had told Keith it transpired he had said

Roughlee. Undeterred, we set off for Roughlee, unaware that Keith had put two and two together and set off for Barley. Missing each other in passing, both drivers arrived at their new car parks and found nobody there waiting. So, they repeated the journeys again missing each other in passing. This sad train of events continued for some time until Keith got an unstoppable nose bleed (probably brought on by stress) and went home!

Similarly, we have had instances of walkers turning up for outings minus an essential piece of equipment, namely their boots! Top marks here to Bob Walsh and Maureen Thornber, although in their defence they did remember their lunches.

John W has twice contrived to misplace his expensive Garmin GPS SatNav device, firstly by leaving it on a fence post, and secondly on the roof of his car! Fortunately, on the first occasion he managed to retrace his steps the following day and incredibly find the device. Unfortunately, on the second occasion, no such luck, and his pride and joy probably now lies buried in a foot of mud in the environs of Higham.

My own particular forte is taking the wrong direction, but I cannot claim to be the sole possessor of this uncanny knack. However, I can say that on all our outings (to date) we have all managed to make it back to base, perhaps a little later than planned, but nevertheless home. Perhaps the most spectacular mis-direction was made by the usually Mr Reliable, 'Sherpa' Ed Walton, who now has a hill in the Trough of Bowland, known to the Burnley Contingent as Mount Walton, to commemorate the event.

These musings got me thinking that perhaps we should have a badge motto that we could incorporate into the splendid Dotcom Walkers badge (see photo somewhere in the book). For those of you reading in black and white, the badge is made up of elements that epitomise the group and Lancashire in particular. We have the large brown walking boot with black walking poles that symbolises what we do, the red rose of Lancashire and the iconic Pendle Hill. I was thinking along the lines of incorporating into the design something like the SAS's 'Who Dares Wins'. Or perhaps Julius Caesar's famous 'Veni, Vidi, Vici', translated as 'I came, I saw, I conquered'. Maybe more fitting for us would be 'We came, we walked, we talked, we ate, we went to the pub'. On second thoughts that maybe too long. Oh well, feel free, all suggestions welcome.

It's Thursday 22nd February and once again we are headed to Calderdale for another 'Weir Wander' billed as Warland to Watergrove reservoir. As previously mentioned this is a slightly longer walk than usual but undeterred 11 eager walkers and 'Button the Wonderdog' are off to an early start. A nice gentle 'loosener' along the Rochdale canal to warm up, then from The Summit pub a steady uphill climb. That accounts for one eager walker - Geoff Ashworth - currently not operating on full power, who retraces his steps back to the lay-by and we suspect the Burger van that is situated there.

It's a lovely day no hint of rain, weak sunshine and light breezes, perfect winter walking weather. On up via Pasture House, Ringing Pots Hill and crossing Turn Slack Clough to join the Pennine Bridleway and some spectacular views. Lunch is taken at Watergrove reservoir and I make that 5.1 miles in to the walk. The weather stays kind as we trek on up Ramsden Rd and take the track over the moor on the Long Causeway to Middle Marsden. Then a sharp right skirting

Cranberry Dam and on via the TC Way and Lower Allescholes, Moorhey Wood before dropping back down to Warland. The route finally panned out at 10.0 miles but all completed it none the worse for wear.

The 'Wandering Weirs' have excelled with this one and truly splendid moorland ramble, no doubt enhanced by the perfect weather. I don't think it would have been half as much fun in the rain. Just time to head back to the Rifle Volunteer and a pint of Reedley Hallows Brewery, Filly Close Blonde. A perfect end to a perfect day.

At last! I hear you say, its time to get back to the important stuff, the football! News in the week is of an easing of the crippling injury situation. Long term absentees Stephen Ward and Chris Wood play in a behind closed doors game against Blackpool. They are also joined, after what has been over half a season's absence, by goalkeeper Tom Heaton. Hopefully all will soon be back in contention to play vital roles as we approach the business end of the campaign.

Bizarrely as players start to return to the fold, we learn that manager Sean Dyche is now injured and will be out for the rest of the season! The boss has, in his own words, ruptured his quad. I don't like the sound of that. However, it transpires to be a muscle in his thigh. Apparently, the injury occurred as he was participating in a warm weather training session with the team in Portugal. He is now unable to run, but thankfully will be able to stand in his technical area berating the fourth official for 90 minutes. Perhaps somebody should tell Mr Dyche that he's not as young as he used to be and perhaps he should leave it to the lads. I'll let somebody else make that suggestion though rather than me.

Back to the action, and thankfully a proper kick-off time.

Game 28 – Saturday 24th February 15.00 – Burnley v Southampton

It's three weeks since the last Premier League action at the Turf, so I was quite looking forward to this one. A home game against a team in the bottom three would also appear to give us a good opportunity to end the ten-match run without a win in the league. So, on another lovely sunny, but cold winters day, perfect for football, all was set fair. Or so I thought.

The team news revealed a recall at left back for Stephen Ward, and a place in centre midfield for Ashley Westwood, as we reverted to a 4-4-1-1 formation. Sam Vokes was dropped to the bench for the game against his hometown club.

What followed in the next 45 minutes can best be described as disappointing and more realistically as dire. Two teams apparently devoid of any real creativity cancelled each other out in an extremely scrappy affair. Once again, we saw the Clarets set up with 'inverted' wingers Johann Berg Gudmundsson (JBG) and Aaron Lennon both operating down their unnatural flanks. I have to say this is not my favourite tactic as it invariably results in the player checking inside the full back on almost every occasion to get onto his preferred foot. Consequently, the momentum of the attack is slowed, and the eventual cross is arcing towards the goalkeeper rather than away. Wouldn't it be nice to see the winger take the full back on and whip in crosses from the goal-line, a far more effective ball in my humble opinion.

Suffice it to say little goalmouth action was seen at either end. Probably the best chance of the half fell to Jeff Hendrick, playing in his attacking midfield role behind Ashley Barnes. It's fair to say that Hendrick has not been enjoying the best of form in recent weeks and his lack of confidence showed as he wanted too many touches instead of firing off a shot. Already the crowd around me were of the opinion that this game would be the prime contender for the last slot on Match of the Day.

The highlight of the afternoon so far was my half time trip to make use of the toilet facilities, so unproductive had been the first period. I had hoped to see a bit more adventure from the Clarets against a team in a serious relegation battle, but what we got was the now familiar safety-first approach. Once more it felt like the intention was not so much to go out and win, but rather to go out and not lose.

The second half started in much the same pattern with perhaps a little more intent coming from the Saints. It was difficult to see where a goal was going to come from, but then as often happens one came from nowhere. Lennon's cross from the left was beyond the far post but met by JBG whose tight angled shot was palmed out by the keeper. The ball came out and was returned goalward by Jeff Hendrick's head, but as the Saints keeper seemed to have the ball covered, Barnes bundled it home from close range. It was a scrappy goal that typified the match as a whole. Three quarters of the game gone and a precious lead against pretty innocuous looking opposition. Surely the time now to be bold and go and win the game.

Our visitors, their perilous position suddenly made even worse, not surprisingly ring the changes from the substitutes bench. One of these, Josh Sims, pretty quickly brings the save of the game from Nick Pope who at full stretch tips his piledriver onto the post and away. Our own substitutes, who prior to the goal were looking ready to be introduced, are now of course all sat back down. Surely 1-0 up and entering the last 20 minutes, it's time to introduce some fresh legs and go snatch number two and with it all three points. Not us, instead we hand the initiative to the visitors as we look to defend our slender advantage.

Then as time is almost up on 90 minutes, the inevitable happens albeit yet again in controversial circumstances. Firstly, Referee Bobby Madley gets in the way of Westwood as he tries to intercept the ball in midfield. Sims puts in a cross from the right flank which is headed back across goal. As the ball drops Saints striker Marco Gabbiadini appears to pull Kevin Long to the ground before turning and firing home. Bloody Hell!

Once again, a disputed late goal has cost us valuable points, and the winless run stretches to 11 matches. However, once more due to the inconsistency of the teams below us, we retain 7th place. With more performances of this nature that position won't be maintained for much longer. Our style of play has of late become increasingly one-dimensional, and our strike force is feeding off scraps. In my humble opinion the loss of Robbie Brady is largely responsible for this. He was the one player who looked to make things happen, not always successfully, but his attempts to try something different rubbed off on his team mates and made us more unpredictable.

We are lacking a player who can 'pull the strings' out on the pitch and this could have been addressed in the

January transfer window. What we required was a 'playmaker', but what we acquired instead were two more conventional type wingers, Aaron Lennon and on-loan Georges-Kevin Nkoudou. Whilst Lennon has established himself in the side it's difficult to justify the decision to bring in Nkoudou. The reluctance to give him any time on the pitch is baffling, and with the lead and 20 minutes to play, that was surely the time to try something different. Still, what do I know? With 10 games left in the season and a 10-point cushion from the relegation spots, we are almost assured of Premier League football next time round. We are currently victims of our own early season success, as we the fans, have perhaps embraced unrealistic expectations.

By the way, we did qualify for the final spot on MOTD, even breaking the convention of the lowest scoring game being last up. Watford's 1-0 home victory over Everton took the penultimate slot. That just about says it all!

Result - Burnley (Barnes 67) 1 - 1 (Gabbiadini 90) Southampton

Burnley Team

Pope, Lowton, Mee, Long, Ward, Gudmundsson, Cork, Westwood, Hendrick, Lennon, Barnes

Subs Not Used - Lindegaard, Bardsley, Taylor, Marney, Nkoudou, Vokes, Wood

Southampton Team

McCarthy, Soares, Stephens, Hoedt, Bertrand, Romeu (Boufal 75), Lemina, Ward-Prowse (Sims 68), Tadic (Gabbiadini 81), Redmond, Carillo

Subs Not Used - Forster, Hojbjerg, Pied, Bednarek

Attendance – 20,982

Season To Date – Played 28, Won 9, Drawn 10, Lost 9, Goals For 22, Goals Against 25, Points 37

League Position after Game 28 – 7th

Tuesday 27th February and we awake as promised to a blanket of snow. Yes, the 'Beast from the East' has arrived in Burnley, as cold air from Russia brings a significant snowfall. Before 7.00 a.m. I have received both a text and an email from Dotcom group leader Bob Clare announcing the cancellation of today's walk. Once again, the curse of Nigel Hext has struck. Nigel was to lead a walk from Witton Park, Blackburn taking in some of the Witton Weavers Way. However, not for the first time has one of Nigel's walks been weather abandoned. On three previous occasions his planned route on Waddington Fell have been aborted. Come to think of it the last walk he led ended with one Dotcom walker hospitalised with a broken ankle! Probably just as well we didn't go. Perhaps he should be Nigel Hex, not Hext.

MARCH

By Thursday 1st March the 'Beast from the East', no not Brian Jensen, has really got a grip on Burnley. Having had to suffer from a rare walk cancellation on Tuesday, the same fate befalls Thursday's planned expedition. In view of the extremely inclement weather, Captain Mainwaring had planned a route starting from St James Church, Briercliffe, taking in Catlow and Walton's Spire before returning via Coldwell reservoir to The Sun Inn, Haggate. Being very local, especially for me, it meant a minimum of travelling in the hazardous road conditions.

Unfortunately, heavy overnight snow coupled with strong gusty winds led to 'white-out' conditions in Harle Syke on Thursday morning. Undeterred, my extremely conscientious wife set off on foot in blizzard conditions for her place of employment. As I helped her on her way I suspected that today was not a day for the hills. A quick phone call with the Captain and it was 'match postponed'. I'm sure it was the right decision despite most of us wishing to walk. In these conditions safety must come first.

I opted for a morning in St Peter's Gym although buses were not running up to Harle Syke, instead terminating at Casterton Avenue, so a bit of a walk anyway. On arrival home around lunchtime I found my wife had beat me to it. All sent home from work and told not to come tomorrow. Things must be bad if that bunch of slave drivers are shutting up shop.

It's a similar story for daughter Stephanie up in the wilds of Darlington, no trip to work in Northallerton for the second consecutive day. She wasn't happy, doesn't like missing work and the chance to gossip. To be fair on Tuesday she had fully intended to make the trip, only to be thwarted at the death. Stephanie drives a tiny Toyota Aygo, which is sensibly currently fitted with winter tyres. Her partner, and soon to be husband, Tom, goes for a more-sporty VW Scirocco as the vehicle of choice. As is often the case, the expensive option is totally useless when bad weather is prevalent. Up early to make the tricky journey south, Stephanie was alarmed to find on leaving the house, NO AYGO. Yes, Tom had purloined the car to make his way to Birtley leaving her stranded. Fortunately, she had brought her lap-top home the previous evening and was able to work from there. Tom did make it to Birtley but his normal thirty-minute journey this time took three hours. Some might say justice was done.

Game 29 – Saturday 3rd March, 12.30 – Burnley v Everton

The combination of an early kick off time and the recent spate of bad weather conspire to rule out the usual Saturday morning St Peter's Centre Gym session. Hooray, I can almost hear my wife say as it provides her with the ideal excuse to forego this weekly hour of torture. Instead we opt to drop my car off close to Queens Park and walk back home to Harle Syke via the Brun Valley Greenway. This means that I'll have to retrace my steps shortly after a very early lunch and continue the trek to Turf Moor. However, this will allow a shorter walk back after the game as the car will be handily placed for the return.

The weather has abated somewhat with no significant snow fall in the last 24 hours, though it's still extremely cold. As I make my way through the woods on the Greenway through several inches of snow, I wonder how many fans of other Premier League teams would have the opportunity of such a scenic ramble to the stadium. Allowing myself an hour from home to Turf Moor I note approaching Heasandford Bridge that I'm not making as rapid progress as I thought. Obviously, the snow and underfoot conditions are slowing me considerably. Time to put a bit of a sprint on and as I approach the Turf I am shedding gloves, hat and scarf as I start to overheat. Sub-zero temperatures and overheating, doesn't seem right somehow. Anyway, the injection of pace works, and for you lovers of statistics, I make the ground in 51 minutes 22 seconds, a distance of 2.6 miles, at an average of 3 mph.

The team shows one change from last week, James Tarkowski replacing the perhaps rather unlucky to lose his place, Kevin Long. Once again, we line up in a 4-4-1-1 formation, but this time Sean Dyche has clearly read my mind and 'uninverted' the wingers. Aaron Lennon plays down the right and Johann Berg Gudmundsson (JBG) down the left. Wise move Sean.

It's a lively start and there are three early shooting opportunities all falling to JBG but none really troubling the Toffees keeper. Everton currently on a run of four consecutive away defeats, are showing though that they are no slouches and look confident and tidy going forward. Our defence with 'Tarky' recalled is now arguably back to full strength, but in the early stages is looking anything but solid. Indeed, only a shocking miss from right in front of goal by Theo Walcott keeps the scores level. That should have been sufficient warning of the danger but if it was it went unheeded. On 20 minutes the visitors take the lead with a headed goal from recent signing Cenk Tosun, his first ever Premier League goal.

That's a bit of a sickener as we had been playing well up to that point. What will be the reaction now? On the whole pretty positive and only a brilliant save by Everton keeper Jordan Pickford prevents an Ashley Barnes header from squaring things up. It's now an end-to-end contest, and much improved on last week's turgid affair. Although we could feel unlucky to be behind, Everton, by the same token with better finishing, could have had two or three more goals. I text my daughter Stephanie at half time with the news we are losing 0-1, but that it could be 4-4.

The manager's reaction at half-time is to be a bit more pro-active than has sometimes been the case. It's a decisive move to bring on fit again Chris Wood for Jeff Hendrick, as we revert to a 4-4-2 formation and add a bit more fire power.

The two men up front, Barnes and Wood immediately start to look more of a goal threat, and with ex-Evertonian Lennon and JBG looking dangerous on the flanks, its game on. Again, excellent saves from Pickford thwart us at the start of the second period, and you almost get the feeling it could be going to be one of those days. Not so, on 56 minutes Barnes latches onto a lovely through ball from deep by Matt Lowton. Outpacing his marker and with Pickford opting to stay rooted on the goal line, 'Ash' waits his moment before lashing home. That looked a finish worthy of Harry Kane or Sergio Aguero, and once more Barnes has shown he is more than just a battering ram.

Everton's ambition of the first half has now all but disappeared and as manager Sam Allardyce makes changes, their fans loudly voice their displeasure. Wood and Barnes continue to cause havoc in the Toffees defence, which now looks like it has a soft centre! Ex Claret Michael Keane looks nothing like the player he was here, and I almost feel a little sorry for him. We are going for the winner now and it duly arrives on 80 minutes. Wood climbs highest to head home a JBG corner and the fightback is complete. Everton's stuttering attempt to salvage something from the game is not helped by a rash arm flung by captain Ashley Williams at Barnes. The referee has no hesitation in deeming it worthy of a red-card. What an idiot, the offence being committed in our penalty area at an Everton free-kick. I guess his frustration, after a torrid afternoon with 'Basher', finally got the better of him.

There are no more real dangers as Nick Pope takes a couple of routine catches from high balls into the box, and after three added minutes the points are ours. It's the first win in 12 Premier League games, as well as the first of 2018. Also, it's the first time in a Premier League game under Sean Dyche that we have come from behind to win, and that at the 53rd attempt! The points total moves on to the 'magical' 40, generally considered as guaranteeing league safety. We have reached the same points total as last season and still with nine fixtures to complete.

It's a double over Everton, our first of the season, and the 'monkey is off our back'. Oh, happy day! Once again for those of you that like a good statistic, the match stats were as follows, Burnley first. Possession 55/45, Shots 21/10, Shots on Target 8/4, Corners 10/4, Fouls 9/12. All those shots at goal, I don't think we've had that many all year up till now!

Result – Burnley (Barnes 56, Wood 80) 2 – 1 (Tosun 20) Everton

Burnley Team

Pope, Lowton, Mee, Tarkowski, Ward, Gudmundsson, Cork, Westwood, Hendrick (Wood 45), Lennon, Barnes

<u>Subs Not Used</u> – Lindegaard, Bardsley, Long, Marney, Nkoudou, Vokes,

Everton Team

Pickford, Coleman, Keane, Williams, Martina, Walcott, Davies (Rooney 59), Sigurdsson (Bolasie 83), Gueye, Tosun (Niasse 68), Calvert-Lewin

<u>Subs Not Used</u> – Robles, Baines, Holgate, Schneiderlin

Attendance – 20,802

Season To Date – Played 29, Won 10, Drawn 10, Lost 9, Goals For 24, Goals Against 26, Points 40

League Position after Game 29 – 7th

What a good day all round it turned out to be. On reaching home my daughter informed me that they had provisionally booked the wedding venue, the CB Inn Arkengarthdale, with a date in June 2019. The problem is she now keeps mentioning sums of money that are required for deposits and all sorts of related issues.

The day is rounded off with a birthday bash for my old mate Steve Calderbank who is an invaluable contributor to the production of these tomes. Steve has reached the grand old age of 70, and whilst now resident in Wragby, Lincolnshire, has returned to be amongst life-long friends to celebrate the day. A splendid party at Crow Wood Leisure centre, marred only by the absence of any real ale, topped off a highly successful day.

Steve is no football fan, but in his attempt to be an irritating bugger, decided that he would become a pretend Hull City fan following his move to the 'flatlands'. Since their last relegation and continuing demise, he has long since given up that pretence. How, nice then to see at his party, surrounded by many of the Claret and Blue persuasion, him presented with a Burnley FC shirt with the legend Calderbank 70 emblazoned on the back. I wonder if he'll wear it in bed like David Mellor and his Chelsea shirt. I can just imagine his long-suffering wife Noreen's face!

Exiting Turf Moor after the Everton game, I was surprised to hear the stadium announcement that the next match at Turf Moor would be on the 14th April. A mistake I thought, he must mean 14th March. However, it transpires it is correct. Due to the next home opponent Chelsea's continuing FA Cup run, our fixture with them must be rearranged. That coupled with another International break means no football at the Turf for six weeks! Oh well, looks like garden tidying time coming up.

You may recall a little rant a chapter or two back concerning the lack of support from book retailers to promote these precious works of literature. On Monday 5th March following a very affable meeting with Burnley FC CEO, Dave Baldwin, I can confirm that all being well, this and subsequent volumes will be retailed by the club shop. Thank you, Mr Baldwin, who despite being a Bradford City fan, doesn't seem a bad guy!

I may in the past have mentioned a particular hobby horse of mine, that is the use of wrong words. I have lost count of the number of times I have seen 'of' where it should read 'have'. Then there are the good old favourites, 'their' instead of 'there', and 'were' instead of 'where'. However, on Tuesday 6th March I had the pleasure of being privy to one of the most amusing examples of this art, but this time in verbal usage.

Nearing the end of an uneventful walk at Witton Park, led by Nigel the 'Hex', group leader Bob Clare stopped the not inconsiderable number of Dotcomers to brief them about next week, and to thank Nigel for his efforts. One lady, who shall remain nameless to protect her anonymity, and dignity, obviously catching the mood of the moment, decided to proffer her own personal thanks. To a packed crowd of around 30 walkers she announced that she would, *"like to thank the kind gentleman who had humped her over a stile"*. I don't think I need to say any more about what the reaction to that was!

Of course, she meant helped, but tragically on this occasion chose a most unfortunate alternative. Needless to say, the hunt was then on for whom the 'kind gentleman' might be. A quick look round the assembly, and the rather guilty look on Stuart's face, I think identified him as the culprit. For me it was the highlight of the walk…and probably for Stuart too.

Wednesday 7th March's Daily Mail ran a short column hinting of a possible England call-up for the forthcoming friendly internationals for James Tarkowski and Nick Pope. How ironic would that be if a struggling Michael Keane lost his England squad place to the man who replaced him at Burnley! Not only that but Pope could be in line to take his own team mate Tom Heaton's place in the squad, due to his prolonged injury absence. I can't imagine that at the start of this highly successful season for both players that either had imagined that as a possibility. Let's hope Gareth Southgate has the courage to reward these two for their outstanding efforts.

Back on our travels for the next game as we head for the 'Big Smoke' and an opportunity to maintain our unbeaten run in March. With our 40-point safety cushion comfortably reached it's time to go out and enjoy ourselves, and at what better place than the London Stadium, the former Olympic Stadium of London 2012. Our hosts are having an up and down sort of season, but mostly down, and currently sit in 14th place, 10 points adrift of the Clarets, and only three above the drop zone. Having lost their last two games, both by 4-1 scorelines, and being severely injury ravaged, there could be points for the taking. An early goal would get their nerves jangling so come on you Clarets, there's nothing to lose!

Game 30 – Saturday 10th March 15.00 – West Ham United v Burnley

Its same again for us following last week's victory over Everton. Jeff Hendrick starts and last time's match winner Chris Wood reverts to the bench. My mate John W reports from the ground that there are *"Glum faced Hammers all around the ground, but I'm still smiling"*. The question is will he still be later?

A bright start from the hosts, belying their lowly position, and there's a real determination about them. There's an early scare as Nick Pope saves with his legs from the big Austrian striker Marko Arnautovic. Another chance on 15 minutes goes begging as Manuael Lanzini fires high and wide.

The Austrian national coach is apparently at the game running the rule over Arnautovic and our own Ashley Barnes, who qualifies by virtue of an Austrian grandmother. Unfortunately, Ashley is making little impression in the early stages.

There may be no goals at the London Stadium, but the Radio Lancashire commentators are reporting goals galore from AFC Fylde in their National League fixture with Aldershot. It is 4-1 to Fylde after only 17 minutes and prolific striker Danny Rowe already has a hat-trick!

Back at the 'big game' we are apparently under pressure and getting 'roughed up' a bit. It's 24th November since we last won away, that being a 2-1 victory at Bournemouth, so it's high time we repeated the feat.

The game is opening up now as the half progresses and we come into it a bit more. Then another escape on 38 minutes as Lanzini is thwarted again by a brilliant save by Pope's legs. Meanwhile our friends at Fylde have gone nap and lead 5-1 at half time.

Our Radio Lancashire friends report an 'uncomfortable half' for the Clarets, and we hope for better in the second period. Those hopes are almost instantly rewarded as Ashley Barnes turns a Stephen Ward cross past Joe Hart in the Hammers goal. Only to see the effort chalked off for offside. A close call that one. Where's the Video Assistant Referee (VAR) when you need him?

The next action sees Ashley Westwood yellow carded and by all accounts lucky not to see red. Then around the hour mark we see the expected substitution of Jeff Hendrick by Chris Wood as we signal a more attacking intent.

Back at AFC Fylde they just can't stop scoring and they hit a sixth. Unfortunately, goal scorer Sam Finley celebrates a bit too much in front of the visiting Aldershot fans. His over exuberance earns him a yellow card, which coupled with the one he picked up earlier in the game, gets him sent off. How thick is that!

If we thought Wood's introduction last week had turned the game, then this time it was to have an even more devastating effect. On 66 minutes, the striker chases a Matt Lowton through ball to the right edge of the penalty area. Looking up he lays it across for the onrushing Barnes to fire home another 'Barnstormer', leaving Hart clawing at thin air. Another brilliant effort from our Ashley, Austria here we come!

If John W thought the Hammers looked glum before the start, they now looked a damn sight worse and angry with it. The goal sparks a minor pitch incursion by irate Hammers fans, one being grappled to the floor by home captain Mark Noble. With the shell shocked and distracted Hammers in disarray, the Clarets take full advantage as within four minutes we extend the lead. A neat build up in and around the Hammers penalty area sees Barnes feed Aaron Lennon whose low cross is steered home by the lurking Wood.

That's the cue for a second pitch encroachment by a fan, who for some reason best known to himself, uproots a corner flag and tries to plant it on the centre spot. More disturbingly scuffles break out between fans and stewards as some supporters gather close to the Director's box. The referee consults both managers as to whether to take the players off the pitch. Thankfully it's not necessary and the game is allowed to continue.

With the Clarets now in total control its no surprise as on 81 minutes we go three goals up. Johann Berg Gudmundsson's powerful 25-yard shot is spilled by Hart and Wood following up taps home. Once more a pitch invasion, and co-Chairmen Gold and Sullivan flee the Director's Box for their own safety.

What an unbelievable end to a game in which, we had for the first period at least, been second best. The introduction of Wood had once again proved a masterstroke as he helped himself to two goals and an assist for Barnes's belter. Once again in a very difficult atmosphere the team and management had acquitted themselves with great dignity. At one-point, frightened young West Ham fans had been moved to safety on the Burnley substitutes bench, as our players gave up their seats to accommodate them.

Sadly, our magnificent second half performance had been overshadowed by the disgraceful scenes as the home fans vented their spleen. Match of the Day highlighted the troubles at great length, to the point that the football became of secondary importance. Similarly, the Sunday papers went to town on the hooliganism at the expense of the action on the pitch.

I don't much like West Ham fans they, like Leeds United, have delusions of grandeur. They are stuck in a time warp believing they are still in the halcyon days of Bobby Moore, Martin Peters and Geoff Hurst. The fact is that those days are long gone, along with those players, and they have been replaced by classless mercenaries.

In contrast, we know what we are. A small club that packs a big punch!

We don't have a winless run now, it's now a winning one which has extended to two! Whilst the pundits made great play of the fact that we hadn't won in eleven, we can now point out to the fact that we have only lost one in six. We have already surpassed our highest Premier League points total amassing 43, with still 24 to play for. There's no game now till the 31st March and that away at seemingly doomed West Bromwich Albion. Could we end the month having won every game?

Oh, by the way, AFC Fylde won 7-1, so Mr Finley's dismissal didn't cost them too dearly.

Result - West Ham United 0 - 3 (Barnes 66, Wood 70,81) Burnley

Burnley Team

Pope, Lowton, Mee, Tarkowski, Ward, Gudmundsson, Cork, Westwood, Hendrick (Wood 61), Lennon, Barnes (Vokes 89)

Subs Not Used - Lindegaard, Bardsley, Long, Marney, Nkoudou

West Ham United Team

Hart, Zabaleta, Collins, Ogbonna, Cresswell, Kouyate, Noble, Antonio, Joao Mario (Hernandez 71), Lanzini, Arnautovic

Subs Not Used - Adrian, Evra, Cullen, Rice, Browne, Hugill

Attendance - 56,904

Season To Date – Played 30, Won 11, Drawn 10, Lost 9, Goals For 27, Goals Against 26, Points 43

League Position after Game 30 – 7th

This week's walks kick-off with an always popular Dotcom outing, that being a walk from the Chetham Arms, Chapeltown. I think I may have previously mentioned this pub as being outstanding, and Tuesday 12th March reinforces this view. A lovely walk in good conditions taking in Chetham Close, and Entwistle and Wayoh reservoirs. Topped off with Rag Pudding, Chips and Mushy Peas, and washed down with a pint of Hop Pale Ale from Blackedge Brewery, Horwich. What more could any man wish for!

On the following Thursday I find myself in the unusual role of walk leader. This I must say is not from choice, but more as a result of being 'press ganged' into it by our very own Capt. Mainwaring. I suppose I've nobody else to blame except myself, having foolhardily suggested we walk a route pioneered by the Dotcomers pre-Christmas. The route will be circular from Cotton Tree, Colne then via Trawden, Wycoller and Laneshawbridge. Having only walked the route once previously I am not confident that it will go smoothly, but in Garmin we trust! I have informed all Burnley Contingent walkers I will accept no responsibility for missed turns and mud, and there will be no dawdling. Let's see how they like that! I doubt I'll be asked to lead again.

Thursday dawned in most unpromising fashion and as we assembled close to the Cotton Tree Inn the inevitable rain continued relentlessly. This was unfortunate for Gwen Walton for it was at this point she discovered she had left her waterproof jacket back in Burnley. Undaunted she set off back for it vowing to catch us up on the walk. A quick briefing to the troops at which I instructed them that if I was going to be the 'leader' then they would walk by my rules. No dawdling, no singing by Keith, who only knows one song and of that only the chorus to 'Ilkley Moor bah't at', and no historical monologues from John W.

I fear they took no notice of these instructions, but fortunately being a leader who believes it should be done from the front, I managed to avoid the worst of it. Gwen, having made good speed on her return trip to Burnley, was as good as her word and caught us before we even reached the Trawden Arms. The walk then proceeded largely uneventfully, except the occasional missed turn and after lunch at Wycoller, the rain even gave up. The path between Wycoller and Laneshawbridge afforded us the opportunity to engage in one of our favourite pastimes, Lancashire Mud Skiing. If we could only get it entered into the Olympics I think for sure we would be Gold medallists.

The walk de-brief, after some lengthy discussion as to venue, was taken at the Trawden Arms, and today's tipple was, Settle Brewery's, Attermire. Another beer to receive high recommendation. The Captain's view was that next week I should continue my apprentice leadership course with a walk from Salterforth. However, I will be declining his invitation due to an equipment failure. My Garmin Satnav Map SD card having been returned for repair, and not anticipated back for 10-14 days.

On returning home a quick look at the 'Up the Clarets' website revealed that Gareth Southgate had indeed called up Nick Pope and James Tarkowski to the England squad for the forthcoming friendly internationals. I doubt they'll see much if any playing time, but it is still a great reward for their magnificent efforts this season. Unfortunately, there is no call this time for Jack Cork, and once again Ben Mee is overlooked. This brings the total number of Burnley players called up for England whilst under Sean Dyche's tutelage to five. These being, Tom Heaton, Nick Pope, James Tarkowski, Jack Cork and Michael Keane (now Everton). Quite an achievement!

There's a dearth of football news again this week so I'll have to fill in again with details of the walking week.

Tuesday's Dotcom walk was an outing to Rivington Pike and then onwards and upwards to the now disused TV mast on Winter Hill. Group leader Bob Clare, always full of fun, decided that as he believed Tuesday the 20th March to be the first day of Spring, it was appropriate to visit Winter Hill. The walk took us through what used to be the estate of Lord Lever, latterly Lord Leverhulme. A great philanthropist of his time, and the founder of a great soap empire, his estate however was not immune to an act of latter day vandalism. High up on the Rivington estate is the site of what was once a magnificent villa, now reduced to nothing, burnt to the ground by a suffragette! It's not just football that attracts hooligans.

A decent steady uphill climb to the mast atop the hill in fair weather, and for the time of year, good underfoot conditions, was followed by a far more precarious descent. After a visit to the trig point we set off down the hill on a narrow and steep path made trickier by snow and mud. Fortunately, all 24 walkers made it down in one piece to assemble at the Belmont Road. Unfortunately, we were greeted there by a most unpleasant site, a sign saying the road was now entering Belmont, but underneath a further one saying 'Proud Home of Blackburn Rovers'. Ironically, the sign above it reading, 'Welcome to Blackburn with Darwen' had fallen off! Yes, it had crashed to earth, just like it's football team.

A short drive at the end of the walk took us to another top-class watering hole, the Black Dog at Belmont and well-deserved pints of Joseph Holt's, 'Two Hoots'.

Thursday's Burnley Contingent walk was from the Anchor Inn at Salterforth along one side of the valley to Foulridge and back down the opposite side to Sough, before returning to the pub. Sadly the most notable feature of this walk was the chronic wind affliction of 'Button the Wonderdog'. As we took refreshment at the end of the trek, clearly fuelled by his all-day breakfast of sheep shit, which to Button is akin to an all you can eat buffet, he proceeded to pollute the pub's atmosphere. Farting frequently and extremely malodourously, he made us all wish once more for the great outdoors. The only escape was to cover our noses with our bob caps. an act that renders drinking ale very difficult if not impossible. Nevertheless, we did enjoy an excellent tipple, Caledonian Brewery's, Golden XPA. I think next time Button stays in the Walton's car!

The first game of the international break sees England away in Holland. Unsurprisingly, there is no match action for either Nick Pope or James Tarkowski, and I can't help feeling that they are just making numbers up. The first-choice keepers appear to be Jordan Pickford and Jack Butland, both of whom have conceded 50+ goals in this current Premier League season. Pope's statistics for the season are positively miserly when compared to this pair, but they are still the preferred option.

However, amazingly but mainly due to injuries incurred in the Holland game, 'Tarky' does make the team for the home friendly against Italy. Playing in an unfamiliar role on the left side of a back three, he turns in an excellent performance marred only by a late penalty decision awarded after consultation of the accursed Video Assistant referee (VAR). To my mind it's a poor decision as our man inadvertently steps on the foot of the Italian attacker who has already lost possession of the ball and is tumbling to the ground. There's clearly no intent to foul the player, and the referee in 'live time' correctly awards a corner. The official is then advised by the VAR to study the replay of the incident on screen and changes the decision to a penalty. The resulting free shot is duly despatched and what looked like a second successive victory ends in a draw.

It's ironic really, if the Italian had already 'hit the deck' and Tarkowski then trod on him, nothing would have been given. However, because he was still partially on his feet, though in the act of overbalancing, a rather harsh penalty is awarded. A far more obvious incident occurred in the early minutes of the game, yet this received no VAR intervention or punishment. England centre back John Stones, dillied and dallied on the edge of his own penalty area, before having his 'pocket picked' by the attacker. In panic mode he attempted to redress his error by putting an arm around the 'Azzurri' to impede his progress and enabling him to effect his clearance. Where was VAR then? It seems to me that referee's in 'live-time' are prone to the odd mistake, but it would appear that with all the technological aids available the VAR system is just as fallible.

Game 31 – Saturday 31st March, 15.00 – West Bromwich Albion v Burnley

Away again for the last game in March, this time at what looks like an already doomed West Bromwich Albion. It's an absolute age since the Baggies recorded a rather fortunate 1-0 away victory in the opening home game of the season at Turf Moor. Since then they have found victories exceedingly hard to come-by and going into this fixture sit 10 points adrift of safety with only eight fixtures to complete. The Hawthorns is usually an extremely unlucky hunting ground for the Clarets, our last two visits ending in 4-0 reverses. However, we have already this season laid one or two bogeys, today would be a good day to end that run.

And, end it we did! Another Saturday and another away win in this magnificent season. A team that could only win once on their travels last time round, and amassed a paltry seven points, now with still three games away to play have totally eclipsed last season's effort. With three away games remaining we have already six wins, six draws and only four defeats. The points yield from that little lot being a mind boggling 24!

What looked like it might be a mighty struggle against a team desperate for points, turned out for the first half at least, something of a walk in the park.

Following the success at West Ham United, and with Premier League safety already assured, Sean Dyche decided to stick with the 4-4-2 formation that finished the last fixture in emphatic style. On fire strikers Ashley Barnes and Chris

Wood were charged with the task of adding to their recently impressive tally. The only change to the side that finished against the Hammers being a first start for Tottenham Hotspur loanee Georges-Kevin Nkoudou (GKN), in place of the injured Johann Berg Gudmundsson.

Strangely in a game where we would expect the home team to be pushing us back from the start, this is not the case. Our hosts are sitting deep and allowing us plenty of possession. Enjoying a lot of the ball is debutant GKN, but although his willingness and pace are clearly evident, his composure and decision making are somewhat lacking. I think a lot of which can be put down to inexperience and perhaps trying a little too hard to impress.

Nevertheless, we are on top from the start and on 22 minutes are ahead with another Barnes spectacular when Aaron Lennon received the ball on the right flank from Ashley Westwood and fashioned, a cross into the box. The ball is too high for Wood and seemingly a little behind Barnes. However, Ash adjusts his positioning before launching a tremendous bicycle kick that leaves Ben Foster in the Baggies goal rooted to the spot. What is it with Barnes? The guy rarely scores ordinary goals, they are almost always efforts straight out of the 'top-drawer'.

That's four in the last four games for him, and at a ground where we haven't won since Steve Kindon scored in 1969, we are certainly looking good for the points. There's a distinct lack of fight from our opponents and their lack of confidence is clearly evident. A second goal looked imminent and could perhaps have come via the penalty spot. However, yet again the referee, Lee Probert, failed to spot a blatant shirt pull by Ahmed Hegazi on James Tarkowski. Still we wouldn't want to spoil our unblemished record of not being awarded a penalty all season would we!

The only moment of concern for the Clarets' rearguard comes from a Salomon Rondon header before half time, once again excellently stopped low down near the post by the diving Nick Pope.

Half time 0-1, and all set fair, but still time for Radio Lancashire summariser Stephen Eyre to give young GKN a real rough ride. I can't say I'm a big fan of Mr Eyre, too self-opinionated for my liking. I suggest vociferously to my radio, that he shuts up, and gives the lad a chance.

Not surprisingly the Baggies make a change at the interval introducing winger Matt Phillips at the expense of defender Kieran Gibbs. Nothing to lose for them now and they have to give it a go at least. We are under a bit of pressure for the first 15 minutes of the half, but then start to recover our poise and are back in the game.

On 69 minutes Mr Eyre gets his wish as GKN is replaced by Jeff Hendrick and a suggestion that we may be looking to close out the game at 1-0. That thought is dispelled on 73 minutes as Matt Lowton finds Wood running into the penalty area. His shot hits keeper Foster on the chest and rebounds back out to the grateful striker who nods it back past him for a two-goal lead.

That should be that but with seven minutes to play Rondon gives the Baggies some hope as he gets the better of Tarkowski to fire home. There's some suggestion that our defence is disrupted by an injury to Stephen Ward which could have led to a stoppage of play in the build-up to the goal, but we don't make too much of a protest. Just one or two minor scares as the officials add five minutes extra time, but time runs out and the points are ours, yet again.

That's three wins on the bounce for the rampant Clarets and once again confidence is high. Our mid-season blip is now a distant memory and we look to finish the season on a real high.

Result – West Bromwich Albion 1 – 2 (Barnes 22, Wood 73) Burnley

Burnley Team

Pope, Lowton, Mee, Tarkowski, Ward, Nkoudou (Hendrick 69), Cork, Westwood, Lennon, Barnes, Wood (Vokes 77)

Subs Not Used – Lindegaard, Bardsley, Taylor, Long, Marney

West Bromwich Albion Team

Foster, Nyom, Dawson, Evans, Hegazi, Gibbs (Phillips 45), Livermore, Yacob, Brunt, Rondon, Rodriguez (Burke 74)

Subs Not Used – Myhill, McAuley, Krychowiak, Gabr, McClean

Attendance – 23,455

Season To Date – Played 31, Won 12, Drawn 10, Lost 9, Goals For 29, Goals Against 27, Points 46

League Position after Game 31 – 7th

APRIL

After the completion of a highly successful March programme, three wins from three, its onwards into April with the finishing line in sight. Thursday's team news ahead of the fixture at Watford is a mixed bag. Declared fit again and ready for first team action is club captain, Tom Heaton. That poses Sean Dyche something of a dilemma - does he go with his England international keeper or does he stick with the highly impressive Nick Pope. Not a bad dilemma to have, and my feeling is that Pope will retain the jersey.

On the negative side Tom's replacement as skipper, Ben Mee, is classed as doubtful along with last week's absentee, Johann Berg Gudmundsson. It'll be interesting to see if Dyche continues with last week's experiment of starting Georges-Kevin Nkoudou. If he does I sincerely hope that Mr Stephen Eyre is nowhere near the Radio Lancashire commentary microphones!

A shock (aren't they all?) report in the Daily Mail of Friday 6th April is headlined, 'One child has a rotten tooth pulled out every ten minutes'. Now this is indeed a sad indictment of the nation's dental health. However, I can't help but feel sorry for this poor child who is losing his/her teeth at an alarming rate of knots. By my reckoning the whole set will be gone in something around five hours, and a diet of porridge for life beckons. I'll get my coat!

Game 32 – Saturday 7th April, 15.00 – Watford v Burnley

Here's an interesting little fact, this game will be our third consecutive away fixture, and all will have been against teams beginning with a 'W'. Now, being as the first two have been won, that should be a good omen for this one. And, that's exactly what it turns out to be!

As feared Ben Mee fails to make the match day squad, his place going to ever-ready Kevin Long. Also missing for the second consecutive week is Johann Berg Gudmundsson, with Georges-Kevin Nkoudou (GKN) again filling in. There's a place on the bench for returning keeper Tom Heaton, Nick Pope retaining the gloves. Jack Cork takes over the captaincy in the absence of Mee, just reward for a fine season's work.

A quick-fire start from the Clarets sees Chris Wood head home but the 'goal' is disallowed for offside as we dominate the early exchanges. However, by midway through the half the hosts have found their way back into the game and it's relatively even.

Thankfully, this week there's no Stephen Eyre to carp on about GKN's perceived failings, his place as Radio Lancashire's summariser falling to Chris Boden of the Burnley Express.

The first half can be described as stop-start, as a series of niggly fouls disrupts the game's flow. Nick Pope keeps the Clarets level with a couple of outstanding saves and the break arrives with the scoreline 0-0.

The Hornets start the second period in determined fashion and around the hour mark have the lead. Will Hughes, not for the first time, dances into the penalty area but has the ball taken away from him by Stephen Ward. Unfortunately, the loose ball runs straight into the path of Roberto Pereyra who sidefoots home.

In previous Premier League campaigns that would have been the cue for the Clarets to implode and go on to lose by two or three goals. Not this bunch though! A few minutes to re-assess the options then a decisive substitution. Off comes GKN and on comes Sam Vokes. Within 22 seconds of entering the fray, Big Sam has levelled the scores. A free kick to the Clarets is poorly dealt with by Adrian Mariappa whose header is upwards and back towards his own goal. Vokes is on it in a flash to steer past home keeper Orestis Karnezis.

If I was happy with that, I was a damn sight happier shortly afterwards as on 73 minutes these unstoppable Clarets take the lead. Once again, a free kick floated into the box, a header back across goal by Long and a firm header towards goal by Cork. Karnezis claws the ball out and an almighty scramble ensues, before with the benefit of Goal Line technology, the referee confirms Cork's header has cleared the goal line. About time the technology worked in our favour.

Still some time to play out but with this team, I'm fairly confident we can do it. Despite the five minutes of added time being stretched to seven, much to the displeasure of Mr Dyche, we navigate our way safely to another three points.

A third consecutive away win, a fourth win on 'the bounce' and to cap it all our nearest challengers for a place in Europe next season, Leicester City, beaten at home. Saturday's don't come much better than this. A seventh away win of the season, and a four-match winning sequence not achieved at the top level since 1968. This is a truly remarkable season to savour.

Result – Watford (Pereyra 61) 1 – 2 (Vokes 70, Cork 73) Burnley

Burnley Team

Pope, Lowton, Long, Tarkowski, Ward, Nkoudou (Vokes 70), Cork, Westwood, Lennon (Hendrick 81), Barnes, Wood

Subs Not Used – Heaton, Bardsley, Taylor, Marney, Wells

Watford Team

Karnezis, Janmaat (Okaka 76), Prodl, Mariappa, Holebas, Doucoure (Carrillo 85), Capoue, Femenia, Hughes (Richarlison 85), Pereyra, Deeney

Subs Not Used – Gomes, Britos, Cathcart, Gray

Attendance – 20,044

Season To Date – Played 32, Won 13, Drawn 10, Lost 9, Goals For 31, Goals Against 28, Points 49

League Position after Game 32 – 7th

There's no doubting the fact that the older we get, the dafter we get. At the ripe old age of 66, and with arthritic knees, I have suddenly developed a longing to start running again. Now it's fair to say that the pinnacle of my running career was as far back as the 1980's, culminating in a slow Burnley Half Marathon coaxed round by my fellow Claret John W. Since then, whilst maintaining a reasonable level of fitness, running has disappeared from my regime.

However, I find that I am being increasingly drawn to the idea of having, as they say, another 'go'. I think this stems from the fact that my daughter Stephanie has re-discovered a passion for this particular recreational activity and joined a running club in her new home town of Darlington. She is currently in the throes of building up her stamina ahead of her half marathon debut in Edinburgh at the end of May.

In turn Stephanie's return to the trainers is largely down to her partner, and soon to be husband, who is one of a crazy breed of fell runners whose speciality is ultra-running. These guys run prodigious distances over rugged terrain and all for fun! Tom's focus is firmly fixed on the ultimate challenge of the Bob Graham Round, one of the classic big three mountain challenges in the UK. The run involves traversing 42 Lakeland fells in a 24-hour period, first achieved by the late Bob Graham of Keswick. I think Stephanie has come to the conclusion that if you can't beat 'em, join 'em.

Now, can I just say that my ambitions are considerably humbler than Tom's. I would however like to achieve a level of fitness which would allow me to accompany Stephanie in some of the shorter distance events, such as an occasional 10K race. With this in mind I am setting myself a target of hopefully entering, and completing, the Langdale Christmas Pudding 10K Run. This event is held annually in the Lake District and will this year take part on 8th December 2018. This event which at its peak attracts 1000 runners, has the added bonus of a Christmas Pudding presented to all finishers. Now there's an incentive!

With the target set it's time to start some serious training and testing of the knees. My first session, a modest 25 minutes on the treadmill to assess the joint's reaction. Next, it's the big step back into the great outdoors, I'll keep you posted on the progress.

Last Saturday's terrific comeback win at Watford, coupled with Leicester City's unexpected home defeat by Newcastle United, opened up a six-point gap between the two teams. That brought the prospect of European football at Turf Moor tantalisingly closer. With the sides down to meet this coming weekend, as they say in the Westerns, we are heading for a showdown.

A victory for the Clarets would put us nine points clear of the Foxes with only a further 15 points on the table, a commanding position. A draw would maintain the six-point gap meaning we remained in pole position. A defeat would mean the race for seventh place was wide open and must be avoided if at all possible. Fingers and toes crossed!

A couple of walks to report this week. Tuesday's Dotcom outing following the Easter break was a fairly straightforward affair. An ascent to Darwen Tower from Sunnyhurst Woods, then a descent to Roddlesworth Woods for lunch then back via Tockholes. It was a pretty uneventful walk starting in damp weather but finishing dry. The temperature I have to say a little disappointing for April. However, not as disappointing as the lack of an after-walk pint, due to the lack of a suitable open pub at the end. Oh well, better luck next time.

Next up was a Burnley Contingent Thursday walk from Penistone Hill, via Bronte Falls to Top Withens, then back via Stanbury. A bit of a cock up due to malfunctioning mobile phones led to a later than planned start. As we made the journey from Laneshawbridge towards Haworth the mist got thicker and thicker. Bloody Hell its 12th April!

Arriving at the start, slightly behind the rest of the party, I learn that John W and Pete Seavers have come to the rescue of some clearly disorientated Australians. Our Antipodean friends are clearly unaccustomed to thick moorland mist. Anyway, all should be well as our two colleagues point them off in the direction of the shrouded Penistone Hill. Slightly worrying however is the fact that they too were headed for Top Withens and for the rest of the day we saw nothing of them! Mind you we saw precious little of anything at all as the mist stuck doggedly to the moor for the whole seven-mile round trip.

If anybody comes across a couple of bewildered and bedraggled looking Aussies, please turn them upside down and point them in the right direction, which must be South from here. I presume they made it back OK, we certainly did and adjourned for a well-earned beer break at the Wuthering Heights pub in Stanbury. Always a pleasure to visit this hostelry and a very palatable pint of Farmers Blonde courtesy of Bradfield's Brewery Sheffield gratefully consumed. We must come back one day and see where we actually walked.

Thursday's news on the injury front is not good, rumour has it that Ben Mee may well have to sit out the rest of the season with a shin injury. This is exactly the same injury that curtailed his season last time except this time it's the other shin. A big loss is Ben, however, Kevin Long as shown himself a capable deputy when called upon. The problem will be if Long or James Tarkowski were now to pick up an injury as central defence is the position with least cover.

Its Friday 13th, traditionally a day to be dreaded for bad luck, but not so for Sean Dyche as the club announce he has won the Barclays Premier League 'Manager of the Month' (MOM) award for March. A thoroughly deserved honour if ever there were one, and the first for Sean in the Premier

League. Let's hope the MOM curse that often blight the recipient doesn't strike us this weekend.

Game 33 – Saturday 14th April, 15.00 – Burnley v Leicester City

At last! After a seemingly interminable wait of some six weeks Premier League football returns to Turf Moor. Not since the victory over Everton way back on March 3rd have we seen a ball kicked in anger on the hallowed turf. What's more the weather has decided to take a turn for the better, and it's not even raining!

As anticipated Ben Mee fails to make the squad and it does look as though his season has ended prematurely, Kevin Long again deputises. Also missing is Georges Kevin Nkoudou and his place is taken by the returning Johann Berg Gudmundsson (JBG). We make our seats just as the game kicks off in sunshine, with the ground full to capacity and the home crowd buoyed by four consecutive victories, there's a cracking atmosphere. The Clarets are 'at it' from the off and to the delight of approximately 90% of the crowd, we have an early lead. A ball played through to Ashley Barnes sees our man of the moment, turn and play an incisive ball into the path of Chris Wood running in the inside left channel. Ex Leicester City man Wood's right foot shot is blocked by Kasper Schmeichel but the ball runs loose to Woody who fires home with his left foot from a tight angle. What a start in a game being billed as a Europe qualifier.

If that was good it gets better on nine minutes as Wood harries Harry Maguire into conceding a corner. JBG takes it perfectly and the ball is met with a powerful header from none other than Long, who nets his first ever Premier League goal for the Clarets. The perfect start, two goals up inside 10 minutes, no wonder the sun is shining.

Unsurprisingly our attacking intensity drops a little after this phenomenal start. The Foxes after taking some time to recover their composure then start to impose themselves. There's no doubting that with the quality of players such as Riyad Mahrez, Adrien Silva and Jamie Vardy they are potentially a strong force. However, displaying our customary defensive solidity we are coping pretty well with their threat. On the two or three occasions when the defence is breached goalkeeper Nick Pope, watched from the stands by England Manager Gareth Southgate, produces magnificent saves to preserve the two-goal cushion.

So, we are in at half time with a comfortable lead and set fair for Europe. I expect a determined start to the second period from the visitors and am not disappointed. Replacing the anonymous Shinji Okazaki with Kelechi Iheanacho at the break, there's an obviously more attack minded approach. With nothing to lose they are committing men forward in large numbers with both centre backs joining the attacks regularly.

I remark to fellow Claret John W that I would prefer to be seeing more of the game being played in the opposition's half, but to no avail and the pressure is building. We seem incapable of keeping the ball up front as Wood and Barnes become increasingly isolated as the wide men JBG and Aaron Lennon are pegged further and further back.

It's no surprise on 72 minutes as Iheanacho feeds Vardy in the box and he finishes powerfully to make it 'game on'. In an attempt to stem the tide, we revert to a more defensive 4-4-1-1 formation as Jeff Hendrick is introduced replacing goal scorer Wood. The change does seem to have some effect, the visitors still pour forward, but we are managing to keep them a bit more occupied at the back. It feels like an age to go yet slowly but surely time ticks on and we are entering the final stages. Barnes, having been yellow carded for a lunge at Schmeichel is replaced by Sam Vokes for the last five minutes of normal time. As the ninety minutes are up the fourth official signals four minutes of added time and these are negotiated successfully to gain an extremely valuable victory.

That's now five straight wins, but more importantly a triumph over our biggest threat to our European dream. That's a nine-point gap between us now and with only 15 points still on the table, surely too many to make up. It wasn't a great performance by any stretch of the imagination, but the two early goals dictated the tactics for the rest of the game. The fairy tale continues in this incredible season and its Chelsea next at the Turf this coming Thursday as the games now come thick and fast. What odds on a double against the current reigning Champions? With this team I wouldn't back against it.

Result - Burnley (Wood 6, Long 9) 2 - 1 (Vardy 72) Leicester City

Burnley Team

Pope, Lowton, Long, Tarkowski, Ward, Gudmundsson, Cork, Westwood, Lennon, Barnes (Vokes 85), Wood (Hendrick 75)

<u>Subs Not Used</u> - Heaton, Bardsley, Taylor, Marney, Wells

Leicester City Team

Schmeichel (Hamer 86), Simpson, Morgan, Maguire, Chilwell, Mahrez, Choudhury, Silva, Okazaki (Iheanacho 45), Vardy, Gray (Diabate 64)

<u>Subs Not Used</u> – Fuchs, Dragovic, Barnes, Albrichton

<u>**Attendance**</u> – 21,727

<u>**Season To Date**</u> – Played 33, Won 14, Drawn 10, Lost 9, Goals For 33, Goals Against 29, Points 52

<u>**League Position after Game 33**</u> – 7th

Sunday's game at St James's Park sees Newcastle United come back from a goal down to defeat Arsenal 2-1. The gap between the Gunners and ourselves is now down to two points, and suddenly we are now eyeing sixth place not seventh! Don't wake me up!

Good news readers! You may recall back in December that I informed you of my interesting ride to Colne on a Burnley & Pendle transport, or Transdev bus, as they may now be called. This was a revelation to me as the bus not only had a display board showing you what the next stop was, but also a verbal announcement of the same information. You may also recall that there were two voices giving out the spiel, one a genteel young lady, and the other a more brutish male.

Well today I can confirm that I now know who these people are! They are Emma and David, and this information I gleaned on another bus trip to Colne. As I looked around the bus my eyes alighted on a picture of the said twosome on an information board advising me that they were the 'Voices of Mainline'. Apparently, these lucky local people were the winners of a competition to become the 'speaking oracles'.

Now, I have to say my impression of the type of people providing the voices from my first trip were somewhat reinforced by their images. Emma looks to be a delightful young lady who concerns herself with light snippets of info, whilst David is a more forceful, no nonsense sort of guy, who you don't argue with.

Can I just say, that contrary to my daughter's opinions, travel on a B&P Mainline bus is a thoroughly pleasant experience, made more so by the aforementioned pair. Oh, and by the way, I'm only joking David if you are reading, you are a credit to the company. Next time you're aboard a mainline bus, just have a look out for our helpful duo.

At last the interminable rain seems to have ceased, and finally the underfoot conditions for our weekly walks are improving. Tuesday's Dotcom walk, a circular from Downham taking in Sawley, Grindleton and Chatburn, would a week or two back have been a morass of mud. This time expertly researched and led by Nigel 'the Hex', it proved a much drier and pleasanter experience. An opportunity here to also try out the admirable public toilet facilities at Downham, which are located in a refurbished stable block, well worth a visit, and free! We finished the day off at the Assheton Arms, Downham with a pint of Moorhouse's White Witch, a very atmospheric pub with a very cheerful and amiable landlord.

Thursday's Burnley Contingent walk certainly surpassed itself in terms of weather, a glorious day spent in unbroken sunshine and temperatures in excess of 20^{0}C. T-shirt and shorts walking for the first (and probably last) time this year. An excellent walk featured in Bob Clare's revised book edition of '100 Walks in Lancashire', was a pleasure from start to finish. The walk starting from Crookfield Rd. car park just off the A675, commences with an ascent of Great Hill, which as Bob Clare would tell you, is not such a great hill. Then heads off in the direction of Winter Hill, and along Spitlers Edge a truly scenic example of moorland ridge walking to Hordern Stoops and on into Belmont. The route back then takes the Witton Weavers Way along good tracks on this day, dry as a bone. It wasn't the only thing that was dry as a bone either after 8.7 miles of desert slogging. Nothing, for it but to head back in the cars to Belmont and a favourite watering hole, the Black Dog. A pint of Joseph Holt's Two Hoots proved just the restorative to get us in the mood for tonight's duel with reigning Champions Chelsea at the Turf.

Game 34 – Thursday 19th April, 19.45 – Burnley v Chelsea

No home game for 6 weeks then two in the space of five days, it's either feast or famine in the Premier League. An unusual evening for football at Turf Moor, I can't recall any on a Thursday, but I stand to be corrected. This is a game re-arranged due to our visitors continued progress in the FA Cup, a semi-final tie with Southampton awaiting them after this fixture at the weekend. A daunting challenge this one, although not enjoying anything like the all-conquering success of last season, the Blues are still a formidable outfit. Smarting from our 3-2 victory at Stamford Bridge in the season's opener, and still pursuing a top four finish to clinch a Champions League spot, we'll have to fight for anything we can get.

After five successive wins its an unchanged line-up for the Clarets, whilst Chelsea make six changes ahead of their FA Cup game. We are thankful to see players of the calibre of Eden Hazard, Cesc Fabregas, Willian, and Ross Barkley on the bench, but their replacements are hardly lesser names. Surprisingly they opt to go with two up-front, Olivier Giroud partnering Alvaro Morata.

It's a most un-Burnley like gloriously warm sunny evening as we get underway. For the first few minutes our friends from the South are clearly bemused by the weather, no doubt expecting the usual sub-zero temperature they encounter here. There's a near capacity crowd and the home fans are certainly making themselves heard, creating a great atmosphere in the stadium. This leads to a few minutes where we completely dominate the possession statistics, without remotely looking like troubling Thibaut Courtois in the Chelsea goal. However, its not long before they remember what they're here for and we say goodbye to the ball for long periods. With Giroud and Morata proving a handful and the imperious N'Golo Kante pulling the strings in midfield, I sense its going to be a long night.

It wasn't long before that feeling got stronger as on 20 minutes the visitors take the lead. Sadly, it's a bit of a soft goal to concede as an innocuous looking cross from the right is palmed out by Nick Pope but straight onto the body of the unfortunate Kevin Long from whom it rebounds into the net. Two goals in two games for Kevin, unfortunately this one in the wrong net! A marvellous reaction from the home crowd though, stunned initially by the goal almost immediately they recover to deliver a mighty roar of encouragement. Now with their tails up Chelsea continue to give us a bit of a run-around for the rest of the first half. Peppering us with shots whilst soaking up any attacking threat we can muster, they are in full control. It's a relief to reach the half time break just trailing by the one goal.

The interval certainly seems to have benefitted the Clarets most and the start of the second period sees a more determined attacking approach from our heroes. The visitors are pushed back and seem content with their one goal advantage. But, on 64 minutes that lead is gone. As Johann Berg Gudmundsson cuts in from the right wing his left foot shot appears to be 'meat and drink' for Courtois before hitting Ashley Barnes on the ankle and finding the corner of the net. If Barnes meant it he's a genius, but the cheeky grin on his face suggests he was trying to get out of the way of the shot and it fortuitously hit him. Who cares? Not the circa 20,000 Burnley fans now on their feet and bringing the roof down.

Unfortunately, as I feared might happen the goal only served to cause our opponents to step up a gear. Almost from the restart they grab the initiative and are pegging us back at will. Crosses are raining in and it feels like only a matter of time before we concede again. In fact, it's just five minutes as a cross from the left has our defence at sixes and sevens. The ball lands at the feet of Victor Moses on the right of the box, with Stephen Ward too far off him he has time to pick his shot and beat Pope at his near post.

To rub salt in the wounds Chelsea then introduce the appropriately named Hazard, at the expense of the profligate Morata who has wasted a golden opportunity one-on-one with Pope. As usual it's a thankless task trying to get the ball from the little Belgian, but thankfully on this occasion he seems a little over elaborate when a simple pass may have brought richer dividends. Sam Vokes is brought on to replace a largely ineffective Chris Wood. Unfortunately, he can't reproduce his recent feat of a goal within 22 seconds, but his more muscular approach does seem to unsettle the Chelsea defence. With time running out Nahki Wells is given the last five minutes to open his Burnley account, but to no avail.

So, the five-match winning sequence comes to an end. However, it was certainly no disgrace to lose to an extremely talented Chelsea outfit. For ourselves to get anything from the games against any of the 'big six' we need every man to be at his absolute best. Sadly, tonight one or two fell short of that, but heads never dropped, and we kept plugging away. Sean Dyche's mantra of maximum effort being the minimum requirement was never more in evidence. The team can hold their heads high and the fans are once again truly appreciative of what is proving a magical season.

Our quest for seventh spot and Europa League football is not seriously damaged as Leicester City are unable to beat relegation threatened Southampton, the game ending in a 0-0 draw. Chelsea can now do us the ultimate favour by despatching the Saints from the FA Cup and almost guaranteeing our qualification. Come on you Blues!

Result – Burnley (Barnes 64) 1 – 2 (Long 20 og, Moses 69) Chelsea

Burnley Team

Pope, Lowton, Long, Tarkowski, Ward, Gudmundsson, Cork, Westwood, Lennon (Wells 87), Barnes, Wood (Vokes 72)

Subs Not Used – Heaton, Bardsley, Taylor, Marney, Hendrick

Chelsea Team

Courtois, Azpilicueta, Cahill, Rudiger, Emerson (Zappacosta 84), Moses, Kante, Bakayoko, Pedro, Morata (Hazard 71), Giroud

Subs Not Used – Caballero, Christensen, Fabregas, Barkley, Willian

Attendance – 21,264

Season To Date – Played 34, Won 14, Drawn 10, Lost 10, Goals For 34, Goals Against 31, Points 52

League Position after Game 34 – 7th

Game 35 – Sunday 22nd April, 13.30 – Stoke City v Burnley

A difficult game expected here as our hosts for the day are currently languishing next to bottom of the table, five points adrift of safety. With only four games to go they are going to throw the kitchen sink at us for sure. An early morning text from Huddersfield Town supporting pal Rob Waterworth reads, 'Come on you Clarets today!!!!!!!'. The Terriers sit three places and seven points above the Potters, but Rob is still nervous. I reassure him that I think they are already safe, but he will not rest till they are mathematically secure. Hopefully we can go some way to assisting them today.

Its going to be a difficult game for me to follow today as we are invited to the In-laws for Sunday lunch and it will be rude to keep staring at the phone all afternoon. I manage to catch some Radio Lancashire coverage before its time to go and learn that we will be fielding an unchanged team from Thursday night.

I have BBC Sports App tuned to the game and the sound set to mute. However, it's not long before I pick up the vibrations that signal an opening goal for Stoke City after a mere 11 minutes. We're in the car now driving towards lunch and I am hoping my change of venue will bring about a change of fortune. It appears from the commentary that we are taking somewhat of a battering as our desperate hosts pile on the pressure. We're certainly not helped by an early booking for Ashley Barnes for a blatant push on Bruno Martins Indi. With Barnes's physical approach to the game that will leave him walking a tightrope for the remainder. He has also buggered up my Fantasy Football chances with a points deduction for the yellow card. I arrive at the In-laws just as we have a free kick opportunity from a promising position, but unfortunately Johann Berg Gudmundsson's kick is saved by home keeper Jack Butland.

That's it for now as we head inside for lunch and I can only hope to feel a tingle in my trouser pocket signalling an equalising goal. No such thrilling sensation but I do manage to snatch a peak at my phone that confirms a half-time score of 1-0. Some not too complimentary comments on the Up the Clarets messageboard match thread suggest that we are way off the pace and a marked second half improvement is required. It looks as though Stoke City in their desperate plight are playing the game at a very high intensity. But can they maintain it?

Well into the three-course lunch now and I feel the slightest stirring in my groin area. Can it be a goal? Who is it for? It would be very rude to look now so there's no alternative but to plough on through the roast beef and Yorkshire pud. My curiosity is killing me and as I polish off the Apricot Frangipane another stimulus below the belt. Is it another goal? Is it the final whistle?

As the lady folk leave the table to attend to washing up matters, a chance to finally put myself out of my misery. A quick look at the phone confirms an Ashley Barnes equaliser and a final score of 1-1. We'll take that! A good result to keep the European dream alive, good result for my pal in Huddersfield, but a poor result for beleaguered Stoke City.

It transpires a much improved second half performance, perhaps coupled with the Potters running out of steam, have saved the day. Good old Ashley has gone some way to redeeming himself by netting a close-range equaliser to help the Fantasy Football cause. A post-match report on the BBC website confirms a more dominant second half performance which could have ended in victory but for a Man of the Match performance from Butland.

Even Better news comes later as Chelsea defeat Southampton in the FA Cup Semi-Final leaving Europa Cup qualification now completely in our own hands. Another good day to be a Claret!

Result - Stoke City (Ndiaye 11) 1 - 1 (Barnes 62) Burnley

Burnley Team

Pope, Lowton, Long, Tarkowski, Ward, Gudmundsson, Cork, Westwood, Lennon (Hendrick 79), Barnes (Vokes 74), Wood

Subs Not Used - Heaton, Bardsley, Taylor, Marney, Walters

Stoke City Team

Butland, Johnson (Zouma 59), Shawcross, Martins Indi, Pieters, Shaqiri, Allen, Ndiaye, Bauer (Ireland 69), Diouf (Campbell 75), Crouch

<u>**Subs Not Used**</u> – Haugaard, Cameron, Fletcher, Sobhi

<u>**Attendance**</u> – 29,532

<u>**Season To Date**</u> – Played 35, Won 14, Drawn 11, Lost 10, Goals For 35, Goals Against 32, Points 53

<u>**League Position after Game 35**</u> – 7th

It's coming to that time of year that all we serious walking types dread. Yes, the return to the fields of the great beasts. Cows and horses can be very intimidating when they gang up on you. Winter affords some respite from the brutes as they are kept in barracks, but Spring marks their return to the lush green pastures.

Fortunately, Spring in this part of the world doesn't come till July so Mid-April means thankfully that they have not yet re-emerged. No, for us at the moment, only the lambs which seem to be plentiful are our only wildlife threat, and even we can handle them. Well at least that's what you'd have thought, but Tuesday's walk threw up some different challenges.

Giving the usual Dotcom walk a miss I headed off with the 'Wandering Weirs' to recce a walk from the Atom panopticon near Wycoller. The walk took us down into Wycoller then back up via Far Laith to cross the Laneshawbridge to Haworth road. It was at this point that our route became somewhat indistinct as we attempted to navigate around a large enclosure of Alpaca! I believe this is not a native species of the Lancashire/Yorkshire border. Whilst warning John W, who was attempting to make friends with our furry companions, that they had a nasty habit of spitting, we heard a not too distant sound of dogs. Spotting the animals John proclaimed that they had a look of wolves, and also a sound of them. At this point the friendly farmer appeared and pointed us in the direction of the footpath. He then informed us that the dogs were indeed, part wolf. Apparently, there is a maximum percentage of wolf that the dogs are permitted to be and one if not all of these were approaching that figure.

At this point he kindly introduced us to the creatures, thankfully I might say safely fenced in. As one chewed the wire fence retaining it I couldn't help but feel they were sizing us up for the next meal. The alpaca farmer then informed us we were the first walkers he had seen coming through there in 12 months. Quelle surprise! With those howling hounds it will be more than 12 months before I venture back that way.

The walk then continued in pleasant enough fashion via Monkroyd and Knarr's Farms and onto Mosside before re-crossing the A6068 at Green Syke farm. I couldn't help but feel that lunch should be fast approaching as we decided to push on by Fleet and Pad Cote Farms to meet the Pennine Way on Ickornshaw Moor. True to form as we decided to stop for lunch the rain decided to start. Time to hurriedly don waterproof overtrousers and eat soggy sandwiches.

Lunch having been consumed we pressed on our merry way and as we hit the Pennine Way I decided it was time for a comfort break close by a conveniently situated Shooters hut. It was then I discovered something wrong in my attire as I fought with several layers of clothing I found I had surplus material in unexpected places. After a few minutes head scratching I twigged the problem. In my haste I had put on my overtrousers back to front! A senior moment I fear.

However worse was to follow, as the rain continued to persist we crossed the sodden moor with even the good path resembling a bog in places. We had it in mind to take the only track going in our direction just beyond Cat Stone Hill, but on reaching the appointed place, no sign of a track. Fearful of crossing the bog ridden moor without a track we carried on down the Pennine Way causing a considerable detour. Eventually we made the Haworth road again emerging at Crag Top. Picking up the Bronte Way around Moor Lodge Farm we headed back via Watersheddles Reservoir and Foster's Leap Farm to the Atom. By this time bedraggled, rain soaked, lame in left knee and right foot, conversation had all but dried up. A nine-mile proposed walk ran out at 11.5, and to round it off, it was too late to go to the pub!

Thankfully Thursday's Burnley Contingent walk was a much more sedate affair. Starting at Clough Foot on the Widdop Road, we took the route up to Gorple cottages then via the Pennine Way to Clough Head before dropping down to Gibson's Mill in Hardcastle Crags. A leisurely lunch taken then on up through Hebden Dale, Walshaw and New Laithe to Holme Ends and back to Clough Foot. No rain, just seven miles and time to head back to the Craven Heifer, Harle Syke for a pint of Worsthorne Brewery's, Some Like It Blonde. I certainly did.

Although the football season still has three matches to run already the transfer rumour mill is getting into swing, with a short summer break due to the World Cup in Russia, and the transfer window closing early this time ahead of the Premier League season, early activity in the market is anticipated. On Thursday 26th Sean Dyche confirms that two loyal and valuable contributors to our recent success, Dean Marney and Scott Arfield, will both be leaving at the end of the season. Scotty is believed to be in talks to join Scottish giants Glasgow Rangers, whist Deano is believed to be heading to Nottingham Forest. We wish both these loyal servants who have given us many happy memories, all the best in their future careers.

Incoming speculation centres around Leeds United centre back Pontus Jansson, a Swedish international. Whilst we are also rumoured to be set to raid almost relegated West Bromwich Albion for not only Jay Rodriguez, but also Craig Dawson and Matt Phillips. Three good players but at this stage pure speculation.

A quick update on my earlier mentioned running progress. Following the treadmill session, I have ventured outdoors for a couple of 30-minute slow runs, so far without any serious after effects. However, I feel unable to commit to the 'Pudding Race' until the Premier League fixture list for next season is out. I think a bit more training is needed yet before I make any commitments.

Game 36 – Saturday 28th April, 13.30 – Burnley v Brighton & Hove Albion

With the season now drawing rapidly to a close we play hosts to the Seagulls in our penultimate home fixture. I confess to not expecting a lot of excitement from this game as recent meetings between the clubs have generally been low scoring, turgid affairs. On that score this one certainly didn't disappoint.

The Clarets, within touching distance of a Europa League place next season, and the visitors, almost but not quite safe from relegation fears, produced a stalemate that won't linger long in the memory. It was an unchanged Burnley team, with a place on the bench for the returning from injury Georges-Kevin Nkoudou. Brighton opted for on-loan striker Leonardo Ulloa in favour of the unpleasant Glenn Murray who had conned the referee into a penalty decision against us in the reverse fixture. Murray had also been involved in the incident which led to James Tarkowski receiving a retrospective three game ban, so not a popular chap in this part of East Lancashire. Another player not favoured by the home crowd was full back Gaetan Bong who had made 'not proven' allegations of racism against 'local lad' Jay Rodriguez in the West Bromwich Albion game. Suffice it to say Mr Bong endured a hostile reaction from the home crowd on every occasion he touched the ball. When you offend one Burnley lad, you offend them all!

The Clarets, looking a little weary, were second to most loose balls in a first half notable for not very much. Our visitors with two formidable centre backs in Shane Duffy and Lewis Dunk were in no mood to give anything away. The only goalmouth incidents of any note came mainly as a result of Johann Berg Gudmundsson (JBG) dead-ball kicks. One an almighty goalmouth scramble with goalkeeper Mat Ryan clawing the ball back from almost over the line. The ball then ricoched around the goal before coming back off a post and being cleared after hitting Dunk's hand. Had the ball crossed the line? My pal John W was convinced it had, but the goal line technology thought differently. As they say John, "should have gone to Specsavers!" Should it have been a penalty, come on this is Burnley, we don't get penalties!

Another shout for handball in the box as from another JBG free kick, Kevin Long's header hits Seagull's captain Bruno Salter on the arm from close range. Again, no change from referee Roger East, and the penalty dearth continues. The only other effort of note a well struck free kick from JBG which beat the wall but not the diving Ryan. As John W remarked, a well-directed shot but a little short on power. That was about it for a poor first half where despite being probably second best we had created the best chances.

If the first period had little goalmouth action to commend it, I think the second half had even less. The visitors started the half on the front foot, but their momentum soon fizzled out. We recovered and looked a little more likely as Sam Vokes replaced the injured Chris Wood who left the pitch with a bleeding foot. Indeed, Big Sam almost repeated his feat of a goal within 22 seconds of his introduction but was just unable to get onto a knock down in the box. At the other end I can think of only one save made by Nick Pope diving low at his right-hand post to keep out a daisy-cutter.

Ulloa made way for the odious Murray who promptly managed to get himself booked within minutes for continuous fouling, and then attempted a trade-mark dive on the touchline. Let's just say his impact on Brighton's attacking threat was negligible. Five minutes of added time were endured, and the game petered out into the no score draw that I had felt a likely outcome from the start. No doubt about this one, it'll be last game up on Match of The Day tonight!

Not a great day then on the pitch but not a bad one in terms of our European qualification hopes. Nearest rivals Leicester City took a 5-0 hammering at Crystal Palace to end their threat. The only team that can now deny us are Everton, 2-0 winners away at fast fading Huddersfield. However, with both sides having two games to play Everton can only match us on points if we lose both and they win both. Even then the goal difference currently stands +15 in our favour, so it would take two heavy defeats and two big wins to overturn it. I think we are there!

Result – Burnley 0 – 0 Brighton & Hove Albion

Burnley Team

Pope, Lowton, Long, Tarkowski, Ward, Gudmundsson, Cork, Westwood (Hendrick 81), Lennon (Nkoudou 72), Barnes, Wood (Vokes 66)

Subs Not Used – Heaton, Bardsley, Taylor, Wells,

Brighton & Hove Albion Team

Ryan, Bruno (Schelotto 89), Dunk, Duffy, Bong, Knockaert, Stephens, Kayal, Izquierdo (March 85), Gross, Ulloa (Murray 67)

Subs Not Used – Krul, Goldson, Locadia, Suttner

Attendance – 19,452

Season To Date – Played 36, Won 14, Drawn 12, Lost 10, Goals For 35, Goals Against 32, Points 54

League Position after Game 36 – 7th

As we are about to leave April and enter the final month of the season a quick word here concerning 'The Bet'. Now those of you who have had the perseverance to stay with these diaries since their inception may recall that there is an annual wager between Preston North End (PNE) fan Jim (Skipper of the Yard) and myself. Well annually that is unless Jim feels he has no chance of winning.

The bet revolves around which divisions the two teams, Burnley and PNE will be playing in after the current season. If both teams will start the next campaign in the same division, Jim wins, if they are in different leagues, I win. Whilst the bet is only small (£10), and the winnings are donated to their respective Hospices by the victor, its still a major matter of honour.

Jim after skipping the bet last season on some concocted pretext, was sufficiently confident to re-establish the tradition this time round. Now can I say that this was not based on his confidence of PNE gaining promotion to the Premier League, but rather his firm belief that Burnley would be relegated. How wrong can you be!

Well I can confidently say with two games to go we will not be relegated. However, thanks to a valuable win at Sheffield United in the penultimate Championship fixture, PNE have an outside chance of making the play-offs. They trail Derby County, currently in the last play-off position, by two points going into the last game. To leapfrog them they must beat relegation threatened Burton Albion at Deepdale, whilst the Rams must avoid defeat at home to similarly threatened Barnsley to claim the last spot.

So, I can't demand my winnings when we meet this week for the Dotcom walk at Hornby and must wait I feel for one more week. Have no fear Pendleside Hospice the money is on its way. Strictly speaking there's really no way I can lose this one, as I have spotted a technical hitch. Should PNE make the play-offs and ultimately claim a much-prized Premier League place, I can still justifiably claim the prize as we will still be in a different league, the EUROPA LEAGUE!

MAY

Tuesday 1st May's Dotcom outing is a long run for the Burnley Contingent as this week it's at Hornby, Nr Lancaster. It's an early start as we are being offered use of the facilities (always essential for ageing hikers) and refreshments courtesy of the Hornby Village Institute. We are there in good time to take full advantage of the tea/coffee and ample supply of biscuits before we set out on the day's business. It's a walk in two parts, the first loop taking us out along the River Wenning to its confluence with the River Lune. Then its up the Lune to Loyn Bridge and back into Hornby via the road.

A second opportunity here for those with weak bladders to once again use the Village Institute's facilities, and for the greedy buggers to raid the local Butchers Shop for Pork Pies. The second loop then takes us in the opposite direction, after a little diversion to avoid an ocean of newly laid concrete, to visit Wray via the Sewage Works aside the River Hindburn at Meal Bank Bridge. You certainly see some sights on these outings!

After a leisurely lunch taken in a field by Hindburn Bridge, for once in pleasant sunshine, we head into Wray to see the annual Scarecrow Festival. This year's theme is films and TV, and once again the villagers have demonstrated their wit and ingenuity with a tremendous display. A chance en-route to get the feelings of one or two North Enders about their prospects of making the play-offs. The general consensus seeming to be that they felt it unlikely but were hopeful. A stop on the way back for a pint at the Station Inn at Caton, a good pub if a little pricey. My beer of the day Kirby Lonsdale Brewery's, Tiffin Gold. The verdict, well worth a slurp and probably should have had more!

It has occurred to me that our forthcoming excursion into Europe (I hope I haven't jinxed it) will mean some alterations to my pre-season dietary training regime. Out will have to go the Pies and Chips, and a more European cuisine will have to be adopted. To this end I have instructed my wife to lay in a supply of Paella, Moussaka and Pasta. However, I have drawn the line at Sheep's Brains which the Turks are very partial to. Similarly, I will be giving the national dish of Azerbaijan, Plov, a miss as I feel it may be difficult to source in Burnley.

Back on the transfer rumours front another name appears on the list, Joe Bryan of Bristol City. This fellow is reputedly a left-back which would seem a low priority given we already have Stephen Ward and Charlie Taylor. However, with a price tag of £6m and some glowing reports of the player, he might be the sort that we are interested in. On Friday 4th May we are then linked with an Egyptian left winger, Mahmoud Hassan who will represent his country in the upcoming World Cup in Russia. If he is half as good as his compatriot Mohammed Salah, he'll do for us. He is currently on the books of Belgian club Anderlecht but has just had a successful season on loan at Turkish side Kasimpasa.

Saturday 5th May and it's a glorious sunny day in Burnley and indeed most of the country. What is more the forecast for the rest of the Bank Holiday is for more of the same. How unusual is that! An afternoon spent doing the garden is crowned with the good news that the result in the teatime fixture confirms our place in Europe next season. Everton, the only team that could catch us, are unable to overcome relegation battlers Southampton at Goodison Park and can only manage a draw. That leaves them five points adrift and only three to play for. WE ARE THERE!

The pressure is off now so hopefully tomorrow we can go the Emirates Stadium and spoil Arsene Wenger's farewell party.

Game 37 – Sunday 6th May, 16.30 – Arsenal v Burnley

Unfortunately, that's not how it turned out at all. I must confess that for some time I had felt that this game had all the makings of a disaster. Arsene Wenger's 22-year tenure as the Gunners manager was coming to an end and this was to be his grand farewell, the last home game of a magnificent Arsenal career. With a huge home crowd determined to give the guy a good send off, we were set up as the 'patsy's' to roll over and let him leave with a big smile. Again, a glorious sunny day, but again the feeling as we took the field that we were the sacrificial lambs being led to the slaughter.

The team news revealed no Chris Wood, whose foot injury from the previous game required stitching and ruled him out of this one. His place was taken by Jeff Hendrick and we reverted to a lone striker with Ashley Barnes filling the role.

Having recently upgraded my mobile phone I decided to follow the action through the live text reporting on the BBC Sports App. My phone had other ideas though, from nowhere were appearing live Google score updates. Not only that but my Fantasy Premier League subscription decided to get in on the act and also started to flood me with information. To top it off, fellow Claret John W with whom I have a WhatsApp Footie chat set up, which also includes John G who is currently soaking up the sun and alcohol in Spain, decided to keep us informed as he watched a live stream via Sportsmania.

So much information coming and all at once, I was finding it difficult to clear the various screens that kept popping up on the mobile. Of course, John W's WhatsApp chat had the edge on the others for speed, and John G was advising that it was now Happy Hour in Espana. I suspect that Happy Hour had been going on for some time judging by the tone and spelling of his pronouncements.

Not such a Happy Hour here though as on 14 minutes the almost inevitable message comes through from John W, 'Arse score'. Followed shortly by 'Basher hurt'. Impossible, Basher is indestructible, but indeed it was true and shortly after he left the field nursing a dislocated shoulder. Sam Vokes came on as his replacement and off we go again.

Next report from John W, 'Footballing lesson. Lennon poor. Back 4 over run by midfielders charging through. Our mids struggling to keep up.' That doesn't sound so promising and I note from the BBC's match statistics that we haven't managed a single attempt on goal after 30 minutes. Also, the communication links are getting even more complicated as I am relaying details to daughter Stephanie currently half way up Ben Nevis.

I'm hoping that we can make it to half time without further damage and as I look at the clock I think we must have. But no, John W, 'It's 2', as they score in added time, followed by 'H/T 2-0 this could get ugly!' I point out to him that it already has.

There's good news at the start of the second half as a report filters through of an attempt on the Arsenal goal, a Sam Vokes header. Perhaps the tide is turning? By this time our Spanish correspondent's contributions are becoming a tad violent and abusive as the cheap as chips Spanish Brandy takes a hold. By his own confession he is 'A bit pist' (sic). So much for the tide turning, we've been hit by a bloody tsunami as goals three and four hit the net and we are not yet an hour in. John G, obviously suffering from some time difference and jet lag declares, 'Time for bed'. By three minutes past six, goal number five has flown in and it's getting embarrassing. I'd join our Spanish amigo if I could, but Songs of Praise hasn't even been on yet!

Still 15 minutes to go, our positive goal difference blown away, and we are being well and truly outclassed. I tell John W to stop sending updates. He says, 'I wish I could. I'm bloody watching it. It's horrible.' I tell him, 'Make them stop. I can't take anymore.' Thankfully God in his Heaven is listening and Arsene has enough goals in his leaving present goody-bag for the day. It's all over at 5-0, what a stinker! There's an ominous silence coming from Spain as the combination of hot sun, cheap booze and utter disappointment have floored our compadre. Oh well, he's just as well out of it.

Sunday for me is usually an alcohol-free day but after that, NO WAY! I drown my sorrows with a bottle of Guiness and a half bottle of Spanish Tempranillo, in sympathy with John G. Sleep well old chum!

What went wrong? Was it the occasion? Was it the fact we had nothing to play for? I think that is unlikely from a Sean Dyche team. Is the loss of key players through injury taking its toll? A team missing Ben Mee, Steven Defour, Chris Wood and Robbie Brady were bound to struggle. Were Arsenal just too good for us? I think there is more than just a grain of truth in that. Arsenal's home record this season is impeccable, and on this day, they were unstoppable.

However, I'm not going to let this result mar for me what has been an absolutely outstanding season of Premier League football. On only three occasions, at Champions Manchester City, at home to Tottenham Hotspur and at Arsenal today have we looked out of our depth. What we have achieved finishing seventh, the 'Best of the Rest' and qualifying for the Europa League is an unbelievable achievement for a club of our stature. Enjoy your day in the sun Mr Wenger, unlike you, WE WILL BE BACK!

Result – Arsenal (Aubemyang 14,75, Lacazette 45+3, Kolasinac 54, Iwobi 64) 5 – 0 Burnley

Burnley Team

Pope, Lowton, Long, Tarkowski, Ward, Gudmundsson (Wells 89), Cork, Westwood, Hendrick, Lennon (Nkoudou 71), Barnes (Vokes 22)

Subs Not Used – Heaton, Bardsley, Taylor, Marney,

Arsenal Team

Cech, Bellerin, Chambers (Mertesacker 77), Mavropanos, Kolasinac, Iwobi, Xhaka, Wilshere (Ramsey 72), Mkhitaryan, Lacazette (Welbeck 72), Aubemayang

Subs Not Used – Ospina, Monreal, Mustafi, Maitland-Niles

Attendance – 59,540

Season To Date – Played 37, Won 14, Drawn 12, Lost 11, Goals For 35, Goals Against 37, Points 54

League Position after Game 37 – 7th

Shortly before our disappointing afternoon at the Emirates Stadium, the concluding round of Championship fixtures were played out. Cardiff secured a return to the Premier League condemning Fulham to the torture of the play-offs. Preston North End despite defeating Burton Albion at Deepdale missed out on the chance to enter the knock-out, the final place going to Derby County. This of course means that I have won 'The Bet' and Pendleside Hospice will be the beneficiary when I can extract the cash from North Ender Jim (Skipper of the Yard).

Tuesday's Dotcom walk, a rerun of the recent Burnley contingent circular route from Thornton in Craven via Sough, would have presented an ideal opportunity to commiserate with our West Lancashire friends. At the same time, I'm sure they would have wanted to congratulate us on our magnificent achievement of reaching Europe. However, the opportunity didn't arise as all the North Enders were conspicuous by their absence! Strangely though Andy L, a Derby County fan, had made this walk, which following medical treatment was one of his rare outings this year. I'll bet he was disappointed by their absence.

Another brave soul who did make an appearance was Nigel our sole Oldham Athletic supporter. Fighting back the tears he struggled on manfully as he relived the ignominy of relegation to League 2 on the last day of the season. To be fair he was very philosophical about it and had no regrets about purchasing his season ticket. That's the spirit. Never mind Nigel, the only way is up. Or is it?

Thursday's Burnley contingent walk was an old favourite and classic Dales walk, Simon's Seat from Barden Bridge. Once again, it's a nice day with a cooling breeze and good underfoot conditions made for perfect walking weather. A gentle start up the River Wharfe towards Appletreewick, then a stiff climb up onto the moor to the Trig point at Simon's Seat. The Trig point is just short of 1600ft. but judging by the reaction of some of the contingent, you'd have though they'd climbed Everest. Still in their condition its probably the equivalent. A leisurely lunch taken sheltering in the rocks from the breeze, then a long descent via moor and forest plantation, through the forebodingly named Valley of Desolation. On this day in pleasant sunshine it was anything but desolate, in fact it was exceedingly pleasant. The last mile or so then follows the Wharfe back through the Bolton Abbey Estate finishing at the Ice Cream Van.

Not for me the van though, after a lovely nine mile stroll it was refreshment time at the Punch Bowl, Earby. Today's libation, Reedley Hallows Brewery's Pendleside, a fitting end to a fine day!

Sunday 13th February sees the curtain come down on another magnificent season for Burnley Football Club. Hopefully we can end the campaign on a high note with victory over Eddie Howe's Bournemouth. It's the final day of the Premier League season and with all the various issues of winners, European qualifiers, and relegation already sorted, it should set the scene for a feast of attacking football. Watch out for a goal glut!

Game 38 – Sunday 13th May, 15.00 – Burnley v Bournemouth

Football on a Sunday again, and I guess it's something we'll have to get used to following our Europa Cup qualification. May has started brilliantly for weather and today is no exception. A lovely sunny day with light breezes and all is set fair to play out the last fixture of the season. Our visitors Bournemouth could be fooled into thinking this is a home game for them with the warm temperatures and blue skies, but alas no beach! Best we can manage is the boating lake at Thompson's Park, but I think that is currently undergoing renovation.

There's a strangely relaxed feel about the final day this year and the weather is certainly adding to it. For once there are more people outside the pub than in and the pre-match pints are despatched in short sleeves, and in John G's case short pants. I think he still believes he is in Spain, probably the effects of that cheap Spanish Brandy. It's a last chance for a meet up as on Monday John W will leave for a six-week camping trip around Spain, arriving back in good time for pre-season.

There's just the one change for the Clarets as Chris Wood replaces the injured Ashley Barnes whose shoulder injury thankfully turns out to be not as bad as at first feared. There's no place on the substitutes bench for the soon to be departed Scott Arfield and Dean Marney. I guess both players don't want to risk an injury as they look to secure new contracts in pastures new. There is a place however for youngster Dwight McNeil, a young man still only 18, who is rewarded for a fine season with the Under 23's.

Unsurprisingly the game starts at a fairly leisurely place with both team's players already with thoughts of long hot days on the beach and cocktails round the pool. We're not making much impression on a solid looking defence and the visitors are enjoying the bulk of the early possession. Nick Pope is called into action on a couple of occasions and responds in typical exemplary fashion to keep us level.

However, as the half wears on we start to gain some momentum. Johann Berg Gudmundsson and Stephen Ward are enjoying some success down the left flank and most of our attacks are coming from this side. In the centre Jack Cork and Ashley Westwood are beginning to get control of the game. Indeed on 39 minutes we lead as Westwood's shot is deflected by Wood and beats the Cherries keeper. Comfortably through to half time then and we end the first period on top.

It's a bright start to the second half as the Clarets go for the killer goal but on this day it's not to be. Around the hour mark Eddie Howe senses he needs to change something, and the substitutions start. On for Bournemouth come Dan Gosling and Callum Wilson, whilst for Burnley Sam Vokes replaces Wood who has again taken a knock. From this point the game starts to open up and our defence previously untroubled in the main begins to look vulnerable. An unwanted feature that has recently crept into our game is the inability to clear the ball effectively often through trying to 'overplay' the action.

On 74 minutes we are punished for that very same fault as Josh King levels the score with a sumptuous curling effort. Suddenly the visitors sense there may be more to be had from this game and up their attacking intent. Well, what at half time looked a fairly comfortable win to end a fairy tale season, had suddenly turned a little sour. However, worse was to follow! As the game entered four minutes added time, and into the third of those, disaster struck. Third substitute Jermain Defoe took advantage of a slip by Kevin Long to set up Callum Wilson to fire home a late winner.

What a disappointing end that certainly took some of the gloss of my day. My misery was complete when on checking my Fantasy Football I discovered I had amassed a paltry 29 points on the day, dropping me from a challenging second to a poor third in the final table. This football management job is not all its cracked up to be! There'll be no termination of my contract with a big pay-off! Nothing for it but to forget the day and remember the highlights of a momentous season. The highest league position since 1974 and back in European competition. Who could be disappointed at that!

Result – Burnley (Wood 39) 1 – 2 (King 74, Wilson 90+3) Bournemouth

Burnley Team

Pope, Lowton, Long, Tarkowski, Ward, Gudmundsson (Wells 80), Cork, Westwood, Hendrick, Lennon (McNeil 90+4), Wood (Vokes 61)

Subs Not Used – Heaton, Bardsley, Taylor, Nkoudou,

Bournemouth Team

Begovic, S Cook, Ake, Mings (Defoe 66), Fraser, Hyndman (Gosling 59), Surman, Daniels, Ibe, Mousset (Wilson 59), King

Subs Not Used – Boruc, B Smith, Pugh, Taylor

Attendance – 20,720

Season To Date – Played 38, Won 14, Drawn 12, Lost 12, Goals For 36, Goals Against 39, Points 54

League Position after Game 38 – 7th

Well, that just about wraps up our fourth and most successful Premier League season. However, some of our lads are not finished yet, Johann Berg Gudmundsson seems to be a certainty for selection in Iceland's World Cup squad. Then on the 16th May fantastic news for Nick Pope as he is selected in the England party to go to Russia. What a dream season for the young man who at the start hadn't even played a Premier League game. More good news from England Manager Gareth Southgate as he names James Tarkowski and Tom Heaton on standby for the squad. I wouldn't want to wish injury or illness on any player already selected but am glad to see more Clarets are ready to fill any gaps should they arise.

The season ends with Manchester City as run-away Champions, Chelsea as FA Cup Winners, Liverpool in a Champions League Final, but best of all Burnley back in Europe. A highest league finish in 44 years is fitting reward for a campaign of non-stop endeavour and no little skill. A magnificent achievement for all associated with the club for which they should all be 'The Proudest Men in Proudsville'!

ON REFLECTION

So, come on dear readers own up, who saw that coming? Hands up those who predicted a top ten finish! How many of you clairvoyants had us down for another European adventure? Not many I wager, not even Nostradamus or Mystic Meg would have gambled their reputations on that. What happened to make the unimaginable a reality?

A quick look at the table below shows a remarkable consistency in league position over the season. The campaign was off to a flier with the away victory at reigning Champions Chelsea. That was followed by the somewhat unlucky home defeat against West Bromwich Albion. From 4th to 12th in the space of a week and a slight suspicion that the victory in the opener may have been a fluke. With a succession of difficult away games to follow, a slide down the table could have been expected. No such thing for these Clarets, the next two away games yielded unlikely points at both Tottenham Hotspur and Liverpool, with a home win against Crystal Palace sandwiched between the two. Normal service or should that be abnormal service, bearing in mind last season's away day difficulties, had been resumed and the ship steadied. After five games we occupied 7th position a spot we occupied for an incredible 27 out of 38 weeks.

Not once after week two did we drop below half way in the table! Incredibly before the half way mark in the season we had lost only twice on our travels, 3-0 at leaders Manchester City and 1-0 at Leicester City. Besides the draws at Tottenham and Liverpool, we went on to record wins at Everton, Southampton and Bournemouth, with further draws at Brighton and the mighty Manchester United! Successive home wins in December against Watford and Stoke City took us to the dizzying height of 4th, and suddenly people started to sit up and take notice. Unbelievably 'little old Burnley' were challenging the elite.

There followed a bit of a slump, coinciding with the loss of key players through injury and a run of particularly difficult home games. Long term absentees were Robbie Brady, probably our most creative player, Steven Defour, club captain Tom Heaton, and record signing Chris Wood. Additionally, James Tarkowski picked up a three-game ban for an off the ball incident with Glenn Murray in the game at Brighton. A run of four home fixtures starting at Christmas and running into the New Year pitted us against Tottenham Hotspur, Liverpool, Manchester United and Manchester City, all members of the 'big six'. Unsurprisingly, results tailed off and we remained winless for 11 fixtures. There were however some very creditable performances in the period not least of which was a battling 1-1 draw at home to Manchester City. Through all this period only once did we slip from 7th position, dropping one place following the home defeat to Manchester United on January 20th. A draw at Newcastle United in the next game took us back to 7th on 31st January a position we held for the remainder of the season.

To maintain such a high placing despite such a lean run highlights two factors. Firstly, the 'big six' with their huge financial resources are virtually untouchable and will continue to dominate the League. They are effectively having a mini competition amongst themselves taking points almost at will from the other 14 clubs. Secondly below them, and indeed ourselves, the other mid-table teams demonstrated a degree of inconsistency which meant they failed to dislodge us.

Our slump was arrested with a home victory and season double over Everton, coming back from 1-0 down to win 2-1. The monkey now off our back, we then proceeded to win three successive away fixtures! We certainly developed a liking for teams beginning with a W. First came a thumping 3-0 win against West Ham United at the London Stadium - a result so enjoyed by the home crowd that they invaded the pitch several times and threatened their own directors! This was followed by victory at what in the past has been a very unlucky Hawthorns. The defeat virtually condemned West Bromwich Albion to relegation. Finally, a third successive away win at Watford, once again coming from behind to take the points. Still not satisfied, we then saw off Leicester City at Turf Moor to make it a resounding five wins on the bounce! This result effectively killed off the Foxes hopes of nabbing our Europa Cup place and we were almost home and dry.

With 7th place virtually assured the season petered out slightly disappointingly with two draws and three defeats from the final five fixtures. A heavy defeat, 0-5 at Arsenal, followed by a late, late goal loss at home to Bournemouth in the final game, couldn't however take the gloss off a magnificent season.

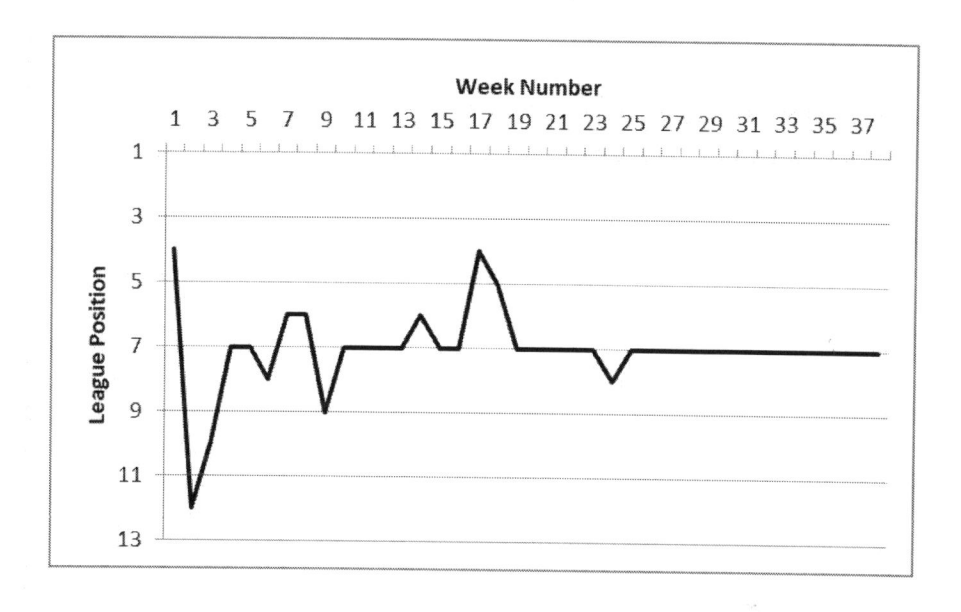

What had transformed a team whom many pundits and football writers considered pre-season relegation candidates into European competition qualifiers? How had we overnight gone from 16th place last time round to 7th this time? No longer were we many people's idea of Premier League misfits, now we were 'THE BEST OF THE REST'!

Without a doubt I think the most significant single factor was the massive improvement in away game results. Our away form was the sixth best in the league - seven wins, seven draws, and a measly five defeats yielding 28 points. Contrast that to season 2016-17 when from 19 away fixtures we accrued a pitiful seven points with just the one victory.

Conversely, we couldn't manage to match the points haul garnered at home this time round. Nineteen home fixtures resulted in 7 wins, 5 draws and seven defeats yielding 26 points, putting us only 14th best in terms of home form. Our tremendous home form in 2016-17 returned 33 points.

In terms of goal difference, we were still in the red to the tune of -3, however much improved on last time's -16. We scored a total of 36 goals, interestingly three less than last time. Significantly though we conceded 16 goals less (39/55). It would appear that our tight defence was instrumental in our vast positional improvement.

Our competitiveness is highlighted by the fact that no less than 20 fixtures we were involved in were won or lost by a single goal. Twelve of these were in our favour with eight against - as Sean Dyche would correctly say *"Fine Margins."* We were really only out of contention in three games, away at Manchester City (0-3) and Arsenal (0-5), and home to Tottenham Hotspur (0-3). No disgrace in losing to these three fine teams all playing at the peak of their game. The best win of the season came at West Ham United (3-0) and it was indeed a victory to savour.

So, what were the contributory factors that brought about this transformation? Without wanting to single out individuals from what was a magnificent team effort there are certainly players who deserve a special mention.

At the end of last season key central defender Michael Keane left for what he must have thought would be greener pastures. The young centre back headed for Everton and Europa League football, no doubt bagging a big pay rise, and earning the Clarets a big transfer money profit. Unfortunately, things didn't quite work out as planned for him and with an early exit from Europe and a struggle in the league, his confidence suffered, and his form dipped. This ultimately cost him his place in the England squad and a chance to go to the World Cup finals in Russia.

His exit created an opportunity for his successor, the patient James Tarkowski, and boy did he take it. Forging a superb central defensive partnership with the ever-dependable Ben Mee, an impressively solid back four began to take shape. Tarkowski's contribution was such that the loss of Keane did not weaken the side at all, and some may argue that it actually strengthened it with the new man's greater ability on the ball. A big fan was England Manager Gareth Southgate, and before the end of the season 'Tarka' had won his first England cap, only just missing out on a World Cup place, whilst making the standby group. How ironic that Tarkowski had inherited the England squad place from his predecessor Keane.

Even more staggering was the impact of goalkeeper Nick Pope. When England keeper Tom Heaton went down injured in the early season game against Crystal Palace, following an accidental collision with Ben Mee, I and many others feared the worst. On the bench was rookie keeper Pope who up to that point had not played a single Premier League game since being signed from Charlton Athletic at the end of our last promotion season. As he made his way into goal to replace the injured Heaton I think its fair to say the lad looked a tad nervous. So, did I!

It wasn't long before he was called into action making a smart save and from that point, with a very supportive home crowd behind him, he never looked back. We went on to win the game and Nick had a partial clean sheet for his debut. Heaton's injury was confirmed as a dislocated shoulder with ligament damage and so a lengthy lay-off was on the cards. What a disaster, club captain and inspirational keeper side-lined for a big chunk of the season. No time for Pope to bathe in the glory of his performance, next up was a rampant

Liverpool at Anfield! A magnificent performance from the young man saw the Clarets come away with a highly creditable point from a 1-1 draw. The Kop fans, always appreciative of a good goalkeeping performance, gave our man a good hand.

From this point Nick grew in stature as he regularly stopped shots that he really had no right to. His fledgling Premier League career took off and by the time Tom Heaton was ready to resume, he was unable to dislodge him from the position. Once again Gareth Southgate was impressed, and with England's goalkeepers suffering a collective bad time, our man forced his way into the England squad and on his way to Russia. What an incredible fairy-tale season for Nick, which as I write is not over yet. What odds on World Cup glory for him? Poor Tom Heaton, who barring the injury would surely have been on his way to the World Cup, did however make the standby goalkeeping position.

The emergence of 'Tarka' and 'Popey' were certainly key factors in our improved defensive tightness, but we shouldn't overlook the importance of some shrewd dealings in the transfer market.

In the summer Jack Cork, a popular player from his previous loan spells with the club, was brought back into the fold signing on a permanent deal from Swansea City. A tidy player Jack who rarely wastes a pass and with an all action style quickly organised the centre midfield. An absolute snip at the price paid for him, his early season displays also brought him a call up to the England squad, and a full debut after being introduced as a late substitute.

One player certainly benefitting from the astute signing of Cork, was the popular Belgian, Steven Defour. After making a big impact following his arrival at the club the previous season, Defour's appearances had tailed off towards the end of the campaign, and it was apparent that all was not well. It appeared that the technically gifted midfielder may not have the heart and stamina to fit the Sean Dyche profile. It looked odds-on that he would leave in the summer at the end of his first season, until a change of heart by the player transformed his Turf Moor career.

It seems that Defour finally understood what our game plan was all about, and he realised that a significantly increased level of fitness was required. To his credit he buckled down, got himself in the best shape of his career, and started the season looking a much more determined and happier player. Linking beautifully with Cork in centre midfield, the pair soon became a force to be reckoned with and the results soon followed. Unfortunately, a knee operation ruled him out for a big chunk of the season, but he has vowed to be back fitter than ever for the start of our Europa League adventure.

Another summer signing coming in and making a quick impression was striker Chris Wood signed from Leeds United before the transfer window closed in August. I always feel that its important for a new striker to get on the score sheet as soon as possible with a new club. Wood certainly did that scoring a late equaliser at Tottenham Hotspur after coming on as a substitute in his first game. This was swiftly followed by an early goal in his home debut, which gave us a 1-0 victory over Crystal Palace. That was him up and running, and his goals came fairly consistently despite missing a number of games through injury. Let's hope next time round he can stay injury free and increase his tally even further.

However, let's not forget that for all the various individual contributions this success was built on camaraderie, team spirit, self-belief and the strength of the squad. We had by the start of the season assembled the best squad of players seen for many years at Turf Moor. We had, by and large, like-for-like cover in all positions and gone was the need to fill round holes with square pegs.

In the full back positions both Matt Lowton and Stephen Ward had outstanding seasons, both making valuable attacking options on many occasions. Neither player was fortunate enough to escape some lengthy injury spells, but when these occurred their replacements Phil Bardsley and Charlie Taylor proved more than capable deputies. Taylor signed in the close season from Leeds United, slotted in for Stephen Ward for a period in mid-season. Unfortunately, this happened to coincide with our winless run, which in no way was down to his efforts. Similarly, the experienced Bardsley also signed in the summer from Stoke City, provided excellent cover for Lowton during his spell out.

Central defence was predominantly the domain of the already mentioned James Tarkowski and Ben Mee. 'Tarka' made 32 appearances pipping club captain Mee by three. Ben unfortunately missed the tail end of the season picking up a troublesome shin injury. More worrying for the fans was his contract situation which with only one year remaining, still remains to be resolved. During their respective absences the spare centre back berth was admirably filled by Kevin Long, who despite his lengthy time as a Claret has found his opportunities limited. This time however he managed 19 appearances, the equivalent of half a season and even managed to add a goal to his tally.

The wide midfielders Johann Berg Gudmundsson (JBG) and Robbie Brady were well supported initially by Scott Arfield, and after the January transfer window by Aaron Lennon, arriving from Everton, and Tottenham Hotspur loanee, Georges-Kevin Nkoudou. Brady was enjoying an electrifying spell of form before a serious knee injury at Leicester City ended his season prematurely. His creativity was sorely missed and we all hope he makes a full recovery ahead of the challenges to come. Similarly, JBG had his best season to date for the Clarets, winning himself in the process the much coveted Up the Clarets website 'Player of the Year' award. Before leaving for his summer World Cup campaign with Iceland he committed to a further contract at Turf Moor and we look forward to seeing him for many years to come.

Centre midfield initially was manned by Jack Cork and Steven Defour, until the latter's mid-season injury, prematurely terminated his season. His place was taken by the ever-dependable Ashley Westwood whose form was good enough to make the change almost seamless. Jeff Hendrick for the most part found himself playing almost as an auxiliary striker when we opted for a 4-4-1-1 formation. It was a role which, if he were being honest, he would probably say was not his most natural. When the formation changed, often during the course of the game where we were trailing, or where we sensed a victory, Jeff would usually be the man replaced by a second striker. To his credit he stuck to his task and chipped in with some vital assists and the odd goal. A perfect example of a player recognising the importance of the squad rather than the individual.

Up front the season started spectacularly for Sam Vokes with two goals in the dramatic season's opener at Chelsea. However, with the signing of Chris Wood he found his opportunities limited, but as with Hendrick, unselfishly accepted his role. Making only nine starting appearances, but a further 23 from the bench he was instrumental in turning some games that appeared lost into draws and victories.

A major contributor and worthy contender for any 'Player of the Season' award would have to be Ashley Barnes. 'Basher', oft maligned, and considered little more than a battering ram, showed a side to his game that surprised many pundits and critics. His aggressive style was certainly there but allied to that was his boundless determination and some impressive link-up play. Added to that was a 10-goal tally that included some absolutely world class efforts. The bicycle kick at West Bromwich Albion and the stunning strike at West Ham United will live long in Claret memories. Indeed, such was the magic and technical ability of most of his strikes that it appeared he only scored 'worldies'. Not true, there were one or two scruffy one's in there as well, notably his effort that earned a point at Stoke City, proving that after all he was only human. I think in my opinion at least he earned himself the description of being a poor man's Diego Costa.

Chris Wood, despite missing a significant number of games (20 Starts + 6 sub appearances) finished as Burnley's top scorer in the league, his 11 goals pipping Ashley Barnes by one. Chris netted on his first appearance of the season and also in the last, hopefully he can carry his goal scoring form forward into what will be for sure a demanding next season.

Completing the striking department were Nahki Wells, signed late in the summer transfer window from Huddersfield Town, and the hugely experienced Jon Walters another summer addition from Stoke City. Unfortunately for both it was a season of frustration, particularly in the case of Walters who was blighted by injury. He managed only one start and four sub appearances, whilst Wells had zero starts and 10 from the bench. In Wells case he was often introduced very late in a game, invariably when we were behind, and with little chance of making any impact. As I write it is uncertain what the future holds for either player, be it here or elsewhere. However, I'm sure that all Clarets will hope that 2018/19 provides both players with more opportunities to shine.

Without doubt the above bunch of players gave us a squad with much more depth, ability, experience and versatility, than in any of our previous Premier League campaigns. The secret of our outstanding success was again based on the great camaraderie and team spirit that the management managed to forge amongst this happy band of brothers. No visible signs of bickering amongst our squad, no disputes fostered by some members earning substantially more than others. We had a collective self-belief and will to win that took many rivals by surprise. It's not always the guy with the biggest pay packet that produces the goods. Ask the fans of Stoke City, West Bromwich Albion, and Swansea City if that is the case! Burnley proved once again the phrase coined by the Greek philosopher Aristotle, *"The whole is greater than the sum of its parts"*.

Of course, even the best orchestras need a conductor, and this is where we are particularly blessed. In Sean Dyche, Ian Woan, Tony Loughlan, Billy Mercer and all the other coaches of the youth and development players, we have as good a team as any. Sean Dyche has become a legend during his tenure as manager. It's hard to envisage any other from the current crop of Premier League managers who could have achieved what he has done on the limited resources available. Not only that, his conduct and professionalism single him out as a rare commodity in an age populated by often unsavoury and megalomaniac 'prima donna' contemporaries. His insistence on doing things honestly and in the right manner, be that a rather old-fashioned notion today, have won both himself and the club much admiration.

It is the management team that dictate the style of play, which sometimes may not be the most attractive, but more often than not, is the most effective. Where would we be without this direction, and most importantly self-belief, that has been instilled in the players? Not heading for Europe that's for sure! His man-management skills, particularly in handling potentially difficult players, are clear for all to see. More importantly he recognises the need to maintain a tight knit squad and this means a thoroughly researched appraisal of potential players personality as well as ability. In everything we do the emphasis is on the team - not the individual. Long may he and his staff reign at Turf Moor.

Anyway, that's enough of singing everyone's praises. What else stood out in a stand-out season?

Well for one thing the fact that we played 38 Premier League games and were not awarded a single penalty! How can that be? I can only put it down to temporary blindness on the part of referees when the Clarets enter the danger zone. Perhaps the most blatant case being Huddersfield Town's Jonas Lossl's downing of Jeff Hendrick as he was about to score at the John Smith's Stadium. The foul was so evident that even his own manager David Wagner conceded it should have been a penalty! I wonder whether it would have been given had Manchester United been the opposition? What histrionics would that have provoked from Jose 'Moaninho'. In time honoured Burnley fashion did we moan? No, we picked ourselves up and got on with it. Perhaps sometimes we are too honest and lack the 'street cred' of some of our rivals, but I for one wouldn't want it any other way.

The high points of the season have to be the opening day away victory at reigning Champions Chelsea, and the home draw with runaway current Champions Manchester City. Who could possibly have believed that on that far off day in August 2017 the Clarets would be 3-0 up at half-time at the home of the Pensioners? I remember at the time sitting in complete disbelief at what I was hearing, and then as only Clarets fans can, wondering if we could hold on! A second half against initially 10 men, and later nine, became a battle for survival as Chelsea finally woke up and realised we were not the pushovers they had expected. A nail-biting second half produced two goals for the hosts, but we stood tall and strong to come away with the three most unlikely points of the season.

The home game against Manchester City had all the hallmarks of a potential thrashing. I recall our first Premier League encounter against them in 2010, 3-0 down in the first seven minutes, five behind at half-time, and eventual losers by 1-6. Our record against the 'Blue Mooners', especially at Turf Moor, is far from impressive of late and against this rampant City side this game could have gone the same way. Outplayed for most of the first period, and trailing by a goal to nil at half-time, the omens didn't look good for us. However, in the second period, aided by some shocking misses from Raheem Sterling, we clawed our way back into the game and fashioned an equaliser on 82 minutes by Johann Berg Gudmundsson. Indeed, but for an exceptional save by the City keeper we may have stolen all three points. Nobody cared, it felt like a victory anyway against these worthy Champions.

A disappointing feature of the season were the early exits in both Cup competitions. After comfortably disposing of the old enemy Blackburn Rovers at Ewood Park in Round 2 of the League Cup, always a delight for all Clarets, we failed at the next hurdle. Drawn at home to Championship team Leeds United we could have hoped to progress but after an interminably long night we went out on penalties.

The FA Cup draw was extremely unkind to us and paired us in Round 3 with Manchester City at the Etihad. Unsurprisingly we were convincingly despatched 4-1, and there ended all dreams of Wembley for another year.

Whilst our focus must always be on winning Premier League fixtures and ensuring our survival and the funding that goes with it, a nice little run to a Cup Final would just be nice for once. Or is that just being greedy? Let's hope 2018/19 can see a bit more progression as we chase glory on four fronts.

Who was my personal choice as 'Player of the Year'? It would be nigh impossible and indeed unfair to single out any one from what was an outstanding team effort. However, the player whose performances gave me the most pleasure was Ashley Barnes. Surely if ever a player epitomises what a Sean Dyche team is all about, it is our Ashley. Selfless, determined, never-say-die and humble, a true Claret hero! His spectacular goals will be well worth the money for a season's video alone. Great effort Ashley!

I think the final say on the 2017/18 campaign should go to the BBC's football man:

Season review – Phil McNulty, BBC Sport Chief Football writer

Pre-season prediction: *"17th Could be some suffering along the way but I think Burnley will stay up."*

Actual Position 7th: *"Magnificent achievement by Sean Dyche and his players. One of the stories of the Premier League season to see this great old club reach the Europa League – European nights at Turf Moor will be special. No praise too high for Dyche, his management team and Burnley's squad."*

I think that says it all!

On a more personal note the highlight of my season was completely non-football related. The engagement of my daughter Stephanie to her partner Tom, has made my wife Julie and myself extremely happy. We look forward to a fantastic wedding day in remote Arkengarthdale in June 2019. Another successful Premier League season will put the icing on that particular cake!

WHAT'S NEXT

So, after having had our most successful season since 1974, and qualifying for European competition for the first time since 1966, what happens next? Will seventh place convince the pundits, bookmakers and many of our own fans that we are now an established Premier League team? Will our increased commitments, as we compete on four fronts, over stretch a club who will still have one of the smallest budgets? Will we be looking hopefully up the Premier League or worryingly down at the bottom?

Who knows? I've seen and heard it debated amongst fans that perhaps the European qualification may turn out to be a millstone around our neck. Certainly, if we progress through qualifying and reach the group stage, we are going to be playing a significantly increased number of fixtures. What we can't afford to do is take our eye of the ball that is Premier League survival. We cannot allow the distraction that is Europe to lead us to kill the goose that lays the golden egg.

Is European football good for Burnley FC? I am firmly of the opinion that it is. As with all things in life we have to try to keep moving forward. If you stand still you will eventually fall back. Progression to Europe was the next step in the impossible dream. The fact is that we may well have taken that step sooner than the Directors and management team could have envisaged. However, as a result of last season's Herculean efforts we are there and must give it as good a shot as possible.

Without doubt we need to increase the squad in both numbers and quality. The effects of cumulative long-term injuries could be seen around the half-way point last time culminating in the long winless run. Without the points cushion earned from the terrific first period, anxious glances downwards could well have been a possibility. That said, we have never been in a better position to attract quality players to the club. With a healthy bank balance, guaranteed income in excess of £100m, a stable management team, and the attraction of European football, we must be an attractive proposition.

Not for one minute do I think we will be looking to attract established international 'Superstars' who might see us as an opportunity for a last big pay-day. I'm sure the emphasis will again be on looking for players firstly with the right character and hunger, who wish to progress their careers at a high level in a system that has been proven to work. Perhaps there are players to be cherry picked from the Championship sides who have missed out on promotion, and conversely those from relegated Premier League sides with the desire to continue to play at the top level. Hopefully the recruitment team are currently pulling out all the stops to get deals done, and players in place for the early return to pre-season training. I'm sure there are an interesting and exciting few weeks coming up.

Of course, there is also a flip-side to our success, wealthier rivals are no doubt casting envious eyes at some of our own players. How will we manage the situation of having two current England squad goalkeepers vying for one position? Tom Heaton and Nick Pope are two excellent custodians. There are teams higher placed than ourselves, with infinitely larger financial resources, that would take them at a stroke. Clearly this is a situation that will require delicate handling if we are to retain both. Thankfully, in Sean Dyche we have the man most capable of achieving this.

Similarly, James Tarkowski's arrival on the international scene will have alerted the mega-rich clubs to his talents. Ben Mee, currently reputedly stalling on new contract negotiations, is another major potential loss that will hopefully be avoided. It is an inevitable fact that our heightened profile makes us vulnerable as victims of our own success.

Of course, the key to what happens next is the retention of the services of Sean Dyche. Thankfully during the course of the last season, the manager committed himself to a longer-term contract than that which he had previously operated on. Although, some would say, contracts aren't worth the paper they're printed on, this hopefully illustrated his desire to be the architect responsible for the continuation of the rebuilding of our famous club. Without doubt he enjoys an autonomy of control at Burnley FC that would be unlikely at any other leading Premier League club. Having said that, Sean Dyche has himself said that his position at Burnley is not a forever thing. Fortunately, at the moment he is still enjoying the challenge that keeping the club among the leading lights of English football brings. The new challenge of European football should ensure that his attention remains fully focused at Turf Moor.

However, his continuing success and increased media exposure, can only serve to make other ambitious and richer clubs sit up and take notice. At some point he will be sorely tempted by the type of offer that will be difficult to refuse. Let us hope that this is still some time in the far distant future. After all, where else in the country does a manager have the accolade of having a pub named after himself? Even better, he has free beer for life at The Royal Dyche! Who could turn their back on that!

On Thursday 7th June Nick Pope became the fifth Burnley player in two years to be capped by England. This honour following that of Tom Heaton, Michael Keane, Jack Cork and James Tarkowski made them the first Burnley players to be capped by the national team since Martin Dobson in 1974.

That is a fantastic achievement for both the players and the club. If this is not an indication of a club on the up, and a cause for optimism in the future, then I don't know what is. Whatever challenges lie ahead we will meet them resolutely and confidently in the time-honoured Burnley way.

BRING THEM ON!